Profit and Gift in the D

Our economy is neither overwhelmingly capitalist, as Marxist political economists argue, nor overwhelmingly a market economy, as mainstream economists assume. Both approaches ignore vast swathes of the economy, including the gift, collaborative and hybrid forms that coexist with more conventional capitalism in the new digital economy. Drawing on economic sociology, anthropology of the gift and heterodox economics, this book proposes a ground-breaking framework for analysing diverse economic systems: a political economy of practices. The framework is used to analyse Apple, Wikipedia, Google, YouTube and Facebook, showing how different complexes of appropriative practices bring about radically different economic outcomes. Innovative and topical, *Profit and Gift in the Digital Economy* focusses on an area of rapid social change while developing a theoretically and politically radical framework that will be of long-term relevance. It will appeal to students, activists and academics in the social sciences.

DAVE ELDER-VASS teaches sociology and digital economies at Loughborough University. Before returning to academic life he was a senior IT manager in the private sector. This book brings together his expertise in digital technology and its use in business with his academic work on economic sociology and particularly the relation of gifts to the conventional economy. His previous publications include *The Causal Power of Social Structures* (Cambridge University Press, 2010) and *The Reality of Social Construction* (Cambridge University Press, 2012).

Profit and Gift in the Digital Economy

DAVE ELDER-VASS
Loughborough University

CAMBRIDGE
UNIVERSITY PRESS

CAMBRIDGE
UNIVERSITY PRESS

University Printing House, Cambridge CB2 8BS, United Kingdom

Cambridge University Press is part of the University of Cambridge.

It furthers the University's mission by disseminating knowledge in the pursuit of
education, learning and research at the highest international levels of excellence.

www.cambridge.org
Information on this title: www.cambridge.org/9781107146143

© Dave Elder-Vass 2016

First published 2016

Printed in the United States of America by Sheridan Books, Inc.

A catalogue record for this publication is available from the British Library

Library of Congress Cataloging-in-Publication Data
Names: Elder-Vass, Dave, author.
Title: Profit and gift in the digital economy / Dave Elder-Vass.
Description: Cambridge ; New York : Cambridge University Press, 2016. | Includes
bibliographical references and index.
Identifiers: LCCN 2016010294| ISBN 9781107146143 (Hardback) |
ISBN 9781316509388 (Paperback)
Subjects: LCSH: Economics–Sociological aspects. | Economics. | Information
technology–Economic aspects. | BISAC: SOCIAL SCIENCE / Sociology / General.
Classification: LCC HM548 .E43 2016 | DDC 330–dc23 LC record available
at https://lccn.loc.gov/2016010294

ISBN 978-1-107-14614-3 Hardback
ISBN 978-1-316-50938-8 Paperback

For Alisa

Contents

Acknowledgements

I would like to thank the many people who have discussed the issues considered in this book with me, both face-to-face and digitally, for the gift of their attention and their ideas. Inevitably I will miss some, for which I apologise, but those of you I can remember are: Aleksi Aaltonen, Margaret Archer, Michaela Benson, Dave Berry, Gurminder Bhambra, Roy Bhaskar, Tom Brock, Gideon Calder, Mark Carrigan, Bob Carter, Daniel Chernilo, Rachel Cohen, Dean Curran, Asaf Darr, Gerard Delanty, Steve Fleetwood, Rob Garnett, Des Gasper, Christian Greiffenhagen, Mark Harvey, Tuukka Kaidesoja, Ruth Kinna, Chris Land, Tony Lawson, Terry Leahy, Paul Lewis, Andrea Maccarini, Lee Martin, Ashley Mears, Jamie Morgan, Graham Murdock, Karen O'Reilly, Lynne Pettinger, Jonathan Preminger, Olli Pyyhtinen, Hartmut Rosa, Sandy Ross, Michael Roy, Balihar Sanghera, Andrew Sayer, John Scott, Dennis Smith, David Thomas, Hilary Wainwright, Erik Olin Wright and the very helpful anonymous reviewers of both this book and the various papers I have drawn on in writing it.

I owe particular thanks to Dean Curran and Aleksi Aaltonen for reading parts of this book and giving me very helpful feedback, to Loughborough University for granting me the research leave that was used to write the vast majority of this book and my colleagues in the sociology group there for being the most supportive colleagues imaginable. As always, my greatest thanks are owed to my wife Alisa for both her tolerance and her encouragement.

Finally, I must thank several journals and their publishers for permission to re-use material from the following articles. None of them are reproduced in full, but sections are scattered throughout the book:

'Towards a Social Ontology of Market Systems', CRESI Working Paper 2009–06, University of Essex, © 2009 Dave Elder-Vass, used in Chapters 4 and 6.

'Realist Critique without Ethical Naturalism and Moral Realism', *Journal of Critical Realism* (2010) 9:1, 33–58, © 2010 Equinox Publishing, used in Chapter 3.

'Giving and Social Transformation', *Journal of Critical Realism* (2014) 13:3, 261–285, © 2014 Maney Publishing, used in Chapters 1, 2, 3, 5, 7 and 10.

'Commerce, Community and Digital Gifts' in Robert Garnett, Paul Lewis and Lenore Ealy (eds) *Commerce and Community: Ecologies of Social Cooperation*, Routledge (2014), 236–252, © 2015 Dave Elder-Vass, used in Chapters 5, 7 and 8.

'The Moral Economy of Digital Gifts', *International Journal of Social Quality* (2015) 5:1, Berghahn Books, © 2015 Dave Elder-Vass, used in Chapters 4 and 10.

'Free Gifts and Positional Gifts: Beyond Exchangism', *European Journal of Social Theory* (2015), doi: 10.1177/1368431014566562, Sage Publications, © 2015 Dave Elder-Vass, used in Chapter 7.

PART I

Diverse economies

1 | *Introduction*

Over three billion times a day, someone types a search term into Google and within a few seconds receives a list of search results on their screen (Internet Live Stats, 2014). This service, delivered entirely free to the user, has become a cornerstone of the work and knowledge practices of a substantial portion of humanity.[1] But the Google Search business model – like many others in the digital economy – confounds and undermines some of our best established ways of thinking about the economy. Although Google makes substantial profits by serving up advertisements alongside these search results, the idea that one can run a successful business by giving away a free service to perhaps a quarter of the human race flies in the face of conventional economics. Yet it also confounds Marxist ideas that economic value is essentially a product of labour: both the delivery of search results and the sale of advertising space alongside them are thoroughly automated processes, in which almost all of the processing required is done by computers not people. Nor does it support conventional ideas of the gift economy, which is usually seen as an alternative to the commercial economy, making personal connections on the basis of reciprocal obligations.

The best-established ways of understanding our economy are the neoclassical tradition that dominates mainstream academic economics and the Marxist tradition that dominates critical politics. For both, despite individual dissenters and substantial differences in the details, the contemporary economy is a monolith: a capitalist monolith, characterised more-or-less universally by the production of commodities by businesses for sale at a profit. For the typical neoclassical economist this is to be celebrated as the most efficient way to run an economy – and extended into whatever benighted spaces have resisted it. For the

---

[1] Google, at the end of 2012, delivered 65% of global web searches (Internet Live Stats 2014), and by the end of 2014 it is expected that 40% of the world's population will be Internet users (ITU 2014).

typical Marxist it is to be criticised as alienating and exploitative, and overthrown by taking control of the state and imposing an entirely different, but equally monolithic, form of economy.[2]

The real economy, however, is far more diverse. It is neither overwhelmingly capitalist as most Marxists assume nor overwhelmingly a market economy as most mainstream economists assume. Both traditions tend to ignore vast swathes of the economy that do not fit with their stylised models, but because their models have thoroughly shaped our thinking they have largely succeeded in obscuring these diverse economic forms from view. This is not a new problem. Feminists, for example, drew attention to the household economy many years ago (e.g. Friedan, 1963; Hochschild, 1989; Molyneux, 1979). But the problem is coming more sharply into focus with the rise of the digital economy, with its proliferation of innovative economic forms.

Our failure to recognise the diversity of our existing economic systems is doubly consequential. On the one hand, it produces a warped and damaging understanding of how the existing economy works; and on the other, it radically limits our ability to think creatively about economic futures. Capitalism as a universal system, if such a thing could even exist, would be utterly inadequate to the challenge of meeting human needs, but this does not mean that the solution is some *other* universal system. If we are to think productively about alternatives we must stop imagining our economic futures in all or nothing terms: capitalism universal vs. capitalism destroyed.

The central original contribution of this book is to propose a new framework that enables us both to see and to analyse a vast range of diverse economic forms, and to illustrate that framework by applying it to cases in the contemporary digital economy. In this framework, which I call a *political economy of practices*, each economic form is understood as a complex of *appropriative practices*: social practices that influence the allocation of benefits from the process of production. Different combinations of appropriative practices give us different economic forms with very different effects on who receives what benefits and harms from the economy. The political economy of

---

[2] Although even some quite orthodox Marxists are revisiting this assumption in the wake of the collapse of the Soviet bloc, for example David Harvey, who has suggested that communists are starting to adopt more anarchist-inflected visions of the future (D. Harvey, 2011, p. 225).

practices examines how the practices concerned interact to produce those effects, but it also takes an evaluative stance, offering grounds to judge which forms are more desirable in any given context.

The appropriative practices at work in a fairly conventional capitalist firm like Apple are very different from the set at work in a gift economy structure like Wikipedia, but some of the most interesting processes in the digital economy are hybrid forms that combine elements of both capitalist and gift economy forms. The digital economy is diverse not only in the sense that it includes both capitalist and non-capitalist forms, but also in the sense that there are multiple varieties of the capitalist form, many of which do not conform to the traditional models, and indeed multiple varieties of gift economy forms, as well as forms that are neither, or indeed a mixture of both. From this perspective, it becomes possible to see our economy as a complex ecosystem of competing and interacting economic forms, each with their own strengths and weaknesses, and to develop a progressive politics that seeks to reshape that ecosystem rather than pursuing the imaginary perfection of one single universal economic form.

This chapter first summarises the book's argument, then discusses its political implications in the current historical context, and ends by saying a little more about what is involved in a political economy of practices.

An economy of diverse appropriative practices

For too long we have thought of the economy in terms dictated by the market paradigm. Many of the terms we use to think and talk about the economy, including not only *economy* itself, but also *production*, *consumption*, and even *labour* have either been derived from the market model or come to be understood in thoroughly market-oriented ways. The economy has come to be seen as those activities in which goods and services are produced for and exchanged in the market. Production, in turn, is separated from consumption by the moment of commodity exchange: if food is cooked before it is bought, for example, that is taken to count as production, but if it is cooked after it is bought, that is seen as consumption, and thus not as part of the productive economy. Human activity is counted as labour only if it contributes to the production of commodities for sale in the market or is done for a wage – and thus belongs in the labour market.[3] Although this concept of the market is not entirely congruent with capitalism – non-capitalist enterprises, for example can produce for the market – it has become the predominant discursive form of advocacy for a capitalist economy. The market concept itself and all these market-inflected terms are part of what J.K. Gibson-Graham call[4] a dominant discourse of the economy in which 'capitalism is the hegemonic, or even the only, present form of economy' (2006b, p. 2). Gibson-Graham argue that if instead we think of the economy as 'fragmented' we 'could begin to see' a vast range of other economic activity (2006b, p. 263).

Part I of this book adopts their concept of the 'diverse economy' (2006b, p. xii) and seeks to extend their argument. They describe a vast range of contemporary economic activity that does not fit the traditional model of the capitalist firm (2006b, pp. xii–xv), including the state sector, commodity production by non-capitalist enterprises such as co-operatives, the self-employed and family businesses, and the many forms of work that occur within the household such as care work and subsistence agriculture/horticulture. I will also stress the importance of the contemporary gift economy, which overlaps with Gibson-Graham's cases but also goes beyond them, including for example charitable giving, volunteering, blood and organ donation, ritual gifts on birthdays and other occasions, assistance to friends, neighbours, co-workers and indeed unknown passers-by, bequests, the creation of digital resources that are then freely shared with others on the Internet (including, for example, web pages, advice offered on Internet forums, Wikipedia pages, videos posted on YouTube, and open-source software), and perhaps most substantially of all, sharing of resources and caring labour within the household.

Including these activities in the economy requires us to redefine the economy in terms that no longer depend on the market, and Chapter 2 will argue, following a number of heterodox traditions, that we should define it instead in terms of *provisioning*: activities intended to meet human needs. This allows us to include non-market provisioning in

---

[3] Engels made an interesting distinction between *work*, which includes all productive activity, and *labour*, which is work done for a wage (Fuchs, 2014, pp. 26–7; Standing, 2014, p. 22).

[4] I use the plural form because this is the pen-name of two writers writing together under a single 'authorial voice' (Gibson-Graham Cameron & Healy, 2013, p. ix).

our definition of the economy, but measuring the scale of the non-commodity economy is problematic: because it is not traded, it is not automatically valued in monetary terms. Yet I will argue that the non-market economy as a whole, far from being marginal, is at least similar in size to the market economy in contemporary global society, and arguably larger than it.

The concept of the diverse economy represents a radical break with both Marxist and mainstream traditions, leading us on to more theoretical discussions of alternative forms of political economy in Part II. Chapters 3 and 4 respectively engage with the Marxist and mainstream traditions and Chapter 5 outlines my proposed alternative.

Whatever its other strengths, the Marxist tradition, as Gibson-Graham have argued from within its fringes, has contributed to the dominant discourse that sees capitalism and the market as more or less universal in the contemporary economy. The pivotal Marxist contribution to that discourse is its concept of *modes of production*, which remains enormously influential not just in the Marxist tradition but in contemporary understandings of modern history. A mode of production, as the term is usually understood, is a form of economic organisation, characterised by a particular set of class relations, a particular way of allocating rights over the outputs of the process of production to the occupants of different social roles. The mode of production is 'the economic structure of society', and history shows successive modes of production as 'progressive epochs in the economic formation of society' (Marx, 1978b, pp. 4–5). In the popular understanding and in many (though not all) readings of the Marxist tradition, today we live more or less globally under a capitalist mode of production, which displaced feudalism several hundred years ago, at least in Europe. While there has been some recognition that particular societies might include multiple modes of production (Marx, 1978c is a classic example), Marxists have tended to marginalise this issue. Typically for Marxists the mode of production is seen as a single form of social relations that either constitutes or dominates all economic practice within a given society or social formation.

This treatment of modes of production as economic forms that dominate a society, while other forms are essentially marginal, is highly problematic – not only because this concept fails to describe contemporary social reality, but also because that failure is politically consequential. In obscuring the diversity of non-capitalist practice in existing society, it directs the attention of those seeking economic alternatives away from the possibility of developing alternative forms within a diverse economy. This monolithic conception of the economy threatens to lead us directly to a monolithic conception of political action, in which control of the state becomes the only route and the wholesale replacement of one economic monolith with another becomes the only destination. If we are to understand contemporary economies more accurately, then, and develop a framework that allows us to think of economic change more realistically, we need to think of the economy in more flexible terms than Marxists usually do.

But mainstream economics is even less suited to this task. Marxism at least historicises its understanding of economic form and recognises that there might be different forms in different societies or social formations, but mainstream economics is built on a model that is inherently tied to one and only one concept of the economy: the economy as a market economy. Its methods assume that we can model all economic situations in terms of demand, supply, rational calculating agents and optimising functions (Keen, 2011). There are a host of reasons to suspect that this is inadequate as an analysis of the market economy itself, and there is a broad range of work from heterodox economists and other social scientists that contributes to this suspicion. But many of these critics miss a crucial point: there are large sections of the economy that do not follow the market model at all, and mainstream economics has no tools to deal with these. Occasionally we see a kind of economics imperialism that seeks to analyse families and other non-market social phenomena *as if* they could be thought of in terms derived from the market (notably Becker, 1990), but this merely confirms the failure to recognise that there might be sections of the economy that cannot be treated as if they were markets, inhabited by rational optimising agents and immune to the effects of wider social forces.

By contrast with both of these models of the economy, this book seeks to develop a more finely grained analysis that can explain the variety of economic forms at work in contemporary society and thus open up the political possibility of favouring some over others without seeking to eliminate their diversity altogether. This is an argument that cannot be developed within economics as it is currently understood by the mainstream but requires a wider trans-disciplinary perspective, drawing for example on economic anthropology's discussion of gift economies, on sociological accounts of economic practices, and on more theoretical work on mechanisms and causal powers that has been developed by critical realist philosophers of social science. Chapter 4 examines not only the mainstream model but also a number of these alternative traditions and what they can contribute to a more coherent understanding of our diverse economies.

While Chapters 2–4 provide important context, many of their central arguments can be found elsewhere in the literature. Chapter 5, by contrast, develops the book's central theoretical innovation, the political economy of practices. The heart of the argument is that we can understand the economy better by seeing it as a diverse collection of economic forms, each of which can be characterised as a particular *complex of appropriative practices* – social practices that influence the allocation of benefits from the process of production. Groups of people adopting these practices form *appropriative structures*, at a variety of levels. The net result of many different kinds of appropriative structure interacting with each other is an economic system that does not behave like either the Marxist model of capitalism or the mainstream economic model of a market economy.

Let me introduce each of the three terms that define the concept of a complex of appropriative practices. First, the term *practices* is used to identify the unit of economic form. A whole economy cannot be the unit of economic form, the sort of thing that can be described as having or being a single economic form, because many different economic forms can coexist within it. Even single social sites or entities cannot be the unit of economic form for the same reason. Within the household, for example, we may find not only a kind of gift economy at work when parents or carers provide food and other goods freely to their children, but also a more commercial form of economy if they pay wages to a nanny or maid to provide caring or domestic services to the household. These are two different *practices*, where a practice is a tendency to act in a certain way, usually a tendency that is reinforced by normative social expectations, and it *is* possible to identify each of these as a distinct economic form.

The concept of practices, however, is very widely used in the social sciences to refer to a broad range of institutionalised human behaviours, many of which are usually not thought of as economic. Kissing and praying, for example, are practices, but not primarily economic practices. I use the term *appropriative* to single out those practices that are elements of economic form. Despite their nominal interest in production, it is the *appropriation* of the product, or of the benefits that arise from its production, that is the real focus of both mainstream and Marxist economy, and thus of our conceptions of the economic. By *appropriative practices* I mean those practices that determine who receives these benefits (not those related specifically to becoming the *first* owner of something, as the term *appropriation* is sometimes used in property theory). Thus, under wage labour, the worker receives a benefit in the form of a wage, and the employer receives a benefit by taking ownership of the product of the labour, so wage labour is an appropriative practice.

Larger patterns of appropriation, however, often depend not on single appropriative practices, but on interacting *complexes* of them. Wage labour, for example, may be combined with a variety of other practices, and the resulting complexes have quite different appropriational outcomes. The classic form of industrial capitalism combines wage labour with private ownership of production facilities and with commodity production – the sale of the product on the market. This combination of three distinct practices typically generates outcomes that cannot be achieved by wage labour alone, and in particular it tends to generate monetary profits for the capitalist. The interaction of many such commodity sales generates a market system, but wage labour need not be combined with commodity production. It could, for example, be combined with state allocation of the outputs to other enterprises, and in this case we would have a different complex of appropriative practices with quite different consequences, not only for the appropriation of benefits, but also for the dynamic properties of the system. Equally, we could have markets and commodities without wage labour, as when households produce commodities using purely family labour.

One would have to classify and analyse a vast range of such complexes, covering a broad sweep of global history, to evaluate the concept of *complexes of appropriative practices* properly. This book does not attempt such a classification: instead it makes an initial case for taking the concept seriously by applying it to a small number of interesting contemporary cases. It also begins to justify the argument that complexes of appropriative practices have systematic consequences, not just for the appropriation of monetary benefit, but also for phenomena that conventional economics tends to ignore, such as satisfaction in work and the development of community. Part III of the book is therefore devoted to examining four different complexes of appropriative practice that have appeared in the contemporary digital economy and to demonstrating some of the benefits of a political economy of practices by showing how it improves our ability to make sense of these cases. None of these cases can be seen clearly when they are viewed through the polarising lenses of the prevailing views of the economy; each of those lenses allows us to see only one dimension – if that – of the economic activity in these diverse economic forms.

Chapter 6 considers one prominent case of capitalist commodity production, the case of Apple. In many ways Apple approximates to the traditional model of the capitalist firm, making a significant share of its profits by creating and distributing material goods. Yet many aspects of its behaviour, and of its effects, cannot be explained by the rather crude conceptions of the market that feature in political advocacy of the market system. It does not, for example, simply compete in existing markets but constantly seeks to control the market, while excluding competitors by the manipulation of legal rights. It is also earning increasing revenues from the sale of immaterial 'goods', raising major questions about the role of both labour and the social construction of property rights in the generation of profit. Nevertheless, elements of the market paradigm do apply to cases like Apple, and it is essential that any innovative model of economic forms should be able to accommodate such aspects as well as those that escape the traditional view.

Alongside the commodity economy, however, the Internet has become the site for a thriving gift economy, exemplified by Wikipedia and open-source software communities. Chapter 7 discusses the appropriative practices at work in Wikipedia: its creation by voluntary labour, its funding by donations, its provision of its product as a free digital gift, and the internal practices that sustain this model. Wikipedia is a nice example of how the technological characteristics of the Internet have created new opportunities for the co-operative production of digital gifts. As such, it illustrates the importance of the contribution of technology, and in particular of non-human material objects, to shaping and enacting appropriative practices, and this chapter briefly introduces the related concept of *sociomaterial structures*. It is also a fascinating example of decommodification, in which new combinations of information, software and culture threaten existing commodity producers.

The interaction between the commodity and gift economies has led to the emergence of a range of hybrid forms, two of which are considered in Chapters 8 and 9. First we consider the model with which this chapter opened. Google's business model for search generates massive profits that depend on it giving things away – search results, email services, and maps, for example – and using those gifts to acquire data about users that allows Google to sell highly targeted advertising. Business models like this, in which wage labour plays a vanishingly marginal role, cannot be explained in terms of traditional Marxist analyses of capitalism, but they also illustrate the inadequacy of mainstream economics: what is the relevance of price competition in a 'market' where the product is free?

Finally, sites like YouTube[5] and Facebook profit from a different kind of hybrid, which I call *user content capitalism*, in which users effectively donate their time to build resources that generate profits for the capitalist owners of the site concerned. Again, we have profit largely without wage labour, but this case also calls into question fundamental concepts of economics, above all the division between production and consumption.[6] Once we move beyond the market, how do we decide which activities are 'economic'? And how desirable are models of production in which users engage in largely unalienated labour but also generate profits for the platform provider?

Different parts of this argument may appeal to different kinds of readers. More academic and more theoretically inclined readers will find Part II of the book important, but the book should also appeal to non-academic readers, who could skip Part II (perhaps returning to Chapter 5 later) and focus instead on the digital economy case studies in Part III. I have tried to make Parts I and III accessible to any educated reader, but Part II may be a little more challenging for readers without an academic background.

Historical context and political strategy

One central message of this book, then, is that we live in a much less capitalist economy than most of us think, with a broad range of other economic forms coexisting already, some of which could be developed

---

[5] Also owned by Google.
[6] This is often known as *prosumption*, a concept I will question in Chapter 9.

further to shift the balance of our diverse economy away from capitalism. But this should not lead us to underestimate or wish away the enormous power that capitalist business exerts in the contemporary world, or the structural consequences that arise from the interactions of many capitalist processes, whether or not the actors involved intend them. There is a nexus of economic, discursive and political power around the interests of capitalist business that is arguably the single most momentous focus of power in the contemporary world.

In the economic dimension, capitalism generates monetary assets on a massive scale (while the gift economy, however large it is as a share of productive activity, does not) giving capitalist businesses enormous power over resources. They are able to translate that economic power into discursive power through their control of the media industry: although the Internet has created new opportunities for user-driven communication, the most widely heard voices are still predominantly those controlled by the capitalist media. The influence of the popular press, TV and radio on how we think about public issues remains enormous, and this is one of the channels through which, for example, the discourse of the economy as purely a market economy has become so prevalent. Equally important, the media has made a major contribution to the construction of a discursive regime in which the reputation of governments is measured by their success or failure in stimulating business growth. Both this discursive power and their economic resources have also given capitalist business substantial influence in the political process in most of the countries of the world, and as a consequence many of those governments have pursued the interests of the business sector in their international as well as domestic policies.

It is in this context that neoliberals have been able to refashion the global economic environment, capturing and employing state power to deregulate private business, privatise the state sector and cut back the provision of public services that do not directly benefit businesses in many of the countries of the world (Klein, 2007; Mirowski, 2013). Neoliberals have both exploited and encouraged globalisation: for example breaking down trade barriers and thus creating the opportunity to shift manufacturing from the Global North to the Global South – or perhaps we should say the Global East – where lower wage levels and looser regulatory regimes allow the extraction of greater profit. One consequence has been to hold down wages in the North and create a class of permanently insecure workers – the precariat – while expanding the class of similarly insecure workers in the destination countries (Standing, 2014).

This is a world in which inequality is rising, as the share of wages in official national incomes falls (Piketty, 2014), with harmful effects not just for the poor but for the entire population (Wilkinson & Pickett, 2010). It is a world in which multinational corporations like Apple, Google, Facebook and Amazon can arbitrage regulatory regimes to pay only minimal taxes on their enormous revenues, avoiding their obligations to contribute to funding the very states they depend upon to protect their interests (Duke, 2012; Duke & Gadher, 2012). It is a world in which the values of the market gradually eclipse all others (Sandel, 2013). It is, increasingly, a world that pays no regard to the needs and problems of human beings who do not command monetary power. And it is, of course, a world that needs to be changed. The massive power of capitalist businesses to defend their interests is a major obstacle to such change, but it is not the only obstacle.

A further obstacle, and the one that motivates this book, is the lack of viable alternatives on offer from many of the critics of neoliberalism. Traditionally different sections of the left have advocated two routes to improving the organisation of our economy: reformist accommodations with capitalism on the one hand, or seizing the state to impose revolutionary change on the other. Neither of these, in my view, is a viable path to a radically better economy. Both derive from the monoliths in our heads: from the view that capitalism is an 'all or nothing' system, and a homogeneous one at that. But once we recognise that other economies already exist all around us, a third option becomes available: to introduce, develop and support progressive economic alternatives within our diverse economy, while seeking to cut back the more harmful forms and aspects of capitalism.

This is a route that Vishwas Satgar has called *transformative* politics, and it has an increasing number of advocates (Satgar, 2014). In the world of political practice, it fits with the outlook of the World Social Forum and the many campaigning organisations linked to it (Mertes, 2004; Ponniah, 2003). In the world of academic theory, it fits quite closely with a number of projects related to alternative economies and solidarity economies (e.g. Hart Laville & Cattani, 2010), but most productively, perhaps, with the logic of Erik Olin Wright's *real utopias* project (Wright, 2010). Wright, though he has a Marxist background himself, is critical of the traditional Marxist tendency to focus on the critique of the present while saying very little about what kind of future we should be aiming at, beyond vague platitudes about communism. Instead he argues that we need to develop clear and detailed alternative proposals which he calls 'real utopias'. These alternatives are *utopian* in the ethical sense that they are visions for 'social institutions free of oppression', visions that expand our imagination about what is possible (Wright, 2010, p. 6). But they are also *real* in the sense that a proposal only qualifies if we can make a good case that it is viable and achievable. What makes Wright's project particularly compatible with the argument of this book is that the utopian proposals he endorses do not advocate a new monolithic economy, but instead offer a range of partial alternatives that could coexist with existing institutions, including economic forms that could plausibly operate within an evolved version of our diverse economy. As Geoff Hodgson has argued, 'If there is a role for utopians... it is not to design one Jerusalem but to understand and imagine a whole set of contrasting and unfolding possibilities, and the social forces that could lead to them' (Hodgson, 1999, p. 154).

Here we have the basis of a viable progressive strategy for the economy: work on many fronts, advance many options, recognise that we have a diverse economy and work towards shifting the balance. This means growing some progressive alternatives but also cutting back some regressive ones. It entails being open to a wide range of alternatives, including the possibility that there might be some valuable continuing role for some forms of capitalism in a more adequate mixed economy of practices.

Capitalism itself is not a monolith; there are many different complexes of appropriative practice, operating in many different contexts, which have often been lumped together under that label. The Marxist discursive strategy of dividing the economic and political spectrum into bourgeois and proletarian, them and us, has made it difficult for thinkers on the left to differentiate between different economic forms that are labelled capitalist, and closed off the possibility of a radical left that evaluates some capitalist economic forms as useful and others as harmful, and differentiates between these in its political strategy. Only the right, it seems, is allowed to recognise the positives in some capitalist forms of business organisation, such as their flexibility, their dynamism in developing new products and services, their success in pushing forward technological development, and their ability to reallocate resources through the process Schumpeter calls creative destruction (Schumpeter, 1994, p. 83). Even the ability of market forms to orient production towards customer demand would be a desirable force in an economy with a less unequal distribution of purchasing power.

The total abolition of capitalism is thus not only unrealistic but also *undesirable*. Once we recognise that capitalism itself is diverse, we can focus on differentiating between those forms that (if suitably regulated) could contribute to an economy oriented to human needs and those which could not. This is an essential strategy not only for identifying desirable ways forward, but also for identifying politically feasible ways forward, because it is unlikely that any strategy that both antagonises the *entire* capitalist power-complex and denies the positive experiences that many ordinary people have with *some* capitalist employers and providers of goods and services could achieve political momentum. Put simply, I am suggesting a strategy that involves distinguishing between good and bad capitalism and bringing the good capitalists onto the side of progressives, or at least to a position where they do not feel threatened by criticism of more harmful forms of capitalism. The alternative is to push all or most capitalist businesses into the same political alliance against progressive change.

Nevertheless, progress towards an economy more oriented to human needs is also likely to require the outright abolition of some forms of capitalist practice and the regulation of others, including some that are backed by, and productive of, enormous financial power. Such changes will surely provoke massive resistance from the businesses affected and their discursive and political representatives. I do not claim to have a solution to this challenge, but I suggest it will involve building political alliances between the advocates of a broad range of different practices in a diverse economy. There is at least some indication of what such an alliance might look like in the shape of the World Social Forum. It is particularly significant that the WSF, unlike most leftist movements in the Global North, is not centred on the labour movement, and thus not tied to the labourist strategy of shifting the balance of power within the wage labour relationship rather than developing economic alternatives to that relationship.

Towards a new political economy

Although the last section strayed into questions of political strategy, it did so only to position this book's argument in the current political and economic context. The primary focus of this work is not politics as such but political economy. Let me tentatively define *political economy* as the scientific, but also necessarily evaluative and thus political, study of economic practices and systems. While the mainstream tradition often presents itself as purely technical economics rather than an evaluative and thus political enterprise, any recommendation arising from economic analysis is always concerned with the allocation or appropriation of resources and benefits between different people and therefore cannot be ethically neutral. Such recommendations always entail ethical evaluations, whether these are explicit or hidden from view. Marxism, by contrast, makes a virtue of claiming the label of *political economy*.

There are thus multiple political economies, where *a* political economy is a more-or-less homogeneous, coherent and comprehensive tradition of work *on* political economy. These traditions arguably share some of the characteristics of Kuhn's *paradigms* (Kuhn, 1970). They build on core theories that are taken to be fundamental to the tradition. They develop their own conceptual vocabulary and structure of argument, which may make it difficult for adherents of different traditions to make sense of each other's arguments, or even to *see* empirical phenomena that do not fit within the categories of their own paradigm. And their adherents are somewhat resistant to revising or rejecting core concepts and theories, finding ways to reinterpret apparently conflicting evidence that prevents it from threatening their belief in the paradigm. On the other hand, the existing traditions in political economy are even more resilient to disproof than the paradigms Kuhn studied in the natural sciences because they have found ways to insulate themselves from mundane considerations of empirical validity. Partly this is done under cover of the sheer difficulty of testing social science theories, but it also happens because adherence to the paradigm is often motivated more by political belief than by scientific considerations.

Today we are faced with only two substantial political economies: the explicitly political economy of the Marxist tradition and the covertly political economy of mainstream economics. The former claims the label of political economy, but the latter is equally political, though it conceals that under a mantle of pseudo-objectivity and mathematics. It provides a framework that accepts and implicitly validates the market economy as the only form of economy, and provides the technical material that underpins the neoliberal political agenda.[7] Both of these political economies must be rejected. As I shall argue later both are scientifically unsound, and both are committed to political projects that are out of step with the needs of humanity.

This book argues that we need a new political economy: a political economy of practices. As with all intellectual developments, it builds on but goes beyond earlier ideas. Bourdieu, for example, has called for 'a general science of the economy of practices, which would treat mercantile exchange as a particular case of exchange in all its forms' (Pierre Bourdieu, 2002, p. 280). Not only drawing on earlier work, but also influenced by some recent political movements, the book contributes to a tradition that is arguably already in formation, by offering a different kind of political economy more suited to our diverse economy and the political challenges it raises.

From the ethical perspective, it advocates a political economy that is also what Andrew Sayer calls a *moral economy*: a political economy that takes an evaluative stance towards 'economic systems, actions and motives in terms of their effects on people's lives' (Sayer, 2004b, pp. 80–1). Such evaluations always presume values or ethical standards upon which their judgements are based, and providing objective justifications for such values is notoriously difficult. Elsewhere (Elder-Vass, 2010a) I have tiptoed through this minefield to support Habermas's claim that we can arrive at good justifications for ethical standards through a process that he calls *discourse ethics*. This describes a process in which ethical principles are provisionally agreed through discussions conducted in a spirit of truthfulness and sincerity, where all those affected are suitably represented, and where differences in power are not allowed to influence the outcome (Habermas, 1993, p. 31). On the basis of global processes of debate that have approximated to this model we have good grounds, at least, to argue that we should value all humans, support those systems and actions that provide for their basic

---

[7] Though neoliberalism has also been inspired by Hayekian economics, which shares the market paradigm but differs from neoclassical economics in some respects.

needs and the capabilities they require to achieve human dignity and oppose those that do not (see Chapter 3).[8] We may be able to justify stronger ethical standards on the basis of the discourse principle: for example, that we should not only meet the basic needs of all but also enable them to achieve their full human potential, or in other words to *flourish*. But the contemporary economic system blatantly fails to deliver even the weaker requirement of providing the basic human needs of all, and it is the responsibility of political economy to investigate why that is and how it could be changed.

The standard presentations of both mainstream and Marxist political economy implicitly concede that we should value all humans, since both invoke some variety of this standard in their discourses of justification. Mainstream economists and apologists for capitalism routinely argue that the market system benefits everyone, and that this provides adequate justification for it. Marxists routinely argue that their objective is a communist society in which the needs of all are met, and that this justifies all manner of instrumental decisions along the way. Yet both employ this standard as a kind of legitimation device, employed to justify a theoretical and political stance and then pushed aside, never to be consulted again. This is not the perspective of moral economy: for a moral political economy, the principle that we should value all humans and provide for their basic needs and capabilities is a criterion to be employed in the evaluation of specific actions, systems and policies.

An ethical perspective, however, is not all that we need: if we are, for example, to evaluate economic forms on the basis of the outcomes that they have for human flourishing, we need to be able to analyse what outcomes they tend to produce and how. A political economy must therefore also be scientific: it must analyse the real social world as it actually functions, rather than substituting highly abstracted models for empirical relevance. Nor can its scientific conclusions be subordinated to philosophical dogma such as the labour theory of value or the teleological conception of history as a series of stages leading towards a faintly imagined nirvana.

As I have argued in my earlier books, drawing on the philosophical tradition of critical realism,[9] an adequate scientific approach to the

---

[8] On the question of capabilities, see in particular Nussbaum (2000, p. 5). Her full list of essential capabilities is provided on pp. 78–80.

[9] Key contributions to critical realism's social ontology include (Archer, 1995; Bhaskar, 1975, 1979; T. Lawson, 1997; Sayer, 1992).

social world requires that we see social events in terms that are similar in some crucial respects to natural events: they are produced by the interacting causal powers of a variety of different entities, which may include material objects, human individuals, and social entities (often referred to as social structures) (Elder-Vass, 2010b). Any given event will be *multiply determined* by a number of different powers, depending on the particular context, and the explanation of such events depends on (a) recognising the full range of causal powers involved; and (b) identifying how each of these causal powers works. By ignoring all but a handful of the factors that influence economic events, mainstream economics simplifies the task, but unfortunately in the process it simplifies out elements that are crucial to understanding the economy. Social forces beyond the swings of supply and demand are the most striking: the economy depends, for example, on culture, on social networks and relationships and on the social construction of phenomena like money and property (Elder-Vass, 2012). A fully adequate account of the economy will sometimes have to take account of these forces, and indeed others, which is only possible in a political economy that seeks to understand the economy as a site of many interacting entities and mechanisms.

Critical realism's ontology thus provides a coherent framework for the scientific tasks of political economy, but this does not in itself solve the substantive scientific questions: every causal power, and every event, requires investigation of the empirical evidence as well as theoretical analysis of the mechanisms involved before an explanation can be developed. To produce not just one explanation but an entire political economy is thus an enormous task. To produce one from scratch would be unthinkably daunting. Fortunately there is already a great deal of material that can be reused and built on. On the one hand, there have always been thinkers who have stood outside the mainstream *and* Marxist traditions: heterodox economists of many stripes, social theorists, economic sociologists and economic anthropologists, for example. These thinkers have generated important material that already casts light on many of the mechanisms at work in various sectors of the economy. And on the other, even some of the work done in the two central traditions can be disembedded from its context and used to construct a more realist analysis of the phenomena concerned. We can simultaneously draw on both of these traditions while rejecting their core assumptions.

This political economy of practices is also therefore a pluralist political economy, in several respects. From the scientific perspective, it recognises a plurality of economic forms that must be analysed in different ways; it accepts contributions from a plurality of traditions of socio-economic thinking; and it accepts the need for a plurality of methods in order to investigate and analyse economic phenomena. From the normative perspective it advocates a continuing diversity of economic forms and the development of a plurality of new ones. And from the political perspective it recognises that there is no end point for the diverse economy, but only a perpetually changing mix of practices and as a consequence we will have a permanent need for political pluralism: a healthy polity of debate over which alternatives should rise in the mix and which should fall.

This book, then, is a step towards a new political economy, an ethical, realist, pluralist political economy, a political economy of practices, which can provide us with the tools to understand, evaluate and indeed see the diverse economy that surrounds us.

2 | *Diverse economies*

Introduction

Most of us have been persuaded, without even realising that persuasion was occurring, that we live in an overwhelmingly capitalist market economy, with just the state sector as a partial exception to the universal reach of the market. Indeed the very concept of the economy has come to be defined in a way that makes it difficult to escape this conclusion. For mainstream economists, 'the economy' is more or less coextensive with the commodity economy – it consists of the production and exchange of goods and services for monetary payment – and for both mainstream and (most) Marxist economists the commodity economy is more or less coextensive with the capitalist economy – in which production is done by profit-oriented businesses using wage labour. This understanding of the economy is a political trap: unless we challenge the view that the economy is by definition a *commodity* economy it is impossible to conceive of *economic* alternatives to the market and to capitalism.

This chapter begins by asking how the discourse of the market economy has been able to permeate our consciousness so thoroughly, but its main purpose is to examine how we can move beyond that discourse. To do so, we must open up our concept of the economy, and I will advocate an alternative definition of the economy as *provisioning*: roughly, as those activities that provide the goods and services that people need. This is not as simple and straightforward as it might seem: as we shall see it is an inherently political definition, but so is the one that I am contesting. It allows us to see, however, that an enormous proportion of provisioning occurs outside the commodity economy, in a whole range of diverse forms, and the chapter will offer a little evidence on the range and scale of those forms. Once we have reconceived the nature of the economy, in other words, it becomes apparent that there is a vast amount of economic activity occurring beyond the market, and the challenge of transforming our economies becomes much more viable. Instead of having to reinvent our economies from scratch, we have the opportunity to build on the alternative economy that is sitting right under our noses. This remains an enormous challenge, but it ceases to be an impossible one, and the chapter closes by discussing strategies for shifting the balance of our diverse economies.

The discourse of the market economy

As Gibson-Graham argue, a certain concept of the economy has become naturalised in public discourse: we are accustomed to hearing, and as a consequence generally accept, that 'the economy' is 'a force that constitutes the ultimate arbiter of possibility' in politics and society, and that 'wage labor, the commodity market, and capitalist enterprise [are...] the only "normal" forms of work, exchange, and business organization' (Gibson-Graham, 2006a, p. 53). Economic discourse, they argue, is predominantly 'capitalocentric' (Gibson-Graham, 2006b, p. 6): despite formal definitions of the economy that might seem to imply a wider focus,[1] non-capitalist practices are essentially ignored or assumed to be subsidiary to capitalism, and activity beyond the reach of capitalist practices is treated as non-economic. Thus, for example these discourses present 'the household as the space of "consumption" (of capitalist commodities) and of "reproduction" (of the capitalist workforce) rather than as a space of noncapitalist production and consumption' (Gibson-Graham, 2006b, p. 8). These discourses produce 'familiar understandings of capitalism as a naturally dominant form of economy, or as an entire system of economy, coextensive with the social space' (Gibson-Graham, 2006b, p. ix).

I suggest that the economy has been naturalised in at least two senses. First, in the sense that we are expected to believe a certain *form* of economy is natural and inevitable – a market form or a capitalist form or both. And secondly, in the sense that the economy so defined is taken to be an objective system in its own right, a force with its own logic and tendencies, more or less independent of our beliefs and actions, that we have no choice but to accommodate ourselves to. Yet the idea of 'the economy' is a remarkably recent development.

---

[1] Such as Lionel Robbins' well-known definition of economics as the study of how we assign scarce resources between alternative uses (Robbins, 1932, p. 16).

According to Timothy Mitchell, the term was not used by economists until the 1930s, 'and only by the middle of the century was the term as it is understood today in general use' (Mitchell, 2005, p. 126). Although many authors played a part in the rise of the term, Mitchell points to Keynes as a significant contributor: 'Keynes's breakthrough was to conceive of the new totality not as an aggregation of markets in different commodities, but as the circulation of money. The economy was the sum of all the moments at which money changed hands' (Mitchell, 2005, p. 135). This concept of the economy, then, is inherently tied to the sale and purchase of commodities, and this link (as well as the territorial demarcation of the economy by the boundaries of the nation state) was strengthened by the development of national income statistics, which measured the volume of these commodity transactions within a given national boundary (Mitchell, 2005, p. 136).

We must not over-estimate the discursive power of academics, however. They may often (though not always) be the sources of innovations, but many innovations fall by the wayside, and wider social forces make a substantial contribution to *which* discursive habits become established. New discourses require wider circles of support to become hegemonic (Elder-Vass, 2011, 2012, chapter 8). National income statistics, for example, may have been invented by academics, but their widespread adoption aligned perfectly with the demands of business interests that government policy be directed towards increasing the size of the commodity economy. National income statistics provide a measure of governmental performance that is ideally oriented to the needs of business, and a convenient focus for media discourse that pressurises governments to serve those needs. It is not an accident that the prevailing discourse of the economy serves the interests of capitalist business so well, nor is it simply a result of the contributions of pro-business economists, but rather a consequence of the power of those businesses to influence the prevailing discursive regime.

It is not just the concept of the economy itself that we have come to understand in market-saturated terms, but also a number of related concepts. Consider the concepts of production and consumption. One might seek to oppose the discourse of the market economy, for example, by arguing that we should define the economy as all productive activities, whether or not what is produced is a commodity. Indeed this is sometimes how the economy is defined anyway. Geoffrey Ingham, for example, suggests that generally 'the concept of the economy is used to refer to the social organizations and institutions that are involved in the production and distribution of goods and services in society' (Ingham, 2006, p. 157). But I argue that the apparently fundamental, naturalised distinction between production and consumption is itself shaped by commodity thinking. In the dominant discourse, production is regarded as those activities that create commodities – goods and services sold in the market – and consumption as the purchase and use of commodities. Outside the framework of the market economy, however, the distinction between production and consumption starts to break down. In the market economy, for example, cooking food counts as production when it is done in a restaurant and thus creates a commodity, but consumption (of the ingredients purchased as commodities) when it is done in the household and creates a meal to be shared (M. A. Glucksmann, 2014). Washing hair counts as production when it is done in a salon for money, and consumption (of shampoo) when you do it for yourself. Remove the market, and where is the distinction between production and consumption in cases like these? As Glucksmann has said, this 'challenges the notion of "production" and "consumption" as watertight realms' (M. A. Glucksmann, 2013, p. 5). At least one Marxist attempt to make the distinction follows the market model precisely: for Humphreys and Grayson, production activities are those that create exchange value and consumption activities those that create (only) use value (Humphreys & Grayson, 2008). Marx himself makes a more promising distinction:

Labour uses up its material factors, its subject and its instruments, consumes them, and is therefore a process of consumption. Such productive consumption is distinguished from individual consumption by this, that the latter uses up products, as means of subsistence for the living individual... The product, therefore, of individual consumption, is the consumer himself; the result of productive consumption, is a product distinct from the consumer (Marx, 1954, p. 179).

Marx begins here by using *consume* in an older sense: 'to destroy, to use up, to waste, to exhaust' (R. Williams, 1976, pp. 68–9) rather than 'to buy'. This enables him to distinguish between productive consumption – which corresponds roughly to what is now called simply *production* – and individual consumption – or simply *consumption* – in terms of the different relation of the output to the agent of the activity. We must take care in reading 'consumer' in the final sentence – here Marx is referring to the agent who is performing productive consumption, or in other words the worker or *producer*. Production, when it takes the form of a service, may well produce a change in the consumer in the usual sense of the term, a change in the beneficiary of the service, but this is not what Marx is referring to. Translating the argument into more accessible terms, we could say that the difference between production and consumption is that production creates a product external to the agent performing the activity, while consumption transforms the agent performing the activity. This suggests a principled line between the two that is independent of the market framework. But this is a *different* concept of production than the one in everyday use today: the usual concept of production is as thoroughly a product of the dominant discourse as the everyday concept of the economy.

While mainstream academic economics and various other pro-capitalist forces have made an important contribution to the construction of this discourse, a further reason for the dominance of this conception of the economy, as Gibson-Graham argue, is that the idea of the economy as an essentially capitalist market economy is largely unopposed: with some honourable exceptions like Gibson-Graham themselves, Marxists are as likely as neoclassical economists to see the contemporary economy as one that is thoroughly saturated by capitalist commodity production, and to dismiss other forms of economy as survivals from a previous age, with no more than marginal continuing significance. David Harvey tells us, for example, that for those who live in 'those societies we call capitalist', it is the flow of capital that provides us with 'our daily bread as well as our houses, cars, cell phones, shirts, shoes and all the other goods we need to support our daily life' (D. Harvey, 2011, p. vi). Both mainstream economists and Marxists routinely frame the contemporary economy as an essentially capitalist one (perhaps with a few minor non-capitalist survivals) swimming as it were in a non-economic sea of social practices that can largely be ignored in thinking about the economy itself.

While Marxist understandings of capitalism were developed to stimulate political action, Gibson-Graham argue that they have now become an obstacle 'contributing to a *crisis* in left politics' (Gibson-Graham, 2006b, p. 1):

Part of what produces the disarray of the left is the vision of what the left is arrayed against. When capitalism is represented as a unified system coextensive with the nation or even the world, when it is portrayed as crowding out all other economic forms, when it is allowed to define entire societies, it becomes something that can only be defeated and replaced by a mass collective movement (or by a process of systemic dissolution that such a movement might assist) (Gibson-Graham, 2006b, p. 263).

Given the absence of such movements and the utter implausibility of such systemic dissolutions in the current historical context, this perspective acts as 'a brake upon the anticapitalist imagination' (Gibson-Graham, 2006b, p. 3): it obscures the possibility, above all, that anti-capitalist alternatives might be developed within the supposedly purely capitalist economy that we already have. Indeed it is not only a cognitive obstacle but also an emotional one: if to imagine incremental alternatives is necessarily fruitless, then there seems to be little point in hoping for anything better than social democratic tinkering in a thoroughly capitalist economy.

Gibson-Graham themselves tend to see the alternative in linguistic terms: they seek to develop 'a language of the *diverse economy*' (Gibson-Graham, 2006a, p. 60) in order to 'disarm and dislocate the naturalized dominance of the capitalist economy and make a space for new economic becomings' (Gibson-Graham, 2006b, p. xii). Gibson-Graham overstate the contribution that language can make, and understate the impact of the systemic forces of capitalism on our options, but the central thread of their argument is both sound and important. There *is* a powerful tendency on both left and right to think of the contemporary economy as thoroughly capitalist; this *does* obscure the existence of a vast range of non-capitalist economic practices in the contemporary economy; and that *does* discourage us from thinking of the development of such practices as a central plank of anti-capitalist politics. But if we reject that discourse we can begin to see the situation as less desperate: we are already surrounded by a range of functioning and in some cases even thriving non-capitalist economic practices, and developing those alternatives is an important part of a viable anti-capitalist strategy.

What *is* 'the economy'?

In these last few sentences I have assumed a different conception of the economy than the commodity-centred version. To talk of non-market economic alternatives is already to think of the economy as something that is not defined by the commodity. But what *is* the economy once we refuse this definition?

Scholars from a variety of heterodox traditions have argued that we should think of the economy not in terms of the market but in terms of *provisioning* or *social provisioning*. In institutional economics, for example, a number of writers have endorsed Gruchy's argument that economics should be 'the science of social provisioning' (also see Boulding, 1973; Dugger, 1996, p. 31; R.F. Garnett, 2007; Gruchy, 1987, pp. 4–7, 21). A number of feminists have also argued for a provisioning-oriented understanding of the economy (e.g. J.A. Nelson, 1993; Power, 2004). In critical realism, Andrew Sayer has argued:

Rather than use 'market' as a metonym for the economy, or a euphemism for capitalism, which always results in the marginalisation and misrepresentation of economic activities not involving market exchange, I shall use economy to refer to all forms of provisioning, including those outside the cash economy (Sayer, 2004a, p. 2).

This concept of provisioning aligns closely with Karl Polanyi's important concept of the *substantive economy*. Polanyi argues that our understanding of the economic has been compounded from two distinct elements, the substantive and formal concepts of the economy.

The substantive meaning of economic derives from man's dependence for his living upon nature and his fellows. It refers to the interchange with his natural and social environment, in so far as this results in supplying him with the means of material want satisfaction (Polanyi, 2001, p. 31).

The formal meaning, by contrast, is linked to the assumption of mainstream economics that the economy is concerned with the allocation of scarce resources as this is done through a market system. It is derived from the economists' formal models of such a system, rather than from the empirical question of how our needs may be met, and some of the resources required to meet our substantive needs may not be scarce at all. The formal concept is essentially the same as the concept of the economy I have been criticising here, and Polanyi also dismisses it, concluding that 'only the substantive meaning of "economic" is capable of yielding the concepts that are required by the social sciences for an investigation of all the empirical economies of the past and present' (Polanyi, 2001, p. 32).

Broadly speaking, we can understand provisioning, or the substantive economy, as those activities that supply what is required to meet the needs of human beings (J.A. Nelson, 1993, pp. 32–4). This replaces an orientation to 'demand' with an orientation to 'need', thus shifting not only the range of activities that are included in the economy but also, and in consequence, shifting our conception of the economy so that it includes the activities required to meet the needs of the poor and our collective needs for public goods as well as those needs that the market economy meets because they are backed by cash. It is arguably a functional definition of the economy: the economy as those activities that fulfil a certain set of needs. So, for example, growing some carrots would count as provisioning and thus as economic whether I did it in my back garden for consumption by my family or whether a farmer did it for sale to a supermarket who then sold the carrots on to me (cf Sayer, 2015, p. 21).

This is certainly an improvement: the economy is no longer defined by the market and thus space is created for alternative non-market economic forms (J.A. Nelson, 1993, p. 33). While I will argue later that provisioning is indeed an appropriate basis for re-defining the economy, we must first recognise that it is by no means a decisive answer to the question, and then understand why it is still appropriate despite being flawed in many ways. The difficulty with the substantive/provisioning approach to defining the economy is that although it succeeds in including some important things that are excluded by the market answer, it fails to provide us with adequate grounds for excluding things that are *not* appropriately regarded as economic. The market answer at least gives us a clear criterion as to what is economic and what is not (though it is rarely applied rigorously: few scholars deny, for example, that the state sector is part of the economy, despite implicitly using the market criterion to exclude other activity). What happens when we remove this? What demarcation line can we put in the place of the commodity relation that would prevent the river of referents of the concept of the economy bursting its banks and spreading across the entire plain of human action?

As should be clear from my earlier discussion, we cannot simply distinguish between production and consumption. Much of what is referred to as consumption under the market model is work that we do to meet a human need and thus impossible to distinguish from production under the provisioning model.

Nor does the concept of 'need' help us much. Nelson, for example, argues for an economics focussed on 'the provisioning of human life, that is, on the commodities and processes necessary to human survival' (J.A. Nelson, 1993, p. 32). This seems like quite a restrictive under- standing of needs – surely we have other needs than just surviving? But once we accept that we do have other needs it becomes difficult to draw a line between genuine needs and mere desires. In a more ethically oriented economy we might wish, for example, to reduce the produc- tion of extravagant luxuries that are purchased largely as a means of displaying status, on the grounds that they do not meet genuine needs, but how do we determine which needs are genuine and which are not? And even if we could find a coherent basis for distinguishing between genuine and false needs, it is not clear that it would be right to exclude the creation of unnecessary or wasteful products *from our definition of the economy*. It is striking that Nelson allows 'the provision of con- veniences or luxuries' back into the subject matter of economics within a page of framing it in terms of human survival (J.A. Nelson, 1993, p. 33). Part of the point of critiquing our existing economy is that it *does* often produce the wrong things, but we can only say so if we recognise such production as a form of economic activity in the first place.

More issues arise when we consider that the products of the market economy include not only material goods but also services and infor- mation. Polanyi makes a thoroughly confused attempt to limit the substantive economy to the satisfaction of 'material' needs (Polanyi, 2001, p. 34), but services are already a major part of the formal economy, and an essential part of provisioning outside it, notably in the household (J.A. Nelson, 1993, p. 32). Including services in our understanding of the economy is unavoidable, but the concept of provisioning provides us with no means for establishing a boundary between services and other human activities. Perhaps we might take inspiration from the quote from Marx cited earlier, and suggest that services, as opposed to non-economic interactions, provide benefits for other people than the person doing the work.

It is not clear, however, how much benefit is required for an activity to count as a service. If I smile at a friend when I see them, this may provide them with some benefit, a little psychic lift for a few moments perhaps – does smiling therefore count as a service? Indeed, as Arlie Hochschild has argued, smiling and similar emotional labour *does* count as a service in the commodity sector (Hochschild, 2012). Even negative emotional labour – the deliberately unpleasant debt collector – is a feature of the commodity economy (Hochschild, 2012). So shouldn't social interaction count as economic outside it too?

The provision of information as a commercial product raises similar issues: if a magazine that provides us with celebrity gossip is part of the economy, why not include the conversation in which I tell you what a mutual friend did last week? Indeed, in our increasingly knowledge-oriented economy it seems very clear that information content is an economic good, and very difficult to see any basis for excluding some information from that definition.

If we accept all of these arguments, the banks are well and truly broken, the plain of the non-economic is thoroughly flooded, and the concept of the economy has been spread so thin as to mean nothing distinctive at all. At this point the provisioning answer to the question 'What is the economy?' seems to converge with a different answer, which is to dispense with the concept of the economic entirely. This is not an illogical position. If we begin by recognising that the existing concept of the economy is arbitrary, political and constructed, then we must surely recognise that any alternative definition of the economy will also be arbitrary, political and constructed, and so it is an error to think we can replace a 'false' definition of the economy with a 'true' one. Instead we might argue that the very idea that there is such a thing as the economy is the problem, that the idea of the economy serves to perpetuate the idea, for example, that certain social activities should have a privileged status as objects of public policy, and thus that the best way forward is to deconstruct the concept entirely and discard it as irredeemably conflated with market thinking.

Logically, this is a coherent argument, but I think it is a strategic error. The market concept of the economy functions politically as an element in a discursive formation that produces the view that no other way of meeting our needs is possible. In offering an alternative, our definitional strategy must be guided by our purposes. My purpose here is critical, driven by the need to recognise that non-market activities can often meet our needs just as well as those activities that are considered *economic* under the market-oriented definitions of the economy. It seems more viable to persuade people that our familiar concept of the economic needs to be expanded in this way than to invent a completely new non-economic terminology to encompass the market and social alternatives to it. This, of course, is a strategic rather than an ontological argument, and as such it is contextually specific – in some other circumstances we might indeed be better off discarding the concept of the economic altogether.

It is also an argument that, unlike the usual concepts of provisioning or the substantive economy, suggests a practical way of delimiting what activities we will call economic: the provision of goods and services through commodity exchange, plus the provision of equivalent goods and services through other social practices. This is still based on the concept of provisioning but provides us with a means of defining the *provisioning economy* with a little more precision. Nevertheless, it is not a definition of an objective social category with natural boundaries – as Nelson says, the boundaries are 'dialectical and fluid' (J.A. Nelson, 1993, p. 33) – but a political and perhaps a transitional way of identifying a field of study and a field of debate. The most thorough-going deconstructionists might object that we cannot be fully free of market thinking when our understanding of the economy is still linked to the market in this way. I agree. But the task we face today is not to be fully free of market thinking; it is to re-establish belief in the possibility of alternative social practices in a context where being fully free of market thinking is literally unthinkable.

The reality of the diverse economy

Once we have opened up our conception of the economy beyond the boundaries of the market, we can begin to see that we already have an economy that is vastly more diverse than the capitalist market monolith implicit in the dominant discourses of the economy. As Hart, Laville and Cattani have said, 'The human economy is already everywhere. People always insert themselves practically into economic life on their own account. What they do there is often obscured, marginalized or repressed by dominant economic institutions and ideologies' (Hart et al., 2010, p. 5). Alongside the commodity economy there is what the economist Kenneth Boulding calls a 'grants economy': an economy, not of exchange, but of one-way transfers (Boulding, 1973). Some of these transfers are provided by the state; some are forced; but a substantial proportion occur in what we may call the gift economy.

The contemporary gift economy is both extremely large and extremely important socially, but it has been badly neglected by the social sciences. Social scientists are often sceptical of claims that the gift economy is significant. But that scepticism, I suggest, derives at least in part from their usually unwitting acceptance of the dominant discourse of the economy. In conformity with that discourse giving, and production for giving, is generally excluded from economists' understandings of the economy without even an acknowledgement that the exclusion has taken place. The exceptions are gifts of money, and products which are produced and purchased as commodities in order to be given as gifts, which are generally of interest to economists only in their role as commodities, and cease to be of interest as soon as they have been purchased by the eventual giver of the gift. In one of the rare cases in which they have taken an interest, Joel Waldfogel dismisses most gift-giving as inferior to cash for use in the market, labelling Christmas gifts as an inefficient waste of resources (Waldfogel, 1993).

More surprisingly, even sociologists have tended to be dismissive of the gift economy. Under the influence of the Maussian tradition of anthropology, sociologists have tended to treat giving as a marginal hangover from a pre-modern precursor to the market economy (as noted by Cheal, 1988, p. 2; Godbout & Caillé, 1998, p. vii; Negru, 2010, pp. 198, 200). As David Graeber has put it, referring to the free gift economy as *communism*, 'The sociology of everyday communism is a potentially enormous field, but one which, owing to our peculiar ideological blinkers, we have been unable to write about because we have been largely unable to see it' (Graeber, 2011, p. 100). Ironically, this has often led sociologists to focus on much the same giving practices as those that marginally interest the economists, the giving of ritual gifts at birthdays, religious festivals and the like and to ignore other important giving practices (both of whom are criticised for this by Adloff & Mau, 2006, p. 96; e.g., Berking, 1999; and Cheal, 1988).

These are serious errors. As we have seen, we cannot conceive of alternatives to the market economy if we fail to challenge the view that the economy is identical with the commodity economy. Once we begin to think of the economy in terms of provisioning, it becomes clear that giving is an economic activity in much the same sense that exchange is an economic activity, and producing to give is an economic activity in much the same sense as producing for sale. And when we look at the vast range of provisioning activity that occurs in contemporary society, we soon find that an enormous proportion of it occurs outside the commodity economy.

That provisioning activity includes, for example, charitable giving, volunteering, blood and organ donation, ritual gifts on birthdays and other occasions, assistance to friends, neighbours, co-workers and indeed unknown passers-by, bequests, the creation of digital resources that are then freely shared with others on the Internet (including, for example, web pages, advice offered on Internet forums, Wikipedia pages, videos posted on YouTube and open-source software) and perhaps most substantially of all, sharing of resources and caring labour within the household.

Measuring the scale of such activity is problematic, since by definition it is not traded and thus not valued in monetary terms. Nevertheless, some hints are available in the literature as to the scale of some of these activities. For a first example, consider charitable giving or philanthropy. This is a worldwide phenomenon. Based on global poll data, the Charities Aid Foundation has estimated that in 2011, 45% of the world population gave help to strangers, 28% gave money to charity and 18% volunteered their time to an organisation (Charities Aid Foundation, 2012, p. 6). For a second, consider what we may call digital gifts. Just one element of this is the creation of free-to-view web pages. Chris Anderson's 'back-of-the-envelope' calculation of the unpaid effort expended on building these suggests that if it was paid at a modest rate it might cost $260 billion a year (Anderson, 2009, p. 168).

These are just tasters, though, for the main course; the most significant set of neglected economic practices, in terms of scale, is work done in the household – not just child care and household chores, but also for example DIY, growing crops and housing self-builds. While it is sometimes forced, more typically such labour can reasonably be regarded as a form of giving to those who benefit from it.[2] To the

---

[2] In a context where women are expected to perform domestic labour and this expectation is backed by powerful gender norms, it may sometimes be problematic whether this is a voluntary act and thus a gift. Clearly some women enter such relationships voluntarily, and some are happy to perform this role, under the influence of these gender norms (cf. Gibson-Graham, 2006b, pp. 224–5). Others may be under stronger compulsion, e.g. from domestic violence, and in such cases their work in the house must be regarded as forced labour rather than a gift. But much domestic labour is not done by women for the benefit of a dominant male partner anyway: much of it is expended on the care of children and the aged, or in single-sex relationships, or by men themselves, or in more egalitarian relationships (Fraad Resnick & Wolff, 1994, pp. 37–8; Gimenez, 1997; Matthaei, 1994, p. 48; Molyneux, 1979).

extent that this is so, we may take estimates of the scale of household labour as indicators of the scale of this set of giving practices (and even when it is forced, it is still not part of the commodity economy). Extensive statistical work has been done on this question, for example by Duncan Ironmonger, who concludes that in the case of Australia in 1992, and on reasonably conservative estimates of the value of household labour, 'half of economic production comes from the household and half from the market' (Ironmonger 1996, p. 53).[3] If these figures are at all representative of the world economy as a whole, and if we add the many other forms of giving practices, it is reasonable to conclude that the gift economy as a whole, rather than being a marginal survival of pre-modern life, is *at least similar in size* to the market economy in contemporary society.

But this is still not the full story of our contemporary economic diversity, because there are also many non-market and/or non-capitalist forms outside the gift economy. Gibson-Graham describe a vast range of contemporary economic activity that does not fit the traditional model of the capitalist firm (e.g. Gibson-Graham, 2006b, pp. xii–xv), arguing that 'if we theorized [the economy] as fragmented... we could begin to see a huge state sector... a very large sector of self-employed and family based producers (most noncapitalist), [and] a huge household sector' (Gibson-Graham, 2006b, p. 263). As they remind us, commodity production need not be done by capitalist businesses: alongside them we find what Laville calls the *social economy*, 'non-capitalist enterprises operating in the market' (Laville, 2010b, p. 230) such as co-operatives, the self-employed, and family businesses producing commodities without the conventional form of wage labour that is often seen as definitive of capitalism and we find state and non-profit enterprises who do employ wage labour but are not motivated by the expansion of capital.

None of this is intended to deny the central role of capitalism in important sectors of the contemporary economy. Capitalism certainly dominates mechanised industrial production, for example, and has driven the development of much of the technology that has transformed human lives over the last two or three centuries. Other

---

[3] Williams comes to broadly similar conclusions about a range of twenty developed economies: between the 1960s and the 1990s, 44.7% of all working time in these economies was unpaid (C. C. Williams, 2003).

commodity producers who compete in capitalist-dominated markets also find themselves subordinated in some ways to their logic, as when demand for the products of non-capitalist producers collapses due to a crisis in capitalist production, or the prices of their products are squeezed when their capitalist competitors shift production to low-wage countries. Nor is it to deny the enormous power of capitalist producers that arises from their sheer accumulation of monetary resources. The gift economy in particular does not accumulate such resources in the same way.[4] Nevertheless, despite its power, capitalism is very clearly not a comprehensive system saturating economic space. Rather, it is a discursively and politically dominant element in a *mixed economy of practices*: not, that is, a mixed economy of the state sector and the capitalist sector, but a far more diversely mixed economy than we are accustomed to imagining.

Real utopias

Once we have recognised that our existing economy is already a diverse mixed economy of practices, it becomes easier to see the value of nurturing and supporting alternative economic practices that provide, not comprehensive alternatives to capitalism, but limited and partial elements in the changing mix of practices in the diverse economy. Such a strategy, by promoting a pluralist understanding of the economy, is already 'a challenge to the monochrome version of the economy that neoliberal ideology describes as inevitable' (Laville, 2010a, p. 81). It may involve simply encouraging alternative practices that already exist (Hart et al., 2010, p. 6), or it may be more innovative. Again, important work has already been done in this area, notably under the banner of Erik Olin Wright's *Real Utopias* project.

A number of books by a variety of authors have appeared in the *Real Utopias* series, but Wright's programme is outlined most comprehensively in his own book *Envisioning Real Utopias* (Wright, 2010). Wright abandons the traditional Marxist approach to alternatives to capitalism, which is largely to leave the future in the lap of the party and/or the anonymous forces of history.[5] Instead, he argues, we need

---

[4] I thank Erik Olin Wright for pointing this out to me.
[5] An approach which has also been criticised, for example, by Andrew Sayer (1995, p. 14).

to think constructively about alternatives, and where possible start developing them now. These alternatives are his *real utopias*. They are utopian in the ethical sense that they are visions for 'social institutions free of oppression', visions that expand our imagination about what is possible (Wright, 2010, p. 6). But they are also real in the sense that a proposal only qualifies as a *real utopia* if we can make a good case that it is viable and achievable. An alternative is *viable* if it would, when implemented, generate 'the emancipatory consequences that motivated the proposal' (Wright, 2010, p. 21), and it is *achievable* if there is a plausible path by which we could arrive at it: real utopias must be what Wright calls 'destinations that have accessible waystations' (Wright, 2010, p. 6).[6] There is a strong resemblance here to Roy Bhaskar's concept of *concrete utopianism*: 'the exercise of constructing models of alternative ways of living on the basis of some assumed set of resources, counterbalancing actualism and informing hope' (Bhaskar, 1993, p. 395; M. Hartwig, 2007, pp. 74–5). Bhaskar's introduction of sets of resources here implies that our utopian constructions should be feasible and viable in plausibly imaginable circumstances, while the reference to counterbalancing actualism suggests the need, as Wright suggests, to 'expand our imagination' beyond what seems possible in the present circumstances. The purpose, Bhaskar writes, is 'to pinpoint the real, but non-actualized, possibilities inherent in a situation, thus inspiring grounded hope' (Bhaskar, 1994, p. 112, fn 1).

There are many attractive features of Wright's project. One is that he thinks carefully through the issues involved in emancipatory social science. It involves, he argues, 'three basic tasks: elaborating a systematic diagnosis and critique of the world as it exists; envisioning viable alternatives; and understanding the obstacles, possibilities, and dilemmas of transformation' and he stresses that 'all are necessary for a comprehensive emancipatory theory' (Wright, 2010, p. 10). A second is that he recognises the inherently ethical nature of both the task of critique and the development of alternatives and explicitly outlines the ethical basis on which he builds: a '*radical democratic egalitarian* understanding of justice' (Wright, 2010, p. 12). Third, and unlike Gibson-Graham, he recognises that capitalism has systemic tendencies

---

[6] Both this attention to viability and achievability, and Wright's explicit enunciation of the ethical agenda underlying his real utopias, develop arguments that have been offered by Andrew Sayer (1997).

to generate harms that are not purely dependent on the accompany-
ing discursive regime (Wright, 2010, p. 37). Fourth, he recognises the
resistance of the current system to change and examines strategies for
addressing the obstacles this generates (Wright, 2010, p. 273). Fifth, he
recognises that the future is open, rather than driven to some inevitable
conclusion by the contradictions of capitalism, and thus that a successful
emancipatory programme would not lead to a kind of perfect steady-
state society but rather to a continuing process of open contingent
development (cf. Bhaskar, 1993, p. 297; Wright, 2010, pp. 107–9).

What makes Wright's project particularly compatible with the argument being developed here, however, is that many of his utopias are
not totalising blueprints, not designs that purport to offer a new
'unified system... crowding out all other economic forms' (Gibson-
Graham, 2006b, p. 263), but medium-sized proposals for the redesign
of social institutions that can be mixed diversely (Wright, 2010, p. x).
Thus it is possible for many of these utopias to be developed as what he
calls 'interstitial processes' (Wright, 2010, p. 323). As Wright points
out, capitalism itself can be seen as 'having developed in the interstices
of feudal society' (Wright, 2010, p. 323). Capitalism was only able to
establish its discursive and political dominance, and only able
to develop to the extent that makes possible its systemic consequences,
as a result of the growth of capitalist practices within an earlier mixed
economy of practices. New economic practices, beyond perhaps simple
shifts in ownership, cannot be created on a large scale overnight and
expected to run smoothly the next day; on the contrary, they need time
to grow and mature. Hence any workable economic alternatives will
almost certainly need to develop initially within the current context.
There is, therefore, a strong parallel between Wright's argument and
the anarchist strategy of 'forming the structure of the new society
within the shell of the old' (Constitution of the Industrial Workers of
the World, cited in Wright, 2010, p. 325) and a major focus of his
project is identifying existing practices that can form the basis of real
utopias.[7] Indeed this vision also converges with more anarchist understandings of utopia in rejecting the idea of a single blueprint to be
imposed universally (Kinna, 2014).

---

[7] Wright does, however, distance himself from the anarchist view that
emancipatory struggles can ignore the state: for Wright, the state too is 'an arena
of struggle' that cannot be neglected (2010, pp. 335–6).

Wright examines both political and economic innovations but it is the economic examples that are relevant to this book. Some of his utopias would require large-scale change driven by state power, such as an unconditional basic income (Ackerman Alstott & Van Parijs, 2006; Wright, 2010, pp. 217–22), John Roemer's proposals for market socialism (Roemer, 1994; Wright, 2010, pp. 247–52), and Michael Albert's 'non-market participatory democratic economy' (Albert, 2003; Wright, 2010, pp. 252–65). Others, however, are based on actually existing economic practices, such as worker co-operatives, which he examines through the case of the Mondragón group in the Basque area of Spain (Wright, 2010, pp. 234–46), and social enterprises, where he focuses on the organisation of child and elder care in Quebec (Wright, 2010, pp. 204–15), and Wikipedia (Wright, 2010, pp. 194–203).

The very idea that such practices can develop within the existing economy clearly depends on the assumption that the economy is in some sense a mixed economy, as Wright recognises. Although he describes capitalism as 'a particular way of organizing the economic activities of a society' (Wright, 2010, p. 34), which seems to imply a view of capitalism as a totalising form, he nevertheless acknowledges that no society is ever purely capitalist, or indeed purely socialist (Wright, 2010, p. 124). He recognises work like domestic labour and volunteering as economic (Wright, 2010, p. 36), and thus as prompting a challenge to the view that we can characterise the economy as simply a capitalist economy. The presence of these other forms, and indeed of state enterprise, 'can be understood as reducing the "capitalisticness" of the economy', and yet he continues: 'to the extent that these variations all retain the core elements of the institution of private property in the means of production and markets as the central mechanism of economic production, they remain varieties of capitalism' (Wright, 2010, p. 36). Wright even recognises that this opens up what he calls 'a knotty theoretical problem': in these circumstances, 'what justifies still calling the system as a whole "capitalism"? How much non-capitalism is needed before the resulting hybrid is something entirely new rather than a hybrid form of capitalism as such?' (Wright, 2010, p. 36). He is unwilling to let go of the belief that our contemporary economy is a capitalist economy, but goes so far as to admit that 'The use of the simple, unmodified expression "capitalism" to describe an empirical case is thus shorthand for something like "a hybrid economic

structure within which capitalism is the predominant way of organizing economic activity"' (Wright, 2010, p. 125), and to recognise that
there is no simple answer to 'the question of what precisely is meant by
the claim that capitalism is 'dominant' within a hybrid configuration'
(Wright, 2010, p. 126).

Wright, then, goes a long way towards recognising what I have
called the mixed economy of practices, but there are still some crucial
absences from his work. First, like most social scientists, he remains
blinkered about the sheer extent of non-capitalist economic activity in
the existing economy, which allows him to maintain the view that the
contemporary economy is fundamentally a capitalist economy. Even
the term 'interstitial' that he uses to refer to alternative developments
within the existing system reveals a sense that those alternatives occupy
small gaps in a predominantly capitalist structure. Second, as a result,
he fails to see the need to theorise *all* economic systems as hybrid. In
this sense he still seems to cling to a version of the Marxist concept of
modes of production as historical stages that will be questioned in the
next chapter. And third, his neglect of the gift economy is also linked to
a neglect of the emancipatory possibilities offered by developments in
the gift economy.[8]

Conclusion

We face a constant stream of talk about the economy and the economic
that assumes, and encourages us to believe, that the economy is or
should be more or less identical with the commodity economy, and
perhaps even just the capitalist commodity economy. But if there was
economic activity before the market, and if it is desirable or even
possible for us to have an economy beyond the market, defining the
economic and the economy *in terms of* the market is an error. We must
think of the economy more widely, and this chapter has supported
arguments for thinking of it in terms of provisioning: the economy, in
other words, is those activities that provide the things that people need.
Although this does not give us a basis for distinguishing decisively
between the economic and the non-economic, it does perform the

[8] Although recently Wright has taken a step towards correcting this by including a
piece by Yochai Benkler in a special issue of *Politics and Society* on the Real
Utopias project (Benkler, 2013).

essential political function of opening our eyes to the alternative ways in which economic activities could be undertaken. Indeed, it helps to open our eyes to the many alternative, non-market and non-capitalist, ways in which economic activities are *already* undertaken, including in particular the enormous contemporary gift economy. That in turn opens the way to political strategies that seek to identify and grow better alternative ways of organising economic activity, such as Wright's real utopias.

Thinking in new ways about the economy will also require us to discard some cherished concepts from existing traditions of political economy, but those traditions nevertheless have important insights that we may preserve and reposition in a different tradition. The next two chapters ask what we must discard, and what we can usefully keep, from those existing traditions if we are to build a political economy that does full justice to the diversity of our actual and potential economies.

PART II

Political economies

3 | Beyond Marxist political economy

Introduction

For the last century and a half, critical approaches to political economy have been shaped and dominated by the Marxist tradition, and any alternative non-mainstream perspective is inevitably compared to and measured against the Marxist approach. But Marxism itself has become an obstacle to thinking creatively about the economy, not least because it is complicit in the discourse of the monolithic capitalist market economy that we must now move beyond. While Marxists have a very different perspective on the economy than mainstream economists, most still take it as read that there is only one economic form of any significance in the world today: a capitalist economy based on wage labour and the sale of commodities in the market. This chapter criticises two of the central pillars of Marxist political economy that have contributed to this perspective: first, the concept of *mode of production*, which has not only encouraged the view that our economy is overwhelmingly capitalist but also encapsulates an overly monolithic conception of capitalism itself; and second, Marx's *labour theory of value*, which in addition to many other flaws, tends to support the obsessive identification of capitalism with wage labour. As a consequence Marxists have failed to recognise that capitalism has developed new forms of making profit that do not fit with the classic Marxist model, including many that have emerged and prospered in the new digital economy.

Like some of my precursors in the search for an alternative political economy, I recognise that there are strengths as well as weaknesses in the Marxist tradition (e.g. Mark Harvey & Geras, 2013, p. 2; Sayer, 1995, p. viii). Marxist political economy has made important contributions to challenging capitalism and remains a major source of intellectual resources. But we cannot make productive use of those resources if we treat Marxism either as holy gospel or as anathema.

This chapter will acknowledge some of the elements of Marxist thought that should be reused in an alternative political economy, but also criticise some of those that must be discarded.

There is already considerable diversity and debate on the issues covered by this chapter *within* the Marxist tradition, and some of the arguments offered here have antecedents within these debates. Unlike those Marxists who have made similar arguments before, however, I regard them as fatal to the larger framework of the doctrine. Where it seems useful I will engage with these thinkers, but I do not propose to cover the whole range of internal Marxist debate on these questions. This chapter is not intended as a contribution to such debates. Instead it seeks, first, to show that as a tradition Marxism is inadequate to the task of building a political economy for today's world and, second, to analyse some of the most fundamental strengths and weaknesses of the tradition as a step towards a more viable synthesis. Before discussing modes of production and the labour theory of value, however, we need to consider what is involved in taking a *critical* approach to political economy.

Political economy as critique

By contrast with the mainstream tradition in economics and indeed some other heterodox traditions, Marxist political economy prides itself on being a *critical* political economy. Marx and Marxists have played an enormously important role in opening our eyes to the systematic harms that capitalism is responsible for, but they have also placed those harms in a wider context: an analysis of the causal processes at work in economies in general and capitalist economies in particular, which starts to explain those harms. To move beyond analysis, however, requires an ethical component to critique, and this section will argue that Marxism has never addressed this adequately.

Other critical traditions have also highlighted some of the harms for which capitalism is responsible, but Marxists have been in the forefront of exposing many of them. Let me divide them into five groups.

First, capitalism systematically marginalises the welfare of those without capital. Workers may be thrown into unemployment and poverty by economic crises, or because the owners of capital find some more profitable employment for it elsewhere. Benefit payments to those made unemployed as a result may be slashed or removed in order to reduce the burden of taxation on the wealthy. Peasants may be driven off their land so that it can be used in capitalist agriculture or mineral extraction, with no regard for the massive disruption to their lives and their unpreparedness for any other way of making a living. Noxious chemicals may be dumped into our living environments because it is more profitable to do so than to dispose of them responsibly.

Second, capitalism is massively inefficient as an economic system (Wright, 2010, pp. 54–65). Its economic crises leave both workers and production facilities sitting idle while needs go unmet for the products they could be creating. Public goods that would meet the needs of the whole population go unprovided because capitalism has no inherent mechanism to fund them, while frivolous goods for prosperous individuals are produced instead. Potentially public goods – such as digital forms of goods like books, music and film with negligible marginal costs – are subject to copyright restrictions that are designed to protect capitalist profit (and only secondarily the incomes of their creators) at the expense of public benefit.

Third, wage labour under capitalism tends to be highly alienated and alienating for the worker, who is deprived of control over their product and their work process and often turned into a machine-like cog in a production process (Marx, 1978a, pp. 70–9), contributing to stress, exhaustion, demotivation, depression, loss of self-esteem and self-belief and loss of hope in the future.

Fourth, capitalism tends to encourage distortions in our values that support the profits of capital at the price of the quality of life of the mass of the population. Michael Sandel has recently documented some of these (Sandel, 2013), but the most pervasive and perhaps the most damaging is consumerism: the belief that we can achieve fulfilment by buying things, particularly things that appear to demonstrate our high status to other people (Wright, 2010, pp. 65–9). Consumerist values legitimate excessive work, unnecessary purchasing, a whole system of production of goods with little real use-value while other needs go unmet, and pointless economic growth. In order to do so, they magnify what Marx calls commodity fetishism (Marx, 1954, pp. 76–87): Possessions come to matter more than relationships, to the cost of us all.

Finally, there are harms that are specific to particular historical variations of capitalism. Most recently, we have seen the neoliberal destruction of public services, in the name of private profit (Klein, 2007), and the effects of financial capitalism in routing more and more wealth to a tiny elite at the expense of providing for real social needs.

The effects of capitalism are not all negative. Marx himself recognised that capitalism was a dynamic force that has pushed forward technology and some aspects of material prosperity in utterly unprecedented ways. We must also be cautious about attributing harms specifically to capitalism. As both Andrew Sayer and Erik Olin Wright point out, some of these harms may also be generated by other versions of industrial society too (Sayer, 1995, chapter 1; Wright, 2010, p. 38). To distinguish between the harms that arise from capitalism and those that do not, we must consider the *mechanisms* that bring those harms about, and here too Marxism has made important contributions to political economy.

Above all, it was Marx who highlighted the insatiable appetite of capitalist businesses for growth in profit – for the accumulation of capital – and who saw that this arose from the inherent logic of capital (Marx & Engels, 1978, p. 476). The demand of investors to receive constantly increasing income from their investments, combined with the power of the market to punish firms that do not keep up with the innovations of their competitors, produces a constant drive to growth in both output and profit. The crisis tendencies of capitalism, its constant drive to increase productivity and lower costs whatever the consequences for workers and the local community, its constant pursuit of new opportunities for profit and expansion into new territories and new business areas, its total disregard for public goods that do not provide opportunities for private profit, and its constant encouragement of more and more consumption through the creation of new 'needs' and massive marketing and advertising campaigns; all of these are a product of this central mechanism. That is not to say that growth would never be an objective of other economic systems, but under capitalism it has become a fetish, an obsession with a socially constructed measure of success, that has come to dominate the capitalist sector of the economic system.

Marx also sometimes shows a balanced appreciation of how different mechanisms interact with each other, recognising like today's realist philosophers that economic mechanisms generate tendencies rather than exceptionless empirical regularities (Fleetwood, 2011). Capitalism's drive for accumulation, for example, creates a tendency for profit to grow, but that tendency need not always translate into the *actual* growth of profit. Other systemic mechanisms identified by Marx, such as a tendency of demand to fail to keep up with production under normal capitalist conditions of growth (or, if it is different, a tendency of production to outrun demand), may frustrate this tendency to growing accumulation. When he writes in these terms, he is consistent with what contemporary realists would recognise as a scientific approach to causality (see Chapter 4), though not all of Marx's accounts of the mechanisms of capital are as persuasive, or as carefully scientific, as we shall see when we examine the labour theory of value later in this chapter.

Whatever we think of Marx as a scientist, a critical political economy cannot only be a scientific enterprise. It is also inescapably a moral enterprise: criticisms like those he made of capitalism are unavoidably founded on a set of ethical or moral attitudes to the world.[1] As Steven Lukes has made abundantly clear, 'Marx's and marxist writings abound in moral judgements, implicit and explicit' (1985, p. 3).[2] Norman Geras makes the same point: 'Normative viewpoints lie upon, or just beneath the surface of, his writings, and they lie there abundantly' (Geras, 1985, p. 62). Marx was inspired by a vision of an ideal society 'in which, under conditions of abundance, human beings can achieve self-realization in a new, transparent form of social unity' (Lukes, 1985, p. 9), and 'his whole life's work is full of critical judgements that only make sense against the background of this ideal of transparent social unity and individual self-realization' (Lukes, 1985, p. 11). This vision, and the critical judgements of existing society that flow from it, have inspired Marxist thinkers, activists and politicians ever since, lying behind the enormous energy and commitment they have devoted to the pursuit of Marx's ideal.

Yet, as Lukes and Geras also point out, Marx and his followers have constantly *denied* that theirs is an ethical enterprise, claiming 'that morality is a form of ideology, and thus social in origin, illusory in content, and serving class interests' and thus 'that marxism is opposed to all moralizing and rejects as out of date all moral vocabulary, and that the marxist critique of both capitalism and political economy is not moral but scientific' (Lukes, 1985, p. 3; also see Geras, 1985, p. 62).

---

[1] I use the terms *ethical* and *moral* interchangeably throughout.
[2] Lukes provides substantial textual evidence to back up both this claim and the one discussed in the next paragraph (1985, chapter 2).

There is some justification for their belief that existing moralities are ideological: concepts of individual rights and in particular property rights, for example, have often been used to justify massive inequality in capitalist societies. And there is considerable justification for their belief that these elements of morality have become established because they support the interests of powerful economic classes. This belief in turn reflects Marx's theory that 'the social, political and intellectual life process' (Marx, 1978b, p. 4) – or superstructure – of a society are ultimately the product of developments in its economic base. At one level, then, Marxists appear to be taking a scientific approach to the moral values that they reject.

Yet the idea that Marxism's critique is not moral but scientific is an illusion and a self-deception that has made a major contribution to the ruthless disregard for human flourishing that marked Stalinism in the USSR and many of the other communist states of the twentieth century (Geras, 1985, p. 85). By *substituting* so-called science for ethics, Marx effectively denied the need to judge political decisions by ethical standards, let alone to consider what the ethical standards of a progressive political movement should be. Thus communists driven by a fundamentally ethical commitment to a better world were induced to believe that the shining vision of an ideal society was justification enough for the imposition of any human sacrifice whatsoever on those who, by the standards of the prevailing version of Marxist theory, were taken to be standing in its way.[3]

The claim that Marxism's critique is not moral but scientific is doubly flawed. At a purely logical level, criticism of existing society could not be founded simply on the 'scientific' finding that its morality is entirely ideological.[4] Even if such a finding could be scientifically justified, it would not entitle us to make the slightest criticism; to do so we would also need grounds to believe that an ideological morality is *wrong*, and this is itself a moral argument. Critique, in other words, rests on moral standards that are *not* supportive of the existing society: we cannot develop a critique of ideology unless we have moral reasons

---

[3] The power of this force is movingly illustrated in the words of Lev Kopelev that introduce Lukes's book (Kopelev, 1979, pp. 32–4; cited in Lukes, 1985, pp. viii–ix).

[4] In saying so, I implicitly reject Roy Bhaskar's arguments for *emancipatory critique* and *ethical naturalism* (1986, pp. 177–80). I have offered explicit grounds for doing so elsewhere (Elder-Vass, 2010a).

for such a critique that are to some extent independent of that ideology. If, then, Marxists believe that ideology is pervasive and also that its critique is possible they are guilty of a failure of reflexivity and a performative contradiction: an implicit claim to moral independence that explicitly denies moral independence is possible.

The recognition that critique is necessarily based on an ethical stance, however, opens up a range of further issues. In particular, it should lead us to ask *what* ethical stance any given critique is based on, and this in turn raises the question of whether the stance concerned can be justified and the wider question of how ethical stances in general can be justified. Marx's stance was for the proletariat, or rather, for what he imagined to be the long-term interest of the proletariat in overthrowing capitalism and replacing it with a dimly imagined communist alternative,[5] but he refused to consider these other issues. Mainstream Marxists have often followed him in believing that any questioning of the ethical issues this raises is simply counter-revolutionary. These are all errors. Not only the long-term objectives of progressive movements, but also their critiques of existing society and their practical political decisions depend on taking ethical positions on a vast range of issues.

As Marx himself recognised, our ethics are socially shaped and that shaping varies over time because it is influenced by a changing social environment. One consequence is that we can never consider ethical claims to be cast in stone, to be so well established that they are beyond dispute. Despite this, I suggest that it is possible – always provisionally – to justify an ethical basis for a critical political economy, by allowing that basis to be opened up to a certain kind of debate. As I have argued in greater depth elsewhere, we can and should base our ethics on the kind of agreement that can be secured in a process that Habermas describes as *discourse ethics* (Elder-Vass, 2010a).[6] Habermas argues that moral reasoning should be a discursive process, one that allows all those who are affected by an issue to participate. To deliver genuine agreement, such a process would require truthfulness on the parts of the participants but also that everyone concerned is freely able to participate, and to have their views considered with

---

[5] DeMartino identifies two key normative principles in Marx's work: his strong antipathy to exploitation and his well-known slogan summarising the ethical stance of communism: 'From each according to his ability, to each according to his needs' (DeMartino, 2003, p. 5).

[6] The remainder of this paragraph, and the next two, draws heavily on this paper.

equal weight and respect, regardless of differences in power. As Habermas puts it, 'If the participants genuinely want to convince one another, they must ... allow their ... responses to be influenced solely by the force of the better argument' (Habermas, 1993, p. 31).

Achieving such conditions in their pure form may never be possible, but Habermas's argument does give us some standards by which to assess actual processes of moral debate. To the extent that such processes are (i) conducted honestly and sincerely; (ii) open to participation by all affected parties or at least their genuine representatives and (iii) not distorted by the differential power of the parties (Habermas, 2003, pp. 107–8), it is reasonable for us to take the ethical judgements made or validated in them as sound – although always potentially open to further revision. And there have been some long-running international processes of ethical reasoning and debate, notably those conducted around the various rights initiatives of the United Nations, that despite their many imperfections have come somewhere near to Habermas's standard in the sense that the views of at least some groups of the less powerful have been effectively heard (Elder-Vass, 2010a, pp. 52–3).[7] As a minimum, the moral claim that we should value all humans is widely accepted as a result. This is a claim, in other words, that in a pragmatic sense meets the requirements of Habermas's discourse ethics.[8]

Furthermore, if we can take the argument that we should value all humans as discursively justified, then it becomes possible for us to construct further ethical arguments that take this as a premise. For example, one plausible argument constructed on this premise is that all humans have basic objective needs such as food, water, clothing and shelter without which they could not survive, hence there is an ethical obligation to support the meeting of such needs (Assiter & Noonan, 2007). A further extension of the principle that we should value all humans is embodied in the *capabilities approach* developed by Amartya Sen and Martha Nussbaum (see Gasper, 2004, chapter 7).

---

[7] The major flaws in the UN's human rights stance, such as its neglect of LGBT rights, arise from failure to open the process sufficiently to the socially marginalised and remain the focus of continuing debate (J. Morgan, 2005; Woodiwiss, 2003).

[8] I should stress that it is because we can reasonably argue that this value has, to the extent pragmatically possible, met the requirements of the discourse principle that I consider it judgementally rational – *not* simply because it is widely accepted.

This approach focuses on what is required in order to provide people with 'a bare minimum of what respect for human dignity requires', arguing that to do this we must provide them with a certain number of 'central human capabilities', such as life, health, bodily integrity, senses, imagination and emotions (Nussbaum, 2000, pp. 5, 78–80). Nussbaum is not seeking to impose this view monologically. On the contrary, she has engaged in 'years of cross-cultural discussion' (Nussbaum, 2000, p. 76), particularly with groups of women concerned with the needs of the poor and powerless in less-developed countries, hence her approach has been reshaped in a process that bears a striking similarity with the requirements of Habermas's discourse principle (Nussbaum, 2000, p. 104).

These kinds of processes can provide us with something that is still missing from the Marxist tradition:[9] 'a fully elaborated ethical critique and alternative' (Mark Harvey & Geras, 2013, p. 61), built on a coherent approach to ethics. We cannot build a case for alternatives to our current economy without having an ethical basis for our critique of what exists today. Still, although an ethical foundation is essential, political economy cannot be built solely on this basis. It must *also* include a scientific element.

Modes of production

The concept of modes of production plays a central role in Marx's attempt to construct a scientific account of economic systems. This is a concept that has often seemed relatively uncontroversial. The argument that capitalism replaced feudalism as the dominant mode of production in Europe, for example, is a staple of sociological accounts of modernity, and the idea that social progress consists in replacing capitalism in its turn remains a central plank of radical politics. But this section will suggest that once we dig deeper the concept is highly problematic.

The classic source of Marx's concept is the 1859 *Preface*, which outlines in one long paragraph Marx's theory of history. After introducing the 'relations of production' and the 'productive forces', Marx tells us that 'The sum total of these relations of production constitutes

[9] Although there have been efforts to extract ethical arguments from Marx's work, notably by George DeMartino (DeMartino, 2003).

the economic structure of society, the real foundation, on which rises a legal and political superstructure and to which correspond definite forms of social consciousness. The *mode of production* of material life conditions the social, political, and intellectual life process in general' (Marx, 1978b, p. 4 emphasis added). And a little later: 'In broad outlines Asiatic, ancient, feudal, and modern bourgeois *modes of production* can be designated as progressive epochs in the economic formation of society' (Marx, 1978b, p. 5 emphasis added). Even in these first two references to the concept a degree of ambiguity can be detected. In the first reference, mode seems to refer rather loosely to the manner in which production occurs (cf. Althusser & Balibar, 2009, p. 235; Cohen, 1978, p. 79). By the second, it has become identified with some specific economic structures that define successive stages in the development of society.

On the whole it is the latter usage that has prevailed in the Marxist tradition. Étienne Balibar, for example, despite his acknowledgement that *mode* has something of the sense of *manner*, identifies modes of production with states of the economic structure, and tells us that 'the history of society can be reduced to a discontinuous succession of modes of production' (Althusser & Balibar, 2009, p. 228). Similarly, in a formulation that makes sense only if modes of production dominate societies, Althusser proposes that different modes of production produce a different 'society-effect' (Althusser & Balibar, 2009, p. 71).

While there has often been some recognition that particular societies might include elements of multiple modes of production, most Marxists have tended to marginalise this issue. As Hodgson puts it, 'Although he acknowledged their real existence, when analysing the capitalist system in *Capital*, Marx ignored all the non-capitalist elements in that system. This was not merely an initial, simplifying assumption. They were assumed away at the outset, never to be reincorporated at a later stage of the analysis' (Hodgson, 1999, p. 124). More recently, the work of Althusser and Balibar examines the relation between the economic contradictions of capitalism and contradictions in the superstructure, but largely ignores the problem of the relation between different economic forms, except as a feature of periods of transition between the epochs of one mode of production and another. Balibar does hypothesise 'modes of production which have never existed in an *independent* form' such as commodity production by individuals, but without any consideration of how they might appear in combination with other modes of production in practice (Althusser & Balibar, 2009, p. 242).

Thinkers in the Althusserian Marxist tradition have sometimes argued that there may be multiple modes of production within what they refer to as a *social formation* (Hindess & Hirst, 1972, pp. 46–7), but they tend to see these as standing in a relation of dominance and subordination. John Harrison, for example, in postulating a 'housework mode of production' (Harrison, 1973, p. 38), 'argues that within a determinate social formation there may be subordinate modes distinct from the dominant, constitutive modes' – subordinate modes that may be vestiges of past modes, initial traces of future modes, or client modes 'created or co-opted by the dominant mode to fulfil certain functions' (Molyneux, 1979, p. 8). Molyneux criticises Harrison for offering an argument that is inconsistent with both Balibar's and more traditional conceptions of the mode of production because this household mode 'could never become generalised' to the whole economy (Molyneux, 1979, p. 17). There is a strong sense here that for most Marxists the mode of production is to be seen as a single dominant form of social relations that either constitutes or dominates all economic practice within the social formation concerned.

From a somewhat different tradition of Marxism, G.A. Cohen, while using the term *mode of production* rather differently, substitutes the concept of *social forms* and uses it in much the same way as these other thinkers use *mode of production*. For Cohen capitalism, feudalism, and the like are successive social forms of economic structure, and although he acknowledges the theoretical possibility of diverse social relations coexisting within an economic structure, he sees Marx as assuming that 'the production relation binding immediate producers will be broadly invariant across a single social formation' (Cohen, 1978, pp. 77–8). Cohen does recognise that there is always likely to be *some* mix of production relations in any given social formation, but immediately trivialises this possibility by arguing that 'In real and stable economic structures, one kind of production relation binding immediate producers is dominant' (Cohen, 1978, pp. 77–8).

This treatment of modes of production as economic forms that dominate a society, while other forms are essentially marginal, is clearly problematic in the light of the previous chapter of this book. As Andrew Sayer has argued, 'actual economies combine several different forms of organization' (also see Hodgson, 1999, p. 147;

Sayer, 1995, p. 182). The coexistence of economic forms is not a purely transitional phenomenon but a permanent feature of all complex economies, and even our contemporary society is one where capitalist economic activity is in the minority. Hence we need to retheorise this space that is currently occupied by an essentially monolithic concept of the mode of production.

Perhaps the most substantial attempts by Marxists to deal with the coexistence of multiple modes of production are those in the development literature. Development theorists, concerned with what they saw as transitions to capitalism, had to consider the question of the transitional coexistence of capitalism with earlier forms. Pierre-Philippe Rey, for example, used the concept of *articulation* of modes of production[10] to refer to such coexistence, and to theorise the ways in which capitalism depends on these earlier forms during its initial development in any given economy (Foster-Carter, 1978, pp. 56–9).[11] Arguments like these seem to imply a third possible definition of mode of production: as an economic form but not one that necessarily dominates the epoch in which we find it. But some Marxists who take this approach continue to treat the whole economic system as *characterised* by one mode. This is the view taken, for example, by Erik Olin Wright, who nevertheless recognises that this creates a problem: 'when you have an economic system that combines capitalist elements with various kinds of non-capitalist elements, what justifies calling the system as a whole "capitalism"?' (Wright, 2010, p. 36, fn 5). This kind of argument seems to require a theory of multiple levels of economic form in any given society (Foster-Carter, 1978, p. 75), though some Marxists are extremely resistant to this idea. For example, world-systems theorists like Andre Gunder Frank and Immanuel Wallerstein have argued that 'there is but a single "world-system"; and it is capitalist through and through' (Foster-Carter, 1978, p. 49).

Disagreements like these are also reflected in disagreements about other aspects of the concept of a mode of production. Marx's discussion in the *Preface* identifies the mode of production with the 'relations of production' in a society, but which *aspect* of the relations of

---

[10] The term *articulation* comes from Althusser and Balibar, though they did not use it to refer to relations between different modes of production (Foster-Carter 1978, 54).

[11] Similar arguments have been made by the regulation school theorists (e.g. Aglietta – see Chapter 5).

production defines the mode of production? As far as capitalism is concerned, Cohen suggests that there are two apparently different – but in practice equivalent – aspects: the first approach is that capitalism can be defined by the use of wage labour; the second approach is that it is defined by the fact that 'production serves the accumulation of capital' (Cohen, 1978, p. 181). Cohen claims that these two aspects are historically found together (Cohen, 1978, p. 182) but he cannot avoid conceding that there are cases where they are not, such as plantation slavery in the Confederate states before the American Civil War (Cohen, 1978, p. 185). The fudge of saying that the two aspects are often found together gives us no help in determining whether this case, in which capital was accumulated by the exploitation of slave labour rather than wage labour, should properly be regarded as capitalist or not. Nor does it help us with many other cases, such as the employment of wage labour by the state to provide free services to its citizens, where we have the opposite case: wage labour without capital accumulation.

Perhaps the most common response to this problem amongst Marxists is to follow Cohen's path and assume that we can ignore the discrepancies, and treat capitalism as the *combination* of wage labour with production oriented to the accumulation of capital. But this response utterly undermines the argument that there is a single mode of production in contemporary societies, or the contemporary world system, as it is abundantly clear (as argued in Chapter 2) that a vast amount of production does not conform with this model. The argument that there is a single mode of production can only be sustained by loosening the definition of capitalism considerably, which is usually done by extending it to include any sort of activity that results in the accumulation of capital. David Harvey offers one version of this approach when he argues that capitalists

take on many different personae. Finance capitalists look to make more money by lending to others in return for interest. Merchant capitalists buy cheap and sell dear. Landlords collect rent because the land and properties they own are scarce resources. Rentiers make money from royalties and intellectual property rights. Asset traders swap titles (to stocks and shares for example), debts and contracts (including insurance) for a profit. Even the state can act like a capitalist, for example, when it uses tax revenues to invest in infrastructures that stimulate growth and generate even more tax revenues (D. Harvey, 2011, p. 40).

But Harvey quickly pushes all these varied kinds of 'capitalism' aside: 'But the form of capital circulation that has come to dominate from the mid-eighteenth century onwards is that of industrial or pro- duction capital' (D. Harvey, 2011, p. 40). And with that he returns to analysing capitalism in the form of wage labour employed in the production of commodities.

Jairus Banaji offers a more considered and consistent version of the argument. He identifies capitalist relations of production with 'the accumulation of capital' and recognises that this means that capitalist activity 'can be based on forms of exploitation that are typically *precapitalist*' (Banaji, 2012, p. 9). Thus, for example, 'modern plantation slavery was certainly a form of capitalism' (Banaji, 2012, p. 353 also see 10, 67–9) – as indeed Marx himself concluded (Banaji, 2012, p. 67; Cohen, 1978, p. 185). Wage labour, then, is only one of the possible 'forms of exploitation' under capitalism, and Banaji also recognises that wage labour may occur outside capitalism (Banaji, 2012, p. 54). There is no necessary reason, though, to assume as Banaji does that non-waged forms of work that contribute to the accumulation of capital are essentially *precapitalist*. As we shall see in the later chapters of this book, unpaid work, freely contributed in the digital economy, can also play this role. Although the industrial capitalism of Marx's day was overwhelmingly based on wage labour, capitalism in its most advanced, as well as its least advanced, forms, does not depend exclusively on wage labour nor can it be defined by the role of wage labour in it.

It thus seems more coherent to define capitalism, as Banaji does, by its pursuit of capital accumulation irrespective of the means: as *'production for the sake of accumulating capital'* (Cohen, 1978, p. 181 emphasis in original). One benefit of doing so is that we can continue to accept the arguments made in the previous section that capitalism is characterised by a number of systemic tendencies that arise from its ceaseless drive to accumulate capital. Nevertheless, this approach to defining capitalism has a number of implications that severely and perhaps fatally disrupt the Marxist concept of a mode of production.

The first is that we do not have equivalent ways of defining other modes of production. What equivalent to 'the pursuit of capital accu- mulation' might define feudalism, or the slave mode of production, or the Asiatic mode, as Marx understands them? Marx discusses a hypothetical case in which a feudal noble employs a wage labourer to produce commodities but for Marx this is not a capitalist activity because 'this exchange takes place only... for the sake of superfluity, for luxury consumption', and thus not for the accumulation of capital (Banaji, 2012, p. 93; Marx, 1973, p. 469). But we could hardly say that feudalism was defined by the pursuit of superfluity or that this distinguished it from other modes of production. Despite this example, feudalism, for Marx, usually appears to be defined by serfdom (Banaji, 2012, p. 353) and the slave mode by slavery, both of which are what Banaji calls forms of exploitation, and indeed forms of exploitation that are consistent with the pursuit of capital accumulation. Once we recognise that capitalism cannot be defined by wage labour, and thus that modes of production are not defined by forms of labour relation, then feudalism cannot be defined by serfdom, nor the slave mode of production by slavery. Or, if they are, they are a different kind of thing than capitalism, and we could have empirical cases that were *both* capitalist and feudal modes, or capitalist and slave modes, simultaneously.

But Banaji's work also seems to cast doubt on other aspects of non-capitalist modes of production. He suggests that the Asiatic mode 'was a sort of default-category, the most sense Marx and Engels could make of societies whose history was largely inaccessible to them' (Banaji, 2012, p. 349). The phenomenon of serfdom, which seems central to the feudal mode, was far from universal in so-called feudal societies (Banaji, 2012, p. 92) and did not appear until six or seven hundred years after the fall of Rome, which supposedly marked the end of the previous, slave, mode of production in Europe (Banaji, 2012, p. 352). And historians now reject the idea that slavery was the universal form of production in the 'ancient economy' (Banaji, 2012, pp. 351–2). Although Banaji's objective is to develop a more sophisticated understanding of modes of production rather than to abolish the concept, it's hard to avoid the conclusion that the concept of mode of production is far too simplistic to characterise economic forms across broad sweeps of history.

If the accumulation of capital can proceed through plantation slavery, through wage labour in factories, and through the sale of advertising placed on free-to-view web pages, to mention only three of the many forms of labour structure it uses, then we must question whether capitalism is a fully adequate concept with which to theorise all the important variations of economic form. At one level of abstraction, all of these forms may indeed share some characteristics – those derived from their character as enterprises oriented to the accumulation of capital. At a more concrete level, however, they are radically different, and both logic and experience suggest that each has very different systemic tendencies. If this is so, then we cannot attribute the dynamics of capitalism in general to forces that arise from only one of these forms. The drive to accumulate, which is the common characteristic of all of these forms, may drive some common tendencies of them all. But much of Marx's analysis including the labour theory of value is based on wage labour in industrial capitalism. In social formations where this is not the predominant form we will need to consider the dynamics that are generated by other forms than wage labour if we are to have a scientific understanding of capitalism.

Nor does extending the definition of capitalism in this way exhaust the diversity of economic form in the contemporary economy because there are also multiple forms of production that are not even capitalist in the sense of being oriented to the accumulation of capital. Subsistence farming, caring work in the household, the provision of health services by the state (where that still occurs), and baby-sitting circles, to name just a few examples, are not capitalist in even this minimal sense. But nor can they be subsumed under some other epochal mode of production.

It seems, therefore, that we need concepts for at least three levels of economic form: (i) the character of the whole economy or world-system, which is clearly not a purely capitalist system but rather one that also encompasses non-capitalist economic forms; (ii) capitalism as a rather varied form of economy that shares the core characteristic of being driven by the accumulation of capital; and (iii) lower level (more concrete) forms, whether capitalist or not, that can be characterised by particular forms of organisation of the productive practices (these are the forms that I propose to theorise using the concept of *appropriative practices*). The second of these is perhaps the closest to a 'mode of production' in something like the terms intended by Marx, though if capitalism is the only instance of form at this level leaves it rather questionable whether we need a generic term for such forms.[12] Perhaps there is a case for retaining the term *mode of production* to refer to rough periodisations of economic practice,

---

[12] If apples were the only kind of fruit, would we need a word for fruit?

but this is not a concept that is sufficiently well defined to bear any more significant theoretical burden.

The labour theory of value

This book develops a framework for understanding and evaluating the appropriation of the benefits from economic activity, and thus competes with equivalent frameworks in the existing traditions of political economy. The Marxist tradition's framework is based on Marx's labour theory of value and exploitation. This section will briefly explain and criticise his theory of value and criticise the ethical structure of his theory of exploitation. Marx's theory has already generated an enormous critical literature (from Marxist as well as non-Marxist scholars) and much of my argument will repeat themes from that literature. My purpose here, however, is not to engage in arcane debates over the details of Marx's argument but rather to explain those concerns that lead me to believe we need an alternative theory, or theories, of appropriation.[13]

The definitive statement of Marx's theory of value can be found in the first chapter of the first volume of *Capital* (Marx, 1954). He begins with the commodity: an item produced for sale on the market. Every commodity, he argues, has two essential factors, which he calls its use-value and its exchange-value (which he usually calls just 'value'). The use-value of a commodity is simply the usefulness it has for us as a result of the ways in which its physical properties enable it to be used. While the use-value of different commodities of the same type can be compared quantitatively, such as the length of two different pieces of linen, the use-values of different kinds of commodity are qualitatively different and thus quantitatively incommensurable. Yet commodities of different kinds can be exchanged for each other, and in doing so a value equation is made between them – x litres of corn is treated as equivalent to y kilos of iron, for example. There is thus a sense in which their values in exchange can be quantitatively compared, even though

---

[13] I use *appropriation* in its lay sense, meaning *to take possession of something*, which is thus roughly equivalent to *distribution*: like a theory of distribution, a theory of appropriation discusses who obtains what benefits from a process. This contrasts with Ellerman's usage of *appropriation* to mean *creating a new property right* (Ellerman, 1991). Ellerman's sense may be in tune with at least some of Marx's own usages of the term, but it is archaic today.

their use-values cannot. Therefore, Marx argues 'the exchange-values of commodities must be capable of being expressed in terms of something common to them all, of which thing they represent a greater or less quantity' (Marx, 1954, p. 45). The only common property that all commodities have, according to Marx, is that of 'being products of labour' (Marx, 1954, p. 45).[14] Marx recognises that they are, however, products of different kinds of labour, and in order to make them quantitatively comparable we must abstract from this difference, and compare them in terms of the amount of 'human labour in the abstract' contained in them (Marx, 1954, p. 46).[15] He continues:

A use-value, or useful article, therefore, has value only because human labour in the abstract has been embodied or materialised in it. How, then, is the magnitude of this value to be measured? Plainly, by the quantity of the value-creating substance, the labour, contained in the article. The quantity of labour, however, is measured by its duration, and labour-time in its turn finds its standard in weeks, days and hours (Marx, 1954, p. 46).

He qualifies this argument, first by recognising that the product of a lazy or inefficient worker who takes, say, twice as long as the average worker to produce an equivalent commodity is not worth twice as much as a consequence. It is not the actual labour time embodied in a product but the 'labour-time socially necessary for its production' that determines its value (Marx, 1954, p. 47). And secondly, by recognising that skilled labour may create more value than unskilled labour, so that the former must be equated to a multiple of the former when we are calculating value.[16] With these adjustments, he can say that the

---

[14] Although he ignores several other equally plausible candidates (Cutler Hindess Hussain & Hirst, 1977, p. 58).

[15] The entire theory depends on this move of abstracting from specific kinds of labour, otherwise like use-values the different kinds of labour are qualitatively different and thus quantitatively incommensurable. But Marx fails to explain why it is *valid* to abstract from the qualitative differences of different kinds of labour when he has argued that it is *not* valid to abstract from the qualitative differences of different kinds of use-value (Cutler et al., 1977, p. 58; Mark Harvey & Geras, 2013, pp. 37–8).

[16] Böhm-Bawerk argues that in making this adjustment Marx uses the different wage rates of different forms of labour to determine their relative contributions to value creation (see Marx, 1959, p. 142) but this means that he is using exchange-ratios to determine value when his theory claims to use value to determine exchange-ratios (Conway, 1987, pp. 88–9; Cutler et al., 1977, p. 63).

value of a commodity is determined by the amount of socially necessary abstract labour power it contains.

Marx inherited the broad outlines of the labour theory of value from an earlier tradition of political economy, and in particular from the English economist David Ricardo (McLellan, 1980, pp. 39, 89). One of his major innovations, however, was to apply the same theory to the value of labour power itself (McLellan, 1980, pp. 90–1). He argued that, just as the value of a commodity was determined by the amount of labour required to produce it, the value of labour power was determined by the amount of labour required to reproduce it: in other words, by the labour power required to produce the commodities needed to sustain the worker in the long term (including the cost of raising new workers, which was born by the worker's family) (Marx, 1954, pp. 167–8, 188). That cost in turn was contingent on social standards, and could be measured by the normal wage paid to a worker (Marx, 1954, p. 168).[17] This in turn gave Marx a way to explain the profits made by the capitalist who employed the worker to produce the commodities: as long as the worker was made to work longer than was required to pay her wages, then the value of goods produced by the worker was greater than the value of her labour power, and *surplus value* was created in the process of production – the total value was expanded, and the capitalist (typically) appropriated this surplus value as profit. This gave Marx an account not only of how the rewards of the productive worker were determined but also those of the capitalist entrepreneur, and both accounts were based on the same theory of value that explained the ratios at which different commodities were exchanged.

Finally, this also provided Marx with his concept of exploitation. Abstracting from various complexities, Marx defined exploitation to mean that a worker is exploited whenever she is paid less than the value produced by her labour, even if she is paid a wage equal to the value of her labour power (Marx, 1954, pp. 208–9). Marx presents this as a purely technical definition of exploitation, implying that no ethical evaluation is involved.

---

[17] As Leahy points out, real wages are actually determined by a broad range of factors, and bear little relation to the labour time that is required to reproduce labour power (2013, p. 4). Once again, Marx's theory falls back on actual prices – this time wage rates – to determine labour value, undermining itself.

Marx's theory of value, however, is highly problematic. Let us first consider a number of issues that relate to its status as a scientific or explanatory theory. The first is that it's not at all clear what it's a theory *of*. One might think that a theory of exchange value would seek, and claim, to explain the prices that are achieved when commodities are exchanged. However, following Adam Smith, Marx did not regard exchange-value as the actual price of a commodity, or even as the rate at which it could actually be exchanged for some other commodity (Kolakowski, 1981, p. 269). But if value is not equal to price, then what is it? This is not explained by Marx, but in the earlier tradition of political economy he makes use of value is seen as the normal level around which the price of a commodity fluctuates, and in a sense the price at which it *ought* to be exchanged (Mark Harvey & Geras, 2013, p. 6; Martins, 2013, p. xiv). Marx seems to exclude short-term price fluctuations from the concept of value, and he spends a great deal of effort in volume three of *Capital* explaining how the equalisation of rates of profit across different industrial sectors can cause prices to diverge systematically from values, but what is never made clear is the precise relation between value and price (Mirowski, 1991, pp. 179–80).

Because the relation of price to value is never clarified the theory of value is effectively immune from any sort of empirical test. If we can never say with precision what the value of a commodity is, then we can never validate the labour theory of what determines that value. But this state of affairs also means that the theory of value is utterly value-less when it comes to explaining the *actual* benefits that workers and capitalists receive from the proceeds of production. Neither actual prices nor actual wages are predicted or explained by the theory, and it is these, rather than some mysterious notion of value, that determine what workers and capitalists receive. A theory that expresses exploitation as the difference between two non-empirical notional values is of no relevance whatsoever to the real world.[18] As Böhm-Bawerk argued many years ago, to be useful the theory of value 'must account for the

---

[18] Nevertheless, Marx's macro-economic theories may not be affected by this problem, because when values are aggregated across the whole economy he sees them as equal to the aggregate of prices, and when surplus value is aggregated he sees it as equal to the aggregate of profit. Conway is therefore wrong to argue that the failure of the labour theory of value invalidates all of Marx's economic theory (Conway, 1987, pp. 82, 85).

exchange relations that actually pertain in capitalism' (Cutler Hindess Hussain & Hirst, 1977, p. 53). Things would be different if it could be argued that value is an underlying force that, although different from price, exerts a determinate and decisive effect on prices, but no explanatory mechanism has been offered to justify such a claim.

A second problem is that the labour theory depends on an utterly implausible ontology of value. Labour time is taken to be able to influence exchange value because each commodity has 'human labour in the abstract... embodied or materialised in it' (Marx, 1954, p. 46). Marx constantly repeats the point that labour isn't just used to produce the commodity but actually 'contained in the article' (Marx, 1954, p. 46), another belief he took over from Ricardo (Arthur, 2001, p. 217). Many contemporary Marxists continue to insist that labour is somehow present as substance in the commodities it has produced (perhaps even as an 'immaterial substance' (Ehrbar, 2007, p. 237)), thus providing an objective basis, within the commodities themselves, for their exchange value (e.g. Ehrbar, 2007; Engelskirchen, 2007). The difficulty that this idea is designed to solve is that price is clearly determined at the time of exchange, but a labour theory of value requires that value be the outcome of the process of production and not the process of exchange: another idea that remains a staple of mainstream Marxism (e.g. D. Harvey, 2011, p. 101). But the idea that labour is somehow contained in an object it has produced is bizarre. Labour is a process, not a substance, and although it may reconfigure the substance of an object, it does not and cannot introduce any new labour substance into it.[19] Value, conceived of as a residue of labour in a commodity, is purely a figment of the value theorist's imagination.

The problem only gets worse once we recognise that is not concrete but abstract labour that Marx takes to determine value (Elson, 1979, pp. 135–8, 159). As Cutler et al have pointed out it is only at the point of exchange that some sort of equivalence is or could be established between the different kinds of labour that have contributed to producing different commodities (Cutler et al., 1977, p. 89). The implication is that abstract labour cannot be a substance that is a part of a

---

[19] A recent trend in Marxist thought known as value form theory has offered a similar argument to mine here, but even some of the value form theorists seem to wish to retain the labour theory of value in some shape (Arthur, 2001).

commodity but is merely a measure derived from the prices at which goods exchange, which is of course exactly opposite to the result that Marx is trying to establish. Mirowski sums up these issues by arguing that Marx 'simultaneously argued for two contradictory versions of the labor theory of value': the substance theory and one that allows the amount of abstract labour in a product and thus its value to be determined by technological and market conditions at the time of exchange (Mirowski, 1991, pp. 180–1).

At times there are hints in Marx that he sees a role for the market in securing some of the factors relevant to his theory (Cutler et al., 1977, pp. 60, 86–7, 91), and if he had abandoned the substance theory of value he could have pointed to one way in which labour input does contribute to the price of a commodity: it forms an element (only an element, but *sometimes* the major element) of the cost of production of the commodity, which influences the prices that capitalists and indeed many other kinds of commodity producers are prepared to accept for their products. Even in the neoclassical theory of supply and demand, there is a tendency for prices to converge on a level at which they cover the cost of production plus a normal level of profit.[20] Whether or not we accept that theory, it is clear that production costs do have an influence on price, though prices can diverge significantly from them due to a variety of factors – gluts and shortages, technological change, monopoly suppliers and the effects of marketing on user perceptions of use-value, for example. Marx, however, cannot appeal to any variant of this model, for two reasons. First, it is a model that sees prices as being determined at the time of exchange, rather than value being created at the time of production. Second, in contrast with Marx's strictly mono-factoral theory of value it is a model in which prices are determined by a range of factors, of which labour input is only one. To accept any such model is to abandon the labour theory of value.

But prices, like other empirical events, *are* determined by a confluence of multiple interacting factors, and the attempt to preserve a monocausal labour theory of value is above all an attempt – an utterly

---

[20] Marx himself toys with such a theory in his discussion of *prices of production* in volume III of *Capital* (this is what is known as the *transformation problem*) but left this unpublished in his lifetime, perhaps because it can be read as undermining the theory of value (1959, chapters VIII–X).

anti-scientific attempt – to deny this (Cutler et al., 1977, p. 19; Fleet-wood, 2001; Mark Harvey & Geras, 2013, p. 7). No monocausal theory of price is viable, and no theory of value that is not also a theory of price can help us to understand actual allocations of benefit rather than some sort of ghostly concept of value that supposedly lies behind them. It is, however, difficult for anyone who has taken the Marxist tradition seriously to escape from the idea that all value is created by labour and therefore to stop looking for the labour that is being exploited whenever a profit is being earned. Even those who do not accept the labour theory of value have often become accustomed to thinking in these terms, and so a real discursive shift is required for the left to escape from this habit and recognise, first, that it is actual prices and not imaginary values that determine who gets what in commodity exchange, and second, that profit is not a deduction from some metaphysical entitlement but just another empirical phenomenon that requires a proper causal explanation.

Further problems arise when we turn to the use that Marx makes of the labour theory in his account of exploitation.[21] Marx argues that workers spend one part of their working day producing the value that is necessary to provide their means of subsistence – or, in other words, to pay their wages – and the remainder of the working day producing surplus value that is appropriated by the capitalist. He defines the 'degree of exploitation' as the ratio between surplus labour and necessary labour and thus regards all surplus value, and thus all the time spent producing it, as exploitation (Marx, 1954, p. 209). This apparently technical definition purports to be an objective definition of a fact but both Marx and his followers consistently treat this account of exploitation as providing the justification for an ethical critique of capitalism – describing surplus value appropriated by capitalists as 'robbery' or 'theft' for example (Geras, 1985, p. 56). In other words, the supposedly technical concept of exploitation is transformed, *without explicit justification*, into the everyday normative concept of exploitation. The political power of this argument clearly rests on *exploitation* being read in its ethical sense, in which 'to exploit others is to take unfair advantage of them' (Wertheimer & Zwolinski, 2013). As a result exploitation in this so-called objective sense is

---

[21] Again, there have been significant debates over this in the literature already (e.g. Nielsen & Ware, 1997; Reeve, 1987; Wolff, 1999).

routinely regarded by Marxists as wrong, though Marx never justifies this claim in explicitly ethical terms.[22]

There is a sense in which the whole of Marxist politics is founded on this basic claim: Marxists advocate a society that is freed from exploitation by the abolition of capital and thus the elimination of surplus value. One of the reasons for the longevity of the labour theory of value is that it appears to provide an objective foundation for this claim (Mark Harvey & Geras, 2013, p. 9). If all value is created by labour, it seems to be assumed, then it follows that those who perform the labour are entitled to the whole of the value created and therefore are exploited in an ethical and not just a technical sense of the term when they are paid less than the value of that product. However, this argument depends on a number of dubious premises. One is that the scientific version of the labour theory of value is true and thus that labour creates value and is the only contributor to value. But as we have seen, value is an imaginary quantity and its nearest equivalent, price, is a causal consequence of many factors, of which the work of wage labourers is only one. Even if we sought to argue that only those people who contributed causally to the production of a commodity were entitled to share in the price realised, we would have to allow that, for example, entrepreneurs who organise the production process and those who plan, build and maintain the public infrastructure used in the production process also deserved a share. Another premise is that whenever people contribute to the production of a commodity they have a moral right to claim a reward proportionate to their contribution (Mark Harvey & Geras, 2013, p. 10). But this is equally weak: for example, producers have moral obligations to contribute to public goods and to the welfare of non-producers such as children and the elderly, for example through paying taxes (DeMartino, 2003, p. 9; Mark Harvey & Geras, 2013, p. 11).[23]

The strength of Marx's theory of exploitation is that it challenges the appropriations of the benefits of production that prevail in capitalist industrial production, and in doing so it pioneered the need for

---

[22] In an attempt to put Marxism on an explicitly ethical footing, DeMartino adapts Marx's critique of exploitation into an explicitly ethical principle (DeMartino, 2003). Though the attempt is problematic, DeMartino's recognition of the need for ethical justifications for any critical politics is to be applauded.

[23] Leahy discusses several related difficulties in Gibson-Graham's account of exploitation (2013).

a political economy that evaluates such appropriations. Any critical political economy must indeed offer a basis for evaluating appropriations, but we need one that goes beyond Marx's in several respects. Marx reduces questions of economic justice down to the single standard that wage labourers deserve the full value of what they produce; but instead we must recognise (a) that there are always multiple potentially justified claims for a share of the benefits of production; (b) that we require explicit consideration of ethical standards rather than an abstract, pseudo-objective general theory in order to evaluate these claims; and (c) that there are many more circumstances than commodity production by wage labour in which issues of appropriative justice arise. In doing so, we return judgements of exploitation to the realm of ethics where they belong.

Conclusion

Marx and his followers have sustained the possibility of a critical political economy for a century and a half, and any alternative political economy will inevitably be measured against the Marxist tradition. But Marxist political economy is built on a series of concepts that have always been suspect, and that today stand in the way of a more adequate understanding of our economy and the potential alternatives to it. This chapter has focussed on just three aspects of these problems.

First, against more orthodox approaches to the economy, Marxists have rightly insisted on the need for political economy to be a critical enterprise, an enterprise that is prepared to question and judge economic structures and policies. But they have also insisted that there can be a purely objective scientific basis for such judgements, and this is both an analytical error and a dangerous illusion. Supposedly objective foundations for critique always embody ethical assumptions, and when we fail to surface them we open the way to disregard for human flourishing on the basis of dogmatically held beliefs about the objectives of politics. Instead we need an openly and reflexively ethical basis for critique.

Second, Marxist understandings of the larger dynamics of historical change have been framed by the concept of modes of production. Against mainstream economics, this has the enormous benefit of recognising that there are multiple possible economic forms and that different forms are found in different historical circumstances. Yet it is strongly implicated in the Marxist habit of treating the contemporary world as a monolithic universal capitalist system that is ultimately modelled on nineteenth century European industrial capitalism. We must replace this with a model of economic form that recognises the real diversity of all modern economic systems, and Chapter 5 will propose such a model.

Third, the labour theory of value and exploitation has demonstrated the importance of an evaluative theory of the appropriation of benefit from the process of production. But, in accordance with the general pattern of Marxist critique, this is an argument built on ethical assumptions that are hidden, unchallenged, behind a masquerade of science. In order to protect the ethical core, the theory reifies the concept of value, an imaginary construction that is isolated from all empirical considerations. Ultimately Marx's concept of value objectifies a moral claim but represents it as a real property of commodities in order to provide the appearance of a scientific basis for the very same moral claim that was built into the argument at the beginning. Instead we must recognise that there is no ethically neutral basis for evaluating the appropriation of the benefits of production, and accept the need for openly ethical arguments on these questions.

These problems are too central to Marxist thought for it to be viable to rescue the Marxist tradition of political economy from them, but there are still elements of the Marxist tradition that we can pick out from the wreckage and reuse in an alternative political economy of practices.

4 | *Mainstream economics and its rivals*

Introduction

Like the Marxist tradition, mainstream economics is deeply flawed, far too deeply flawed to provide the basis for a viable political economy. Yet like the Marxist tradition it contains elements that could be relocated into a different framework and reused productively in an alternative political economy. This chapter will discuss mainstream economics, but also other traditions that offer different ways of thinking about the economy: heterodox traditions in economics, the Maussian tradition of economic anthropology and economic sociology. Although the title of this chapter positions them as rivals, none of these competitors offers a fully worked out alternative, yet they all have something to contribute, both to the critique of the mainstream tradition, and to understanding our diverse economy. Like Marxist political economy each of these traditions discussed is somewhat diverse, and this brief account will inevitably overlook some of that diversity in order to simplify the argument. The objective of the chapter, however, is not to be comprehensive or even balanced, but rather to show why the flaws and absences in existing approaches create the need for an alternative, while also picking out elements that could be used in a new synthesis.

While it will provide some general introductory material about each of these traditions and its strengths and weaknesses, the primary objective of the chapter is to evaluate them with respect to this book's larger argument. Thus it will generally focus on questions of economic form, economic diversity, appropriations and ethics. It will also consider the ontology of the economy and how this is misrepresented in the dominant tradition, which will act as a prelude to the more realist ontology of the economy that will frame the account of appropriative practices developed in the next chapter.

Mainstream economics: the neoclassical core

The mainstream tradition in economics is centred on neoclassical economic theory.[1] Although many and perhaps even most mainstream academic economists no longer adhere to all parts of the neoclassical core, and the mainstream itself is increasingly defined by its commitment to unrealistic mathematisation rather than neoclassicism (T. Lawson, 2014, p. 103), this section will focus on the core and its manifest inadequacy as a theory of the economy and the appropriations that occur within it. One justification for doing so is that although many academic economists move beyond the core in their research, they continue to *teach* the core neoclassical paradigm, which is utterly dominant in, and largely unquestioned in, the leading textbooks of the discipline (see, for example, Keen, 2011, pp. 57–63). Keen estimates that around 85% of academic economists are adherents of the mainstream tradition, and even the dissidents are generally obliged to teach that tradition (Andrew Brown & Spencer, 2014; Keen, 2011, p. 8). The result is that new economists are thoroughly indoctrinated with this as the starting point from which they may move on, and indeed students of economics who leave academia, often to work in roles with significant economic power, leave with the belief that the neoclassical core is both sound and the only viable way to understand the economy (Keen, 2011, p. 22). There have been many critiques of this tradition, and this section will draw on some of them to highlight its key weaknesses and relate them to the specific interests of this book.

The neoclassical tradition is utterly focused on the economy conceived of as a system of markets. Although it occasionally analyses the state (by applying pseudo-market logic to it) it is overwhelmingly an account of a purely market economy, and the central place of the neoclassical model of markets in the mainstream tradition has made a major contribution to the contemporary discourse of the economy criticised in Chapter 2. While there are some mainstream economists

---

[1] I use the term *neoclassical* in the conventional sense, of referring to a continuing tradition in economics that is defined by certain paradigmatic theoretical commitments to be discussed later. Lawson has argued that the term ought to be defined instead in terms based on those of its originator, Thorstein Veblen (T. Lawson, 2014). No doubt Lawson's definition is useful, but the generally accepted meaning is the one I employ here and it is hard to see why we should abandon it in favour of Lawson's alternative (Jamie Morgan, 2014).

whose work is more critical of the current economic system (T. Lawson, 2014, pp. 101–2), few challenge this focus on markets. This simple and no doubt unconscious act of exclusion of other economic forms already makes this a covertly political form of study of the economy.

It is also, though it does not use the term, utterly focused on *appropriation* in the lay sense of the term: on what determines the allocation of the benefits produced in the economic system. It sees all economic action as being motivated by the desire of economic actors, both individuals and organisations, to maximise their own share of the benefits of production (Cowell, 2006, p. 2),[2] and it is centred on a theory of how the resulting interactions in a market system determine the allocation of benefits between actors. Consumers appropriate benefits derived from their acquisition of goods, and producers appropriate benefits in the form of monetary income arising from the sale of their goods or labour. Despite this focus on appropriation, however, the neoclassical tradition claims to avoid taking an ethical stance towards the resulting distribution of the benefits of economic activity. It claims that markets produce the most efficient set of outputs, in the sense of meeting consumers' needs as well as possible with the resources available, *given* the initial distribution of ownership of those resources, while refusing to judge that initial distribution.[3] This, it is claimed, is a purely technical form of optimisation, while the ethical question of the initial distribution of resources is regarded as somebody else's problem. But this argument plays a directly ideological role, in that it is commonly taken not only to describe but also to *justify* the market economy. The general equilibrium model is widely interpreted by mainstream economists to mean that a competitive market system is the most efficient way of organising an economy, since it seems to imply that when equilibrium is achieved, production is as well matched and as efficiently matched as possible to the buying preferences of consumers. This argument is thoroughly implausible (for example, as

[2] I include some citations from current economics textbooks for the benefit of readers who are unfamiliar with economics. Note that the textbooks often qualify statements like these as if recognising the sorts of criticism I will make later – for example Cowell says 'The assumption of selfishness is not essential to economics, but it gets us a long way in formulating problems precisely and... it can be useful in specifying a well-crafted model' (Cowell, 2006, pp. 2–3). They typically then ignore these qualifications as they develop the argument, generally as a consequence of prioritising modelling over empirical relevance.

[3] This is known as Pareto efficiency (Varian, 2010, pp. 310–2).

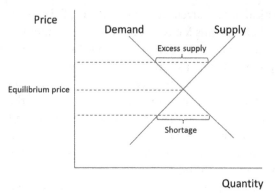

Figure 1: Demand and supply curves.

we shall see later, equilibrium rarely if ever occurs in markets anyway) but it has been central to the neoliberal rationale for privatisation and marketisation which has dominated political discourse over the last few decades. Thus the mainstream excludes economic diversity, not only as an assumption about the nature of the existing economy but also as a prescription for how economies should operate.

Neoclassical economics is thus inadequate as a political economy both because it has very little to say about the economy beyond the market and because of its ethical failings: the pretence of neutrality that acts as ideological cover for its role as cheerleader for the market system. But there is more: as the rest of this section will argue in a little more detail it is even inadequate as a technical theory of market systems themselves.[4]

The core of this theory is a mathematicised model of product markets as interactions between buyers and sellers, which play out to produce equilibrium prices and levels of output of the product concerned. In this model, the collective behaviour of buyers is described using a demand function, often represented graphically as a line or curve (marked 'demand' in Figure 1), which relates the quantity of a product they will buy to the price it is offered at (Varian, 2010, pp. 3–5). Buyers are regarded as highly rational actors who carefully select the mix of products to buy that maximises the benefit they can obtain from the funds they have available to spend (Cowell, 2006,

---

[4] Much more thorough explanations of its inadequacy are available elsewhere, notably Steve Keen's (2011).

pp. 79–81; Varian, 2010, p. 3). Changes in the price of a product will therefore affect the amount of it that they will buy – typically, if the price rises, they will buy less of the product concerned, and vice-versa. In graphical terms, this means that there is a downward sloping demand curve for each product when we aggregate the behaviour of all buyers together (Varian, 2010, pp. 3–6, 270–2).

Unfortunately, this model depends on an utterly unrealistic conception of human individuals and in particular an unrealistic conception of how we make purchasing choices. The model of buyers as rational optimising actors was never developed on the basis of an analysis of actual purchasing behaviour. It is used, on the one hand, because it reflects a philosophical commitment to the idea of human beings as self-centred individualists, and on the other, because in this tradition neat mathematical models are valued more highly than the realisticness of the assumptions upon which they are based. A rare empirical study of consumer preference formation suggests that in fact consumers do not follow any of the rules that would make their choices rational in the ways that the neoclassical core assumes (cited in Keen, 2011, pp. 67–9; Sippel, 1997). Indeed, the kind of careful consideration of all possible buying options that the model assumes is normal would be impossible for any real individual to carry out, because it requires a huge amount of information which it is impossible to acquire and the evaluation of a huge range of alternatives, which is equally impossible given the time constraints economic actors face (Keen, 2011, pp. 70–3; Simon, 1972). We *are* rational beings to some extent, and a viable model of the human actor must recognise this, but we are *also* habitual beings, which helps us to minimise the time we spend on evaluating alternatives, and our habits are strongly influenced by our past socialisation.[5] Buying decisions, then, are only partially influenced by rational optimisation, and even then only a limited range of options is usually considered. Still, when we do consider our options, it seems likely that we have some tendency to spend less on things when they are more expensive (Keen, 2011, p. 65). The net effect is that there may well be a *tendency*, in *certain circumstances* and *certain types of case* – perhaps even widespread circumstances and types of case – for demand

---

[5] For a more sophisticated discussion of the role of socialisation in our decision making in general, see Bourdieu (1990, chapter 3), and on the relation between this and conscious deliberation, see Elder-Vass (2007b).

to respond to price in the way the model suggests, but this is only one of many factors that affect consumers' purchasing decisions.

The collective behaviour of sellers in the neoclassical model is represented using a supply function or curve relating the quantity of the product they will supply to the price available in the market (marked 'supply' in Figure 1) (Cowell, 2006, pp. 50–3). The standard model assumes *perfect competition* in the market, which means that none of the suppliers are big enough to be able to influence the price of the product (while there are also models of monopoly or imperfect competition, where small numbers of suppliers can influence the price, these tend to be treated as exceptional cases). Suppliers too are treated as rational optimising agents, who seek to maximise the profit they can make (Cowell, 2006, p. 10; Varian, 2010, chapter 19). At the collective level, it is argued, this means that that the supply curve will be upward sloping: if the price of a product increases, producers in general will produce more of it.

Supply curves, however, are no less problematic than demand curves. They rest on the assumptions made about the ways in which production costs vary with levels of output, and these too bear little relation to the actual situation faced by many producers. As with demand curves, the assumptions have been adopted to make the model work rather than because they reflect the real economy. Many producers usually have significant spare capacity that they could make use of profitably at the prevailing price, but there is insufficient demand from customers to make full use of this. The neoclassical solution would be to drop their price, but (in the very common case where marginal costs are below average costs) this would often result in them having to sell at a loss. Conventionally producers in these markets sell their goods at cost plus a margin that provides them with a certain level of profit, and it is simply not sustainable for any producer to undercut these prices. In these circumstances the notion of a supply curve becomes somewhat meaningless, since there is not a single quantity but a whole range of quantities that producers are willing to supply at their current price.

The neoclassical model then combines the aggregate demand and supply curves to argue that prices and quantities in the market for a given good will tend to adjust until they arrive at the equilibrium point where the demand and supply curves meet (Varian, 2010, pp. 3, 7–8, chapter 16). If the price was lower than this, the level of demand would be higher than the level of supply, so there would be a shortage of the product, and the price would tend to rise, stimulating more production and reducing demand. If the price was higher than the equilibrium level, the level of demand would be lower than the level of supply, so some goods would be unsold and the price would tend to fall, stimulating demand and reducing production. Changes in price, therefore, move demand and supply along the two curves on Figure 1, until the equilibrium point is reached. While neoclassical economists do recognise certain types of cases in which equilibrium will not be achieved they tend to see these as unfortunate 'rigidities' in the economy rather than as faults in the model.

However, we now arrive at the deepest problems of all for the neoclassical model, which are those raised by its whole orientation to the achievement of equilibrium in markets. The model assumes that there are markets for each product that are large by comparison with individual producers, who therefore cannot influence prices, and, crucially, that within these markets all products will be sold at the same price because if any producer prices higher than the others all buyers will move to the other suppliers. But the reality is that in most markets prices for the same product do not converge at a single level. True, there is *some* pressure in this direction: if the price of tomatoes, for example, was twice as high at one market stall as the one next to it, and the quality was similar, it would seem likely that many buyers would switch to the cheaper stall and as her unsold stocks mounted up the more expensive trader might feel the need to drop her price. Retailers of many types of goods pay close attention to the prices charged by their competitors, and often avoid large variations in order to prevent such situations. Yet variations abound. Two identical candy bars, for example, may sell for very different prices in a budget supermarket, the local corner shop and a motorway service station, even if they are only a few minutes away from each other. Two more or less identical handbags may sell for enormously different prices depending on where they are bought and whether the seller succeeds in representing them as authentic products of a particular manufacturer. And despite the apparent obviousness of my comment about tomatoes, it turns out that in at least one real face-to-face market there is significant price dispersion, and significant loyalty of buyers to specific sellers (the Marseille wholesale fish market, discussed in Kirman & Vriend, 2000). Every supplier of a product is different, and indeed suppliers systematically attempt to make themselves so by pursuing what I will call *preferential attachment*: by providing reasons why buyers should prefer them to other suppliers (Michel Callon Méadel & Rabeharisoa, 2002; Chamberlin, 1956, pp. 56–7, 71; Elder-Vass, 2009; and see Chapter 6; White, 1981). As a result prices for very similar or even identical products often vary considerably (Keen, 2011, p. 117).

If we evaluate actual market systems against the neoclassical model, then, we find that while some are more like the model than others, many fit a pattern that is more or less the opposite of it: instead of homogeneous prices across a 'market', which move dynamically in response to variations in demand and supply, we often find that market systems lead to a diverse set of prices for the same commodity, that are relatively stable over the short term. The consequence is that the mechanisms of demand and supply theorised by the neoclassicals do not even succeed in practice in equalising the price across a given market, let alone bringing it to an 'equilibrium' value. The neoclassical equilibrium model reduces the determination of prices and output levels to an abstract conjunction between two forces, each modelled without regard to the actual behaviour of buyers and suppliers in order to create a superficially well-behaved model, but that model does not stand up once we examine how real economic actors behave. The neoclassical model is only a touch closer to the actual processes of price and output level determination than the Marxist one, but the neoclassical tradition has done a better job of concealing this, to the extent that both scholars and lay actors routinely accept what is perhaps the core obfuscating assumption: that there is a single price for any given commodity at any one time. As we shall see when we come to discuss the case of Apple, a vast range of firms base their entire business strategies on finding ways to charge a *different* price than their competitors do.

Beyond neoclassical economics

In some ways, the neoclassical core is a brilliant intellectual construction, but it simply does not work as a theory of pricing and output determination in the real world. We have already seen one set of reasons for this: that actual buyers, sellers, and markets do not operate in the ways required for the mechanisms to work. But there is also another reason: causality in general does not operate in the way that is assumed by the model. Not only the theory but also the ontology of the mainstream must be rejected. This section examines these ontological problems, but also raises some ethical concerns and discusses the positive contribution that heterodox traditions within economics can make to a more plausible political economy.

The problem here is that the core model assumes that price and output levels can be determined by just three mechanisms: demand functions, supply functions and market equilibration, whereas in reality events of all kinds, including prices and output levels, are the outcome of multiple interacting causes, and the mix of causes varies from case to case. The previous discussion has introduced a small number of complicating factors to illustrate the point: firms, for example, seek to establish preferential attachment of buyers to their products and to the extent that they succeed in doing so they can maintain price differentials over their competitors, undermining both the supply curve mechanism and the market equilibration mechanism postulated in the neoclassical core. But this is just one of many potential complications. Causal systems in general, and social systems in particular, are *open systems*: they cannot be explained by the operation of just one or a few causal mechanisms because all causal mechanisms are subject to interference from others which may on occasion frustrate or alter their operation or consequences (Faulkner, 2007).

Lawson has argued that the defining feature of the mainstream tradition is not its attachment to the neoclassical core, but rather a commitment to what he calls 'mathematical-deductive modelling' as a universal method (T. Lawson, 2014, p. 106). He presents substantial evidence that mainstream economists are *required* to use these methods (T. Lawson, 2014, p. 105), which logically depend on the assumption that the systems being modelled are *closed* systems. We cannot deduce a conclusion from a mathematical model without the infamous *ceteris paribus* clause: the assumption of *other things being equal,* which in practice amounts to the exclusion of causal influences other than those being modelled. The core neoclassical model discussed previously is a prime case: the model assumes that only the three mechanisms it models are relevant to determining prices and output levels. But the technique of mathematical-deductive modelling appears throughout mainstream economics. And because it depends on the assumption of closed systems, it is 'just not appropriate for dealing with social material, given the latter's nature' (T. Lawson, 2014, p. 108).

This does not mean that mathematical models have no useful role at all to play in the analysis of economic systems (T. Lawson, 2014,

p. 107). In particular, they may be useful for describing how individual mechanisms operate – what Hodgson has called a *heuristic*: 'Their purpose is to establish a plausible segment of a causal story, without necessarily giving an adequate or complete explanation of the phenomenon to which they relate' (Hodgson, 2009, p. 181). There is room for debate over which comes first, the understanding of a causal mechanism or its mathematical description (T. Lawson, 2009a, p. 208). But the important issue here is how such models are *used*. First, they must be closely based on the actual nature of the actors whose behaviour they model, unlike the supply curve and market equilibration models of the neoclassical paradigm (T. Lawson, 2009a, p. 211). Second, they cannot be used to predict empirical outcomes, because empirical outcomes always depend on the interaction of many such mechanisms and heuristic models describe only one or at most a few.

Instead of these over-ambitious attempts to explain complex empirical events in terms of simplistic but convenient mathematical models, we need methods of study that respond to the actual nature of causation and the actual nature of the social phenomena being studied. To do so we must combine two explanatory processes. On the one hand, we need to identify particular mechanisms that contribute to a wide range of actual events, examining how those mechanisms operate to produce certain tendencies or causal powers – a form of study known as *retroduction* (Elder-Vass, 2010b, p. 48; T. Lawson, 1997, p. 24). On the other, we need to examine which mechanisms interact, and how they interact, to produce particular events or particular classes of event – *retrodiction* (Elder-Vass, 2010b, p. 48; T. Lawson, 1997, p. 221).[6] Careful attention to retrodiction as well as retroduction helps to sensitise us to the question of when – in which circumstances, defined by which sets of other interacting mechanisms – particular mechanisms are more or less effective. By replacing deductive mathematical modelling with a mix of retroduction and retrodiction, we can start to make allowances for the complex interactions of multiple mechanisms that operate in practice. This is a model of explanation that is always provisional, always open to the possibility that new mechanisms may be discovered or developed, and one that rarely produces neat mathematical formulae to describe the operation of the

---

[6] For a detailed discussion of the methodological issues this raises, see Elder-Vass (2007a) or Elder-Vass (2010b, pp. 64–76).

world. But it is one that allows us to develop massively more plausible explanations of social events – and incidentally, one that allows us to theorise not just market exchange, but the whole range of economic activity in our diverse economies.

While the neoclassical arguments are false as mathematised descriptions of invariant relationships between causal factors and events, many of them are based on accounts of mechanisms that may operate to some extent in some circumstances, and that may be of value in an alternative political economy once they are relocated into a less deductivist framework. Thus, for example, there are good reasons to believe that demand for a product often, though by no means always, falls when the price rises. Similarly there are good reasons to believe that market economies are *to some extent* responsive to the wishes of buyers, because producers adjust their output and productive capacity, roughly and with lags, to what they can sell at the prevailing price.

This last argument, however, is advanced in a much stronger form in popular ideological uses of neoclassical theory, where it plays a central role in the ethical defence of market systems. This defence justifies market systems on the grounds that they adjust output to the needs of the population. In reality, however, output is not adjusted to the needs of the population in general, but only (and highly imperfectly) to those needs that are backed with purchasing power, because the only demands that the market responds to are those that are made by people with the resources to buy things. In other words, the needs of the rich are served far more fully than those of the poor. This could only be justified if the distribution of wealth and income was itself justified, and neoclassical theory has also been used as a resource to justify *this* claim. Some economists have argued that everyone who supplies an input to the productive process, whether it is land, labour or capital, receives an income that is proportional to the marginal productivity of their input (an argument developed in the nineteenth century by JB Clark: Keen, 2011, pp. 129, 185), and this is commonly translated into the claim that they get what they deserve given their contribution to the productive process. Once again, this is a thoroughly ideological position, and one that bolsters the existing economic system, but one that cannot be justified, for a number of reasons. Consider just three. First, real market economies never do reach anything like an equilibrium position, so incomes never are adjusted to marginal contributions. Second, the model assumes that the existing patterns of ownership of land and capital, and thus the rent and profit that they attract, are themselves justified, when in practice they are the outcome of a vast range of processes, including speculation, inheritance and indeed crime, as well as direct contributions to the process of production. Third, the neoclassical version of the argument that income should be proportional to one's contribution to the process of production is no more justifiable than the Marxist version: what is to become, for example, of the young, the old, the disabled and those who are unemployed through no fault of their own?

Like Marxism, then, the economic mainstream has a covertly ethical theory of appropriation; like the Marxist version it begins from the assumption that income should be proportional to one's contribution to production and combines this with a thoroughly untenable method of measuring these contributions. Instead we need an explicitly ethical theory that evaluates appropriation on an open basis that is sensitive to a variety of ethical arguments. Without going into detail, I suggest that any broadly acceptable theory must be sensitive to both needs and contributions. There are multiple sorts of ethical claims, and in any given circumstance we might reasonably expect a number of them to be relevant. Once we recognise this, we can no more have a formal deductive model of fair distribution of income than we can have a formal deductive model of how the economy works.

Alongside the mainstream and Marxism, there are also several heterodox strands of economics, including Austrian, evolutionary, feminist, institutional, post-Keynesian and Sraffian schools (see Keen, 2011, chapter 18 for an overview). These vary enormously in their analytical techniques, their evaluative orientation and their topical foci, but Lawson argues that they do have one thing in common: whether they recognise it explicitly or not, they reject the technique of mathematical-deductive modelling of closed systems as the only acceptable way of doing economics (T. Lawson, 2014, pp. 107, 113). This does not mean that they reject mathematisation entirely, but they do not see it as the only acceptable technique for economics, and this is arguably because they do not see the economy as a closed system.

As a consequence, all of these traditions make useful, though different, criticisms of the mainstream and offer more realistic accounts of varying elements of the economy. Thus, for example, the Austrians recognise the dynamic nature of market economies and dispense with any belief in equilibrium states as either possible or desirable – though most continue to advocate market systems as aggressively as the neo-classical mainstream (Keen, 2011, pp. 445–9).[7] Post-Keynesians stress the need for economic models to be realistic, and take account of uncertainty, monopoly and the influence of monetary and financial factors on the economy (Keen, 2011, pp. 449–50). Feminists dispute the neoclassical model of economic actors as isolated selfish amoral individuals (England, 1993; Julie A. Nelson, 2006) and the exclusion of non-market economic activity, particularly in the household (Fraad Resnick & Wolff, 1994). Similar themes can also be seen in heterodox re-evaluations of the work of Adam Smith, reclaiming his legacy from the market ideologues by showing that he thought beneficence and cooperation just as important as commerce (Robert F. Garnett, 2014). Institutionalists see markets not as abstract clearing processes that magically equate supply and demand but as social institutions that operate in varying ways depending on the organisational and cultural context (Hodgson, 1988). A viable alternative political economy would draw on some or all of these traditions, though also on more mainstream elements that have been developed in more recent years in a diversification from the neoclassical core, such as behavioural economics, which seeks to explain economic behaviour on the basis of realistic and empirically tested models of human psychology (Kahneman, 2012).

The common thread that unites these different elements is that they can be integrated under the banner of a realist approach – whether or not this is how the authors working in these traditions see them – because they are based on examining how the economy actually works and because each element can be used to help theorise one particular mechanism or set of mechanisms (retroduction), and then employed, in conjunction with accounts of other mechanisms, to explain particular events of classes of events (retrodiction). As Tony Lawson – the leading advocate of a realist approach to economics – has pointed out, many different economic theories are potentially compatible with a realist ontology, though this in itself does not make those theories right (T. Lawson, 2009b, p. 344). One of the aims of this book is to contribute towards a substantive account of the economy that is based on a realist ontology but also seeks to integrate work from other traditions.

---

[7] Though there are also left Hayekians who advocate varieties of market socialism (Burczak, 2006).

Mauss's anthropology of the gift

A number of those traditions come from outside economics. Scholars from several other disciplines have made important contributions to our understanding of the economy, contributions that have often been framed as critiques of the neoclassical tradition, and there is considerable scope for combining ideas from these different disciplines in the construction of an alternative perspective (Andrew Brown & Spencer, 2014). This section will consider the contribution of Marcel Mauss to economic anthropology and the next will discuss economic sociology. One advantage that both share is that unconstrained by the mathematical-deductive modelling framework of mainstream economics, and in line with the wider concerns of their disciplines, they have taken far more open views of the forces at work in the economy, views that recognise the variety of forms that an economy might take and the ways in which those are shaped by institutional and cultural forces.

Economic anthropology has been shaped by the work of Marcel Mauss, or rather by a single short book dating originally from the 1920s, the *Essai sur le don*, published in English as *The Gift* (Mauss, 2002). Mauss examined anthropological evidence relating to social practices in Melanesia and amongst native Americans, and historical evidence relating to pre-feudal Europeans, and on the basis of this argued that in pre-modern economies the market is marginal. Instead, these societies depended on cycles of deferred gift exchange, which worked in a very different way from the market but nevertheless performed some of the equivalent functions of economic circulation. For Mauss this was a way of criticising the market fundamentalisms of his day, in particular the idea that only markets can coordinate economies, and the utilitarian claim that all economic decisions are, or should be, made by rational calculation of self-interest (Douglas, 2002, pp. x, xviii; Mauss, 2002, pp. 41, 96–8).

These gift economies, he argues, depend on cycles of giving which take the form of deferred exchanges. They are characterised by a strong set of social obligations to give, to accept gifts and above all to reciprocate gifts: to return something else of equivalent value at a later date (Mauss, 2002, pp. 3, 16–17, 50–5). To return an equivalent immediately was unacceptable in most social situations. This was tantamount to refusing the gift, by transforming the cycle of giving into an instantaneous exchange that conformed instead to the logic of barter (Bourdieu, 1990, p. 105; Godbout & Caillé, 1998, p. 10). To do so was to undermine the very point of the gift, in which the transfer of goods was secondary to a more fundamental purpose: the creation of a network of social obligations that served to stabilise social relations. The recipient of the gift accepted not only the material gift but also an obligation to reciprocate at some point in the future, an obligation that constituted a social tie between recipient and giver. The implication, as Mary Douglas makes clear in her foreword to the English translation of Mauss's book, is that there can be no free gifts, because in the gift economy every gift generates an obligation to reciprocate (Douglas, 2002, pp. ix–x). Mauss's argument thus sees economic transactions as being driven by systems of normative obligation as opposed to (or as well as) rational utilitarian calculations of interest.

However progressive Mauss's intentions, attempts to apply his model of the gift to contemporary societies have had unfortunate consequences. Mauss's insistence on the centrality of reciprocity has been extended uncritically to contemporary giving, but his analysis of gift exchange does not necessarily apply to modern giving (Elder-Vass, 2015b). As Testart has argued, the practices he analysed corresponded more closely to the modern practice of lending than that of giving (1998, pp. 101–2). Seeing gifts as a form of deferred exchange potentially reinstates the utilitarian idea that calculation of self-interest is the motor of these transfers (Graeber, 2011, p. 90), and unites theories of the gift with conventional economics of the market as varieties of exchangism (Elder-Vass, 2015b; Pyyhtinen, 2014, chapter 2).

Bourdieu's work on giving is a prime example of this tendency (notably 1990, pp. 97–106). Initially he proposes to analyse the practice of giving from two points of view, which he seems to suggest are equally significant (Adloff & Mau, 2006, p. 103). On the one hand, there is the subjective point of view, the point of view of the actor, from which perspective giving is seen as an act of pure generosity, with no expectation of return and no calculation of reciprocity. On the other, there is the objective point of view, the view of the observing scholar: that careful comparison of giving relationships over a longer period of time reveals that reciprocity does occur, and to such a well-matched extent that it is inconceivable that the actors had not engaged in some degree of calculation. But far from giving these two views equal weight as understandings of the practice of giving, Bourdieu proceeds to label the actors' point of view as a misrecognition of the nature of giving. Both are equally important, he says, but not because he takes the actors' point of view seriously as an account of giving. On the contrary, the actors' view is important because it provides an ideology of giving, a misrepresentation of it that allows it to function effectively in the building and maintenance of relationships despite the fact that in reality reciprocity rules (Bourdieu, 1990, pp. 105–6). The so-called subjective view, it turns out, is treated by Bourdieu as part of the object: as a phenomenon that contributes to the overall effect of the practices of giving and not at all as an account of giving that we should take seriously in its own right. Thus Bourdieu produces a thoroughly alienated and alienating account of giving: alienated because it reduces giving to a kind of rational calculating exchange, and alienating because it encourages us all, lay actors included, to treat it cynically as merely a hidden variety of the pursuit of self-interest. As Osteen puts it, 'Bourdieu constantly criticizes economism, arguing that it fails to capture the nuances of transactions as perceived by the actors... And yet his description falls victim to such economism by implying that the economic truth is the most basic one' (Osteen, 2002, p. 24).

A second consequence of the Maussian perspective is that giving is sometimes seen as a kind of pre-modern alternative to the market; a mode of economic transfer and social integration that is replaced by the market in modern societies (Mauss, 2002, p. 59). With the rise of the market, it therefore seems that the gift becomes economically marginal (Adloff & Mau, 2006, p. 99; Negru, 2010, pp. 198, 200; Zelizer, 1994, p. 77) (though Mauss himself insisted on its continuing symbolic importance: see 2002, p. 83). As Benkler has pointed out, 'There is a curious congruence between the anthropologists of the gift and mainstream economics today. Both treat the gift literature as being about the periphery, about societies starkly different from modern capitalist ones' (Benkler, 2004, p. 332). A number of sociological treatments of giving have fallen into the trap of seeing contemporary giving as nothing more than the exchange of presents on ritual occasions such as birthdays and religious festivals: as, in effect, a residual survival from pre-modern society in a ritualised form of relatively marginal significance to our personal relationships.

This perspective, however, obscures the existence and significance of a vast range of other forms of giving that continue to be of vital importance in contemporary societies, not just in building and sustaining relationships, but also as a crucial element of economic provisioning (Godbout & Caillé, 1998, p. 11; Negru, 2010). The range of giving practices and their frequency varies in different cultural contexts, but may include, for example, gifts to formal charities, gifts to beggars, religious donations, volunteering, doing small favours for strangers, giving blood and organs, leaving bequests, buying drinks for friends, giving away unwanted goods (e.g. via services like Freecycle) and giving presents on ritual occasions such as birthdays. Perhaps the most significant of all, though, is giving within the family or household. Almost all of us depend utterly in our childhood on the provisioning of our needs by our parents or carers, and indeed such giving often continues on even into adulthood. For Godbout, for example, 'the family is the primary site for the gift in society' (Godbout & Caillé, 1998, p. 29).

Furthermore, much of this giving is not reciprocal giving. Giving to one's children, for example, is not motivated primarily by the expectation that one will receive a material return of equivalent value from them at some point in the future (Cheal, 1988, pp. 8, 57–8; Godbout & Caillé, 1998, p. 24). This is nicely illustrated by Daniel Miller's account of shopping, which he suggests is 'primarily an act of love' (Miller, 1998, p. 18) directed on the whole towards the benefit of other members of one's household (Miller, 1998, p. 12). Such gifts are more plausibly seen as *positional* rather than reciprocal: they are not given because of an obligation to reciprocate or to initiate a process of reciprocation but because their givers are in a social position which carries a normative expectation to give such gifts, e.g. the position of parent (Elder-Vass, 2015b). Likewise, giving to charity is not motivated by the expectation that the recipient will make a return, and on the whole there are only rather weak positional normative expectations to give such gifts. As we will see in the following sections, many digital gifts carry no sense of any obligation at all.

Even when there are elements of reciprocity in gift-giving practices, exchangist readings of reciprocity may be utterly wrong. If, for example, I receive a birthday gift from you and a few months later I give one to you, the observer may see this as a case of one gift obligating a reciprocal return, a kind of deferred exchange. But this may be a complete misreading of the second gift: rather than being the completion of a deferred exchange of material equivalents, the second gift, and indeed the first one, may be understood, and understood rightly, by the participants as affirmations of commitment to their relationship with each other. The logic in such cases is not a logic of reciprocity of objects, in anything but the most superficial of senses, but a logic of mutual recognition and relatedness of people (Schrift, 1997, p. 2). There is a kind of empiricism or even behaviourism involved in seeing a sequence in which one gift is followed by another that flows in the opposite direction and defining this as reciprocity. When such events are interpreted as deferred exchange, in opposition to the self-understandings of those involved, this privileges the analyst's exchangist theoretical preconceptions over the understandings of the actors.

Even apparently reciprocal gifts, then, may not fit the exchangist assumptions that are characteristic of the hegemonic discourses of neoclassical economics, and instead should be understood as parts of a *moral economy*, an economy of transfers that are products of emotional commitments, social relationships, and the normative environment rather than the pursuit of individual material profit. Mauss is thus important for a number of reasons. Not only does he provide substantial evidence that economies need not be run on market principles, but he also demonstrates that economic actors always operate within a cultural context that shapes their motivations, expectations and actions. As long as we avoid exchangist interpretations of his work, he steps further outside the market tradition than any other major thinker about the economy.

Economic sociology

Like heterodox economics, economic sociology has many strands, though there is a clear common theme: attention to the relationship between the economic and the social – and thus a clear potential for fruitful collaboration (Andrew Brown & Spencer, 2014). At least two of these strands, centred around the work of Karl Polanyi and Mark Granovetter, respectively, have approached this question using the concept of *embeddedness*.

Polanyi argues that the economy is 'embedded and enmeshed in institutions, economic and noneconomic' including for example 'monetary institutions or the availability of tools or machines' and 'religion or government'. He continues: 'The study of the shifting place occupied by the economy in society is therefore no other than the study of the manner in which the economic process is instituted in different times and places' (Polanyi, 2001, p. 36). Polanyi's argument, amongst other things, is a critique of mainstream economics. On the one hand, he attacks its conception of the economy as 'analytically autonomous' from social influence (Krippner & Alvarez, 2007, pp. 221–2), stressing instead that it is always embedded in and dependent upon a specific institutional context. On the other, he attacks its ahistorical and total-ising conception of the economy as always and entirely a market economy. Economies, he argues, may be instituted in different ways – they may be shaped by or embedded in very different organisational and normative contexts – with three main alternative 'forms of inte-gration' (Polanyi, 2001, p. 36). He labels these 'reciprocity, redistri-bution and exchange', corresponding roughly to gift economies, state control of the economy, and market economies (Polanyi, 2001, p. 36). Any one of these may be dominant in a particular economy, but he also recognises that they may often be mixed (Polanyi, 2001, p. 40). Polanyi is thus an important precursor of the argument of this book. He criticised what he called the 'economistic fallacy' – 'an artificial identi-fication of the economy with its market form' – and called for a wider frame of reference for thinking about the economy that supersedes this fallacy (Polanyi, 2001, p. 49).

The idea that the economy cannot be autonomous of social influence is also important for understanding market forms themselves. Polanyi himself paid relatively little attention to market behaviour at the micro level (Krippner & Alvarez, 2007, pp. 221–2), but sociology gives us numerous ways of developing the argument. Exchange is fundamen-tally an institutional process. For example, what is exchanged when we purchase something is not merely a material object but *property rights* in it, and such property rights always depend on the larger legal and normative institutional regime. When we purchase a commodity, we acquire a socially recognised and normatively enforced right to the exclusive use of the item concerned, or at least to some of the uses of the item concerned. Every market transaction is an exchange of insti-tutionalised rights. Furthermore, the entire process of exchange is normatively framed and constrained (in ways that may vary from one social context to another). We are guided, for example, by social norms that regulate what kinds of things may be exchanged, who we may or should not purchase from or sell to, the actual conduct of the sales process and obligations to provide accurate information regarding the goods concerned. Buyers are motivated, in part at least, by desires that are themselves normatively influenced – we may feel obliged to wear smart clothes, for example, and thus to replace them frequently. Even practices on how to price commodities are institutionalised (M. Harvey, 2010).

This dependence of the economic upon the social has been a constant theme of economic sociology (see, for example, Smelser & Swedberg, 2005), and is also the focus of Mark Granovetter's rather different account of embeddedness. Granovetter is particularly interested in the role of social networks in enabling economic exchanges. Neoclassical economics assumes that the identity and history of an individual is irrelevant to the process of market exchange, which is taken to be determined purely by questions of price and the utility of the commodity being exchanged. But Granovetter focuses on the dependence of exchange on trust between the transactors. Without such trust, for example, he suggests that it would be foolish to pay a stranger for five dollars' worth of goods with a twenty dollar note: we only do so because we trust that even strangers will return our change because they follow certain standards of morality (Granovetter, 1985, p. 489). But more often, he suggests, and for transactions where the consequences of dishonesty would be more serious, we rely instead on a history of social relations: we trust people because we have dealt with them before without problems, or because we are aware of their reputation. Reputation depends on us belonging to shared social networks, and here he gives the example of a community of diamond merchants who were comfortable making high value contracts on the basis of a shake of the hand because they belonged to a community that monitored and discussed each other's behaviour and thus provided strong evidence of trustworthiness (Granovetter, 1985, pp. 490, 492). By contrast with the neoclassical view that actors 'behave or decide as atoms outside a social context', he argues that their action is 'instead embedded in concrete, ongoing systems of social relations' (Granovetter, 1985, p. 487).

Granovetter's influential account of embeddedness is rather different from Polanyi's, focusing on interactions at the micro level rather than the macro institutional context. While it adds a further sociological dimension to our understanding of economic action, it has often been criticised on the grounds that it ultimately leaves mainstream economists' accounts of the market untouched. Rather than contesting their accounts, it seems to set out some sociological preconditions that are required for markets to work in the ways posited by the neoclassicals. Beckert suggests that there is 'an implicit acceptance of what Polanyi calls the formalist definition of the economic' – that there is a purely market economy, distinct from the social in which it is embedded (J. Beckert, 2007). The implication 'is that there is somewhere a hard core of market transacting that exists apart from society' (Krippner & Alvarez, 2007, p. 231). But to accept the existence of such a core would concede too much to mainstream economics.[8] It is not enough to say that economic activities are embedded in a social context. The economy is not something distinct from the social and embedded in it, but rather an aspect or a subset of social practice, and thus social through and through. Instead we need to see 'the economic process as an organic part of society' (Smelser & Swedberg, 2005, p. 6). This means that sociological theories of the economic need to be thoroughly articulated with whatever can be rescued from economics itself (Smelser & Swedberg, 2005, p. 20), but the terms of that articulation are crucial (Sparsam, 2013). We cannot import mathematical-deductive models from economics but we can synthesise the contributions of both disciplines to understanding economic mechanisms in the context of a realist understanding of social causation and explanation.

More recent contributions to economic sociology remain diverse, and many have useful things to contribute to our understanding of the economy, but this pattern of leaving the mainstream economists' accounts of the economy largely untouched while wrapping them in what is arguably a protective blanket of sociological context continues to be common. Perhaps the most striking examples are provided by scholars from science and technology studies associated with actor-network theory, led by Michel Callon.[9] Callon and Muniesa suggest we should think of markets as 'calculative collective devices' that 'allow compromises to be reached, not only on the nature of the goods to produce and distribute, but also on the value to be given to them' (M. Callon & Muniesa, 2005, p. 1229), and they examine the particular configurations of things and operations that, they believe, enable these calculations to occur. They see this as an improvement on the

[8] Approaches like this seem to leave sociology as a kind of '"left-over" science' that allows economics to define its own scope and feeds off the scraps that it refuses to touch (Curran, 2014, p. 1048).

[9] I have criticised actor-network theory in Elder-Vass (2008, and 2015a).

economic conception of a market as 'an abstract space in which aggregate demands and supplies encounter and cross one another' (M. Callon & Muniesa, 2005, p. 1239). As they rightly say, this conception has been combined with a remarkable lack of interest in actual empirical markets amongst mainstream economists (Nee, 2005, p. 56), but their own approach is no more balanced or comprehensive. Not only do they ignore the systematic structural consequences of markets, but also many of the sociological influences that have been painstakingly documented by earlier economic sociology. Their market actors are merely 'calculative agencies' (M. Callon & Muniesa, 2005, p. 1236), a concept that is suspiciously reminiscent of rational optimisation, though detached from specifically human decision-makers, and there is little or no evidence of institutional influence, normativity, socialisation, *habitus*, power or emotion in the explanation.

A final and more promising strand of recent economic sociology is the growing attention that it has bestowed on the gift economy. Although in the past the sociological literature on the gift has been overshadowed by the influence of Mauss, and in particular by exchangist readings of Mauss like Bourdieu's, discussed previously, there are increasing signs of recognition that giving is an economic activity in its own right with a range of roles and motivations. The classic source here is Richard Titmuss's famous study of blood donation, first published in 1970, which sees the gift-based system of blood donation as a more effective way of providing for this need than alternatives based on the market (Titmuss, 1997). More recent studies have focused, for example, on the complex institutional structures that have grown up around giving, notably in the areas of organ donation (K. Healy, 2006), philanthropy (Barman, 2007; McGoey, 2015; Sanghera & Bradley, 2015) and politics (Lainer-Vos, 2013), the ways in which giving is marked off from the realm of exchange (Zelizer, 1994, chapter 1), the normative influences on giving (Caplow, 1984; Elder-Vass, 2015b), and the sometimes rather porous boundaries between the gift and the market (Bird-David & Darr, 2009; McClain & Mears, 2012; Pettinger, 2011). While these authors take a wide range of perspectives on giving, the very fact that giving is coming to be seen as a significant concern of economic sociology indicates a growing sense of the diversity of economic activity.

The growth of the digital gift economy has also stimulated considerable academic and often critical work, though this is not focussed in any single discipline, and I will make extensive use of this in the later chapters of the book. To mention just a couple of examples, the legal scholar Yochai Benkler has made important contributions to understanding peer production as an alternative economic form, and the Marxist media scholar Christian Fuchs, though I shall criticise some of his work later, has produced valuable work on the entanglement of the digital gift and commodity economies (Benkler, 2002, 2004, 2006; Fuchs, 2008).

Economic sociology, then, provides considerable material that is relevant for explaining the operation of the economy. It may, arguably, provide 'microfoundations' for an alternative political economy (Jens Beckert, 2013), but it falls short of offering explanations that compete with those offered by mainstream economics. Nor does economic sociology have a clear ethical or critical stance; it is often concerned with questioning economics, but much less often with questioning the way our economy operates.

Conclusion

Academic analyses of the economy are primarily analyses of market systems, and these analyses are deeply divided. Amongst economists, there is a tendency to neglect the personal and sociological factors that shape the behaviour of market actors, and to assume that these can be safely abstracted from in analysing the causal consequences of market interactions. Often their assumptions – most strikingly the common assumption that market actors are purely rational, calculating, optimising agents – are strikingly unrealistic and yet they persist, in part because they make it possible to produce mathematically tractable models of market interactions. Amongst sociologists, there is a tendency to focus on the social factors that shape the behaviour of market actors, while discounting the possibility of a systematic analysis of the consequences of market interactions. This may produce more realistic accounts of market behaviour, but it leaves sociologists poorly equipped to explain the economic effects of markets. Economists thus end up with unrealistic models of markets, and sociologists end up unable to explain the causal impact of markets.

We need to bridge this gap with an analysis of economic phenomena that combines a realistic sociological explanation of the behaviour of economic actors and an analysis of how such behaviour produces systematic economic effects. Such an analysis has the potential to be both more credible than economists' models and more productive than sociological critiques of those models. This book, however, does not just seek to build a better theory of the economy, a theory that might in principle be politically neutral. It is a critique not only of theories of the economy but also of the market economy itself. Hence it not only explains but also evaluates economic practices.

Andrew Sayer's conception of *moral economy* offers a framework for just this sort of enquiry. On the one hand, drawing on the work of E.P. Thompson, *the* moral economy as an object of study is comprised of 'all forms of provisioning, including those outside the cash economy' (Sayer, 2004a, p. 2) rather than being confined to the market economy (Hann, 2010; Thompson, 1971, 1991). The economy is also, for both Sayer and Thompson, a *moral* economy because it is not driven only by the pursuit of individual self-interest (though self-interest is one factor) (Sayer, 2004b, p. 80). Other factors, including for example emotions, caring and normative or cultural influences also influence economic actions (Sayer, 2003, p. 353). But the role of normativity in the economy is still greater than this: norms are also *constitutive* of economic institutions, such as property, which depends utterly on a set of norms regarding the rights of people with regard to those resources over which they stake property claims (Sayer, 2011, p. 249). Such institutions are also protected by discursive structures that are used to legitimate them (Sayer, 2011, p. 249) – and these too are normative (Elder-Vass, 2012, chapter 8). To make the connection to my argument here clear, we need only recognise that norms produce *practices* and thus both property (amongst other economic institutions) and its legitimation depend on practices.

Moral economy, however, is also the name for a kind of inquiry, which assumes both an analytical mode and a normative mode. In the former, it is 'the study of the ways in which economic activities, in the broad sense, are influenced by moral-political norms and sentiments, and how, conversely, those norms are compromised by economic forces' (Sayer, 2004b, p. 80). In this sense, it may be regarded as a variety of economic sociology, or perhaps as a refusal to subject the study of the economy to traditional disciplinary boundaries at all. In the latter, normative, mode it takes an evaluative stance towards 'economic systems, actions and motives in terms of their effects on people's lives' (Sayer, 2004b, pp. 80–1) while also being reflexive about 'the standpoints from which these critiques are made' (Sayer, 2004b, p. 81; also see Sayer, 2015, pp. 18–22). Moral economy is thus ethical and political as well as scientific, and in this sense this book is a work of moral economy. Moral economy, however, is not a fully fledged tradition of economic thought, but rather an orientation to thinking about the economy, and thus thoroughly compatible with drawing on material from a range of other traditions. The next chapter moves on from the examination of earlier traditions that has occupied us for the last two chapters, to the constructive phase of building a new framework for understanding diverse economies.

5 | *Complexes of appropriative practices*

Introduction

Economies are not monoliths but diverse mixtures of varying economic forms. To understand and evaluate economic phenomena, then, we need to be able to describe and analyse these varying forms and the ways in which they operate, both independently and in conjunction with each other. This chapter develops a framework for analysing economic form that is tied neither to ideological preconceptions about markets nor to a teleological narrative of epochs dominated by single modes of production. Instead, in the central theoretical innovation of the book, it introduces the concept of *appropriative practices*, and argues that we can understand different economic forms more productively as *complexes* of appropriative practices.

In describing these practices as *appropriative* I focus attention from the outset on the ways in which they produce a variety of different benefits – and indeed negative consequences, which I shall call harms – for those who participate in them. This is the ultimate focus of all political economy: who (or which groups or types of people) gets what from our economic system, why does it turn out this way, how should we evaluate these appropriations and indeed how could they be improved? This is necessarily a political and a moral debate but one that must be based on a sound understanding of the causal structures involved.

The framework accommodates diversity by recognising not only that there is a broad range of appropriative practices, but also that appropriative practices may be combined with each other in a variety of different complexes, and that the same practice may contribute to different economic forms when it forms a part of different complexes. It is these *complexes* of practices, I argue, that are distinctive economic forms, with different systemic consequences. Strictly speaking, though, it is not practices or complexes that act causally; these practices have to be combined with people and things to form social structures like households, firms, states and other forms of collective to give us the entities that interact to produce economic phenomena. In the contemporary world many of these structures coexist, compete and interact to generate an economic system that does not behave like either the Marxist model of capitalism or the mainstream economic model of a market economy.

The chapter builds slowly to its core innovation. It begins by examining why *practices* are the most coherent unit of economic form, then says a little more about what practices are and how they work. Then it moves on to the concept of appropriation and what sorts of practices we may call *appropriative* ones. Finally, it discusses the issues raised when we examine how multiple appropriative practices interact with each other in *complexes* and illustrates them briefly with reference to different varieties of capitalism and hybrid forms.

Practices: the unit of economic form

The concept of *economic form* is highly abstract. It refers to different ways of organising economic activity, but without entailing any commitment to a specific theory of economic forms. By contrast, the concept of *mode of production* also refers to different ways of organising economic activity, but carries with it a set of theoretical commitments – in effect, a commitment to Marx's theory of history. Thus *mode of production* would be one possible concretisation of the more abstract concept of *economic form* and this chapter develops an alternative concretisation: *complex of appropriative practices*. The mainstream tradition, by contrast, does not have a substantive concept of economic form in general, but assumes that there is one and only one normal and desirable economic form: the market economy.

A theory of economic form, such as the theory of modes of production, can be characterised in at least two dimensions. First, we may ask what *unit* of activity it relates to: if economic forms are to be distinguished from each other, then there ought to be some reasonably well bounded kind of thing or class of activities that could be described more or less unambiguously as having one specific economic form. Second, we may ask what *aspect* or aspects of organising economic activity it picks out as significant, as differentiating one economic form from another. This section considers the units.

The traditional identification of modes of production with historical epochs implies that a mode of production is a feature of a whole social formation, in other words, the unit of form is a whole society – and indeed the mainstream conception of a market economy also implicitly identifies economic form with whole societies. The concepts of *social formation* and *society* are problematic when they imply methodological nationalism, that is, that societies are bounded by state borders (Chernilo, 2007, chapter 1), although increasingly scholars think of *society* and *social formation* in global terms. But whether we use *social formation* in the national or the global sense, it is clear from the arguments of Chapter 2 that economic processes are far too diverse in the contemporary economy for the social formation to be a viable unit of economic form. Because there may be multiple economic forms within a society or social formation, the unit that can be identified unambiguously with a *given* economic form must be a smaller unit than the whole social formation.

Those Marxist thinkers who have sought to develop the argument that there might be multiple modes of production within a given social formation have tended to think of the unit of economic form as what we may call a *site*, or perhaps more accurately, a *social entity*. Thus, for example, the domestic labour debate often seems to have been conducted on the assumption that capitalism operates within commercial businesses, whereas some other economic form, if there is one, operates within the household. Although the concept of the household is typically identified with the space of the home, and that of the commercial business may be identified with the space of the factory, shop or office, these identifications with geographical sites are somewhat crude. Thus, for example, when an office worker works from home she is engaged in activity on behalf of the business that employs her rather than household activity, and when a housewife shops in a supermarket she is engaged in activity on behalf of the household rather than work for the business that operates the shop. A more plausible version of the argument, therefore, identifies the *social entity* as the unit: in these cases the geographically spread business or household. Gibson-Graham, for example, generally argue in this way: they identify privately owned firms as capitalist, and a whole range of other social entities such as family businesses, households and co-operatives as non-capitalist (e.g. Gibson-Graham, 2006a, pp. 65–6).

Yet even this is unsatisfactory. Not all activities within the household can plausibly be seen as cases of the same economic form, and not all activities within commercial businesses can be seen as capitalistic.

One way of making this argument would be to suggest that different economic forms operate in *different* households, as is implicit in Fraad, Resnick and Wolff (1994) (note that they avoid the term *mode of production*). There is some value in this argument, but it still misidentifies the unit of analysis. Even within one and the same household multiple economic forms may be at work. Thus, for example, some households mix work done without direct renumeration by family members with work done as wage labour by outsiders working as nannies, housekeepers, cleaners or gardeners. Miriam Glucksmann, for example, documents a variety of mixes of paid and unpaid domestic labour in her study of women workers in 1930s Lancashire (2012, chapter 3). Similarly, within commercial businesses wage labour is accompanied by activities that can more plausibly be regarded as parts of a gift economy: most notably the work that workers do to assist each other (Sayer, 2004a, p. 10). Entanglements of the commodity and gift economies in the digital environment also illustrate the point: when a salaried programmer in a profit-oriented commercial software company spends time writing code for free open-source software, for example, it is not clear that this can be neatly filed away under 'capitalist mode of production' (Elder-Vass, 2015c).

I propose, therefore, that the unit that we can characterise as belonging clearly to a specific economic form is neither the social formation nor the social entity, but rather the *practice*. A *practice* is a tendency to act in a certain way, usually a tendency that is both reinforced for the individual and standardised across individuals by normative social expectations, although other factors can also contribute to the standardisation of practices, notably standardised material objects. Returning to the case of workers helping each other out while they work as wage labourers for a commercial business, the practice of wage labour and the practice of appropriating surplus as profit are capitalist practices in this context, while the practice of assisting one's fellow workers is not. Similarly, in the case of salaried programmers writing open-source code, the practice of wage labour may be capitalist, as is the practice of selling support services at a profit, but the practice of writing open-source code is a gift economy practice.

Practices are primarily the product of social norms: standardised expectations about how we should behave. Norms in turn are primarily the product of endorsing and enforcing behaviour by members of social groups that I call *norm circles* (Elder-Vass, 2010b, chapter 6,

2012, chapter 2). For every social norm and corresponding social practice, there is a group of people – the norm circle for the norm concerned – who are prepared to act in support of the norm, whether by praising and/or rewarding those who conform to the norm, or by criticising and/or punishing those who do not. Those who are exposed to their actions in support of the norm will realise, whether consciously or not, that they face a normative environment in which there is some pressure and some incentive to conform to the norm concerned, and this will tend to increase their tendency to conform to the norm themselves. Thus, for example, queuing is a practice that is strongly normativised in certain cultures. In certain contexts where more than one person is waiting to access a service, it is expected in these cultures that they will 'form a line, ordered by the time at which the individuals joined it... with the understanding that the first person in the line will take the next turn to access the service' (Elder-Vass, 2010b, pp. 146–7). If they do not,

they are likely to face strong negative sanctions, particularly from those who are already participating in the queue, but often also from those staffing the service points concerned... There is, in other words, a norm circle for queuing and the power of the norm circle tends to influence individuals to form queues, to observe the norms of queuing within the queue and to endorse and enforce queuing norms in queuing situations (Elder-Vass, 2010b, p. 147).

Each norm has its own norm circle, and these may be diversely intersectional. Normativity, then, is not produced homogeneously for all of us by 'society', but rather in a variegated fashion depending on the size, range and strength of the many different norm circles that operate within it. Furthermore, the size and influence of different norm circles varies over time, producing normative change in society. And that influence is also related to other forms of social power: those norm circles whose members have significant social power and in particular significant discursive power (such as newspaper editors and owners, politicians and public intellectuals) may exert more social influence than others. The practice of wage labour, for example, is produced by a complex of norms which are backed by powerful actors like capitalist companies and the state, and their influence over the practice arises in part because of the imbalance in power between employers and employees.

Furthermore, normative practices underpin much more than just simple interactions like queuing. All property, for example, and therefore much of the appropriation that occurs in modern economies, depends on complexes of norms such as 'you may not take an object that belongs to another person without their permission' (Elder-Vass, 2012, p. 72). In such cases several different norms may interact to create what John Searle calls *institutional facts*: facts that depend on how we collectively think and talk about them (Elder-Vass, 2012, chapter 4; Searle, 1995, p. e.g. 27–8, 2010, p. e.g. 93–6). Property is only property because we collectively accept that it is so, and in particular because we collectively endorse and enforce the norms and practices that make it so. Such practices are bolstered by law, but law itself depends on, and can be seen as a form of, normative endorsement. Property is by no means the only institutional fact that is fundamental to the appropriation that occurs in modern societies. Money is another (Searle, 1995, pp. 32–6, 2010, pp. 101–2). Without normativised practices relating to the acceptance of certain methods of payment and standards of valuation used in pricing, for example, money literally would not exist (Elder-Vass, 2015d). Many of the fundamental elements of modern economies, in other words, are ontologically dependent on social processes, and in particular on normativised practices, that are ignored by both mainstream and Marxist economics. If and when those social processes change, our economies change. And practices are equally fundamental to other forms of economy: Mauss's account of so-called gift economies, for example, was an account of the economic practices observed in them. This dependence of *all* form of economy on practices is one of the factors that makes them a suitable unit of economic form in general, unlike for example markets, which are institutionally specific to certain kinds of economy and not found in others. And it is this dependence that makes it possible for a political economy of practices to be more general than the political economies criticised in the last two chapters.

Appropriative practices

There are many different kinds of practices, many of which are not primarily economic.[1] The concept of *appropriative* practices that is

---

[1] For example, discursive, linguistic and epistemic practices (Elder-Vass, 2012, chapters 6, 8 and 11).

central to this book's argument picks out a specifically economic subset, using *economic* in the sense discussed in Chapter 2, that is, those practices that are concerned with provisioning our needs, either in the form of commodities or through goods and services that could have been supplied as commodities. Appropriative practices are related to – and ultimately dependent on – the production of goods or services (defined broadly, to correspond to this broad definition of economic) but their defining feature is that they are concerned with the allocation of the benefits (and indeed harms) that arise from production to individuals or social groups. In a sense this is a functional definition, as it picks out a specific set of practices on the basis of their tendential effects rather than, say, some common feature of their structure, mechanisms or the actors involved: it includes all those *practices that significantly, systematically and more or less directly influence the allocation of the benefits of production.* I include the terms *significantly, systematically* and *directly* because all practices may have some small or occasional or indirect influence on who receives benefits, and here the focus is on those that have the most substantial and consistent influences. Speaking more loosely, we may say that appropriative practices are those practices wrapped around the process of production that determine the allocation of its benefits. Thus, for example, sharecropping is an appropriative practice that governs the distribution of the crop produced by a certain class of agricultural workers.

When any term is reused for a new purpose, there is a danger of its meaning being confused with earlier uses, and in this case there are at least two confusions to be avoided. First, as noted in Chapter 1, *appropriation* is sometimes used in the economic tradition to mean the first conversion of something unowned into something owned: into property. Second, the everyday sense of *appropriation* sometimes has the connotation that the person who receives a benefit actively *takes* it, and it is not my intention to suggest this. Unfortunately alternative terms tend to have directly opposite and equally unsatisfactory connotations – *allocative* and *distributive* can both seem to imply that the person who provides a benefit actively determines who receives it. *Transfer* is perhaps more suitable in this respect, as it is more neutral about who is in control of the process, but appropriative practices do not necessarily take the form of transfers. Let me be clear, then, that my use of the term *appropriative* neither refers to the initial creation of property nor carries any implication as to who is in charge of the practice. I should also make clear that my use of the term does not in itself imply a specific ethical judgement about the practices concerned, unlike the occasional use of the term *appropriative practices* in cultural and religious studies, where it generally seems to indicate disapproval of the practice concerned (e.g. Welch, 2007). Indeed, one virtue of the term is that in using it I seek to distance myself from the connotation that appropriations by anyone other than the producer of the product concerned are necessarily *exploitative* (cf. Cohen, 1978, p. 332 and see Chapter 3 in this book).

One consequence of adopting this approach is that it is not only acts of production in the narrow sense in which the Marxist tradition understands them that are moments of appropriation. In particular, appropriation also depends on acts of transfer: transfers of products and sometimes of money. These transfers may take the form of exchange but there is no necessity for this to be the case. The serf's transfer of a share of their product to the landlord, for example, is not an exchange; nor is the transfer of a parent's caring services to their child, but both are moments of appropriation that re-allocate benefits.

The concept of *benefits* plays an essential role in this account of appropriation. Benefits are ultimately personal and psychological in nature, and should be distinguished from the benefit-carriers that produce them. In moments of appropriation benefit-carriers are transferred or implemented, leading to benefits (or harms) for the individuals concerned. Thus, for example, in wage labour, the worker receives a benefit-carrier in the form of a wage, and the employer receives a benefit-carrier by taking ownership of the product of the labour. For another example, in a commodity purchase the buyer receives a benefit-carrier in the form of the commodity and the seller receives a benefit-carrier in the form of monetary payment. Benefit-carriers may be measurable and commensurable – we can compare, for example, how much money different people earn. Benefits, by contrast, are not, although sometimes we may wish to compare benefit-carriers as a proxy in evaluating the distribution of benefits. Workers may obtain some satisfaction merely from receiving their wage, but on the whole they need to convert their wages into commodities and then make use of those commodities in order to obtain actual benefits. Nor can these benefits be equated to use-values in Marx's sense. Use-values are possessed by objects and an object's use-value is its capacity to meet a certain generic need. The use-value of a coat, for example, is that it can be worn to keep one warm and dry, but the *benefit* is actually *being* warm and dry. Use-values can sometimes be measured in cardinal terms: two bicycles, for example, have twice as much use-value as one, but benefits cannot: there is no numerical relation between the benefits and/or harms someone obtains from owning two bicycles as compared to owning one. Benefits thus share some of the features of the concept of *utility* employed by utilitarian philosophers and main-stream economists, but not others. In particular, benefits are not one homogeneous property but vary in character from case to case. Nor can we make ordinal evaluations of different sorts of benefit by assum-ing that individuals prefer the benefits arising from a chosen course of action to those arising from an unchosen course, since this would depend on the assumptions of complete information and full rational optimisation of choice that were rejected in Chapter 4.

Benefits from production arise when some material process creates an effect that the affected individual values, and thus depend on a conjunction between a benefit-carrier and a valuation. The same benefit-carrier may be valued in different ways, according to different principles, in different circumstances, according to what benefit it is intended to realise. This resembles the phenomenon Gregory has called 'value switching': 'people can switch from one value regime to another as, for example, when gold is purchased as a commodity, given as a gift to a daughter and passed on to descendants as a family heirloom' (Gregory, 2000, p. 110). Value switching implies that people are more complex than the self-interested utility maximisers of mainstream economics. It is possible, for example, that 'the drive to give is as important to an understanding of humanity as the desire to receive' (Godbout & Caillé, 1998, p. 19). The gift of gold to a daughter, for example, may generate psychological benefits for the donor – pleasure in increasing the status of the daughter, for example – as well as for the recipient. Appropriative practices, then, need not be zero-sum phenomena.

The relation of benefits to principles of valuation, and indeed to material and social circumstances, also entails that the same benefit-carrier may count as a benefit in some cases and a harm in others. A bland simple meal may be a benefit for someone who is starving, or for a religious ascetic, but a harm for a prosperous gourmand. Perhaps the most striking case of this is *work*. The act of production may be a source of alienation and unhappiness, or of fulfilment and pleasure, depending on the circumstances and the principles of valuation applied to it by the worker. The difference between the two is arguably a product of the social organisation of work and the culture of work. The physical nature of work is also a key factor, but one that can operate in very different ways depending on these other two. The social organisation of work may thus be seen as an appropriative practice, not just in terms of its consequences for incomes but also in terms of its consequences for the work process. In other words, not only wages but also work itself are benefit-carriers whose benefits or harms depend upon principles of valuation.

Since appropriation is the allocation of benefit, this dependence of benefits on valuation also means that appropriation itself depends on how people value the consequences of economic activity. Therefore we cannot even *describe* appropriation without at least implicitly recognising a standard of evaluation, though this does not imply that we must agree with the standard concerned. We can recognise, for example, that a currency speculator receives a psychological benefit from making a large monetary profit on a deal without accepting that *we* should value such benefits according to the speculator's implicit standard of value.

There are thus two sets of principles of valuation implicit in a moral economy of appropriative practices: those employed by the actors themselves and those deployed in evaluating appropriative practices and outcomes. To accept those employed by the actors themselves for the latter purpose (as mainstream economics implicitly does when it adopts utility theory as a device for justifying allocative outcomes) is to abandon the possibility of taking a critical stance towards the economy. Moral economy thus appeals to other standards, though it may also recognise that there are multiple valid principles of valuation – as Boltanski and Thévenot's discussion of regimes of justification implies, for example (Boltanski & Thévenot, 2006). We must justify the standards that we use for such valuations or at the very least make them explicit, as I sought to do in Chapter 3, rather than taking some implicit standard as adequate without careful consideration. As Boltanski and Thévenot argue, a great deal of moral conflict is ultimately concerned with *which* principle of valuation should be applied to some activity or outcome.

This book focuses on *appropriative* practices because the distribution of the benefits of the economic system is precisely what political economy is about, and appropriative practices are precisely those that affect these issues. This orientation to the distribution of economic benefits is common to all traditions of political economy. Mainstream economics is focused on who gets what from the economy, and so is Marx. Of the two, only Marxist political economy has a theory of economic form, but despite naming economic forms modes of *production*, Marx's focus too is on the appropriation of benefit. For Marx, also, as we saw in Chapter 3, this is very much an evaluative enterprise, but appropriation in Marx's scheme is linked far too directly to exploitation.[2] As a consequence of the labour theory of value, any appropriation of product by anyone other than the producer is seen as exploitation (see Chapter 3). But once we have rejected the labour theory of value, the possibility of exploitation can once again become an ethical question, to be judged by asking whether any given appropriation or appropriative practice is just or fair.

Complexes of appropriative practices

The most significant economic forms are not defined by single appropriative practices. Rather, they are interacting *complexes* of them. Thus, for example, the pursuit of capital accumulation by the employment of wage labour to produce commodities, which I shall call *canonical capitalism* (due to its role in Marx's system) is a complex that combines at least three practices: capital accumulation, wage labour and commodity production. Wage labour alone is not enough to give us canonical capitalism, since people may work for wages in a variety of non-capitalist contexts such as government deparments.[3] Nor is commodity production enough to give us canonical capitalism, since commodities may also be produced by individuals working alone, in family businesses that do not pay wages, or in co-operatives (Gibson-Graham, 2006b, p. 263; Sayer, 1995, p. 181). We may even have *both* wage labour and commodity production without canonical capitalism, notably in state-run enterprises. Canonical capitalism is thus defined by a certain *complex* of

---

[2] Marx also uses the term *appropriation* but usually to refer to the process of production itself, which he regards as an appropriation of nature by the producer (Althusser & Balibar, 2009, p. 238).

[3] For a contrary Marxist argument, discussed later, see (Cohen, 1978, pp. 181–3).

appropriative practices rather than by any specific appropriative practice.[4]

This concept of a complex of appropriative practices, I argue, has several advantages over competing understandings of economic form. Both the neoclassical orientation to markets as the only significant economic form, and the monolithic conception of a mode of production are inadequate for theorising the range of economic forms in diverse economies. This section will examine some of the ways in which the concept of complexes of appropriative practices allows us to theorise social relations more flexibly.

The first is that there is no difficulty in theorising the coexistence of multiple economic forms. There is no longer a conflict, for example, between the belief that capitalism is an important element of the contemporary economy and the recognition that it governs only a minority of productive processes, and thus there is no longer a need to obscure the significance of the gift economy or indeed of other non-capitalist economic forms that coexist relatively stably alongside capitalism. Given this, we can reject the attempt to reduce all contemporary class relations to capitalist appropriation of the product of wage labour that is characteristic of the most vulgar Marxism, and start to theorise the social relations and practices of appropriation that characterise these other complexes. We need not, for example, ignore the appropriation of caring services by children in households because Marxism implies that this would make children exploiters of their parents, but rather examine the complex of processes in which this occurs as an economic form in its own right. We can escape from the hidebound pigeonholing of all social relations into what Folbre and Hartmann have called 'a formulaic set of class processes' (1994, p. 59) – those few patterns that Marxists believe have dominated epochs.

As well as examining the coexistence of multiple complexes of appropriative practices within the economy we now have the tools to examine such coexistence within specific sites or social entities. The fact that commercial firms are the site of capitalist practices is no longer a theoretical obstacle to recognising that they may also be the

---

[4] When multiple norms and the resulting practices interact systematically, powerful social structures can emerge. For another type of case, see (Elder-Vass, 2012, pp. 69–73).

site of other forms of appropriative practice. Nor is the argument that households are the site of gift-forms of appropriative practice compromised by recognising that they may also be the site of wage labour, whether it is capitalist (e.g. when an agency supplies cleaning staff) or not (e.g. when a self-employed cleaner contracts to provide a service). The household, in this perspective, becomes the site of moments of appropriation that operate within the frames of a variety of different complexes of appropriative practices. It is, we may say, a mixed economy of practices in its own right. Struggles within the household over the division and control of domestic labour may then also be theorised as struggles over the mix, struggles over which complex of appropriative practices is to prevail in which circumstances.

Relaxing the requirement that an economic form must correspond to the dominant form of an epoch also makes it easier to theorise varieties of a form. As I argued in Chapter 3, following Banaji, capitalism is characterised by a central preoccupation with the pursuit of capital accumulation. This in itself is an appropriative practice, but one that can be implemented in many different ways, and each of these is a distinct complex in which the practice of capital accumulation is combined with other appropriative practices. This allows us to postulate varieties of capitalism in which this general form is combined in a more concrete complex with further appropriative practices. Thus, for example, we might distinguish between private capitalism in which the capitalist is an individual, and joint-stock capitalism in which the ultimate rights to control capital and share in its appropriation of profit are distributed across a larger group through the practices of shareholder voting in general meetings and dividend distribution. These two forms of capitalism might have quite different systemic tendencies if, for example, the joint stock form tends to suppress other orientations than capital accumulation more thoroughly than the private form. Or, as was noted earlier, we could distinguish between canonical capitalism, based on wage labour, and plantation capitalism, which combines capital accumulation and commodity production with slavery. Not only would these require very different ethical evaluations, but they might also have different systemic characteristics: plantation capitalism, for example, might be more prone to shortfalls in demand for mass produced commodities.

Marxist thinkers have made some such distinctions already. As Jessop argues, for example, 'there is no logic of capital but a series of logics with a family resemblance, corresponding to different modes of regulation and accumulation strategies' (Jessop, 2001, p. 105). We must avoid, however, seeing these different forms of capitalism as being defined by what remnants of previous systems they have carried over (cf. Hodgson, 1999, pp. 148–51). There is no standard form of capitalism, with other forms as corruptions or imperfect realisations of it, but rather many different practices with which the drive to accumulate may be articulated to form a variety of different but equally capitalistic complexes of appropriative practice. As suggested in Chapter 3, then, we can retain the concept of capitalism while replacing the concept of modes of production with a more flexible model of economic form.

Just as capitalism can take many different forms, many of the practices that appear as elements of capitalistic complexes can also appear in non-capitalist complexes. The failure to recognise this has caused endless confusion in the Marxist tradition. Cohen, for example, as we saw in Chapter 3, argues that there are two 'equally standard but logically distinct Marxian definitions of capitalist society', a structural definition based on the use of wage labour and a modal definition based on the orientation of production to the accumulation of capital, but argues that 'what satisfies each definition also satisfies the other' (Cohen, 1978, p. 181). Cohen, in other words, argues that capital accumulation depends on wage labour, and wage labour necessarily serves capital accumulation, and indeed spends the next ten pages trying to prove this, even discussing plantation slavery and still concluding that capital accumulation and wage labour necessarily go together. Cohen's argument, however, is constrained by his commitment to the idea that the unit of economic form is a whole society, and he thus feels able to dismiss other economic forms as marginal or transitional. Once we reject this idea, we can see that wage labour can indeed form part of non-capitalist economic forms. Thus, for example, a family that pays wages to a nanny or a gardener, or a university providing free education that pays a salary to lecturers and other staff, does not thereby become a capitalist enterprise: we have wage labour but neither commodity production nor the accumulation of capital.

It may also be useful to think of some complexes of appropriative practices as hybrid forms. Hybridity can mean that a case is synchronically (simultaneously) an instantiation of two different forms, or that it has been derived diachronically (historically/genetically) from the combination of two different forms. In the synchronic sense all complexes are hybrids of the various practices that compose them, but by labelling one set of such complexes as capitalist we create the further possibility of a more specific type of hybrid form: one that is simultaneously capitalistic and also instantiates some other form. As I have argued, the practice that is decisively capitalistic is an orientation to accumulation on the part of at least one set of actors. Even in canonical capitalism, however, not all classes of actors are oriented to capital accumulation: in the classic case, the capitalist is, but the proletarian is oriented to earning a wage for the purpose of surviving and perhaps sustaining a family. Thus the presence of actors who are not oriented to accumulation is not enough to make a form hybrid.

To get hybridity, we need other *types* of economic form as well as the capitalist type. Although I have questioned whether there are other coherently identifiable *modes of production* than capitalism, there can still be other types of complex of appropriative practices. One candidate is suggested by the idea of the gift economy: there is a wide variety of complexes of appropriative practice in which voluntary transfers of goods or services are made without any expectation or obligation to make a return transfer. Some complexes are hybrids of both capitalism and the gift economy because they include both the practice of capital accumulation and the practice of making transfers of goods or services as gifts. Such hybrids are decisively capitalist and yet simultaneously the sites of more progressive practices.

One group of such hybrids, for example, employs what I have called *inducement gifts* (Elder-Vass, 2014). Inducement gifts (discussed in more detail in Chapter 8) are given in order to induce a commercial transaction, or a series of such transactions, that are collectively of greater value to the giver than the original gift. Unlike many other giving practices, which often represent economic forms that we may see as alternatives to, or in competition with, contemporary capitalism, inducement giving is giving turned to the service of capitalism. Anderson, for example, describes the strategy adopted in the United States in the early twentieth century to market Jell-O, a gelatine-based food product. Unable by law to sell their product door to door, the company's salesforce gave away recipe books with recipes for using the product instead. The result was to encourage consumers to buy the product in order to try out the recipes (Anderson, 2009, pp. 9–10).

This kind of gift has long been a fairly widespread phenomenon in commercial economies, but it is one that has been given a new lease of life by digital developments, as we will see in Chapter 8. Inducement gifts are certainly still gifts; but they are equally certainly embedded in a capitalist complex of appropriative practices and thus a hybrid form of gift and capitalist economies.

The approach advocated here also has potential advantages for considering the systemic effects of different economic forms. One of the most valuable features of Marx's work on modes of production is his examination of the mechanisms through which capitalism produces systemic effects such as the drive to growth, a tendency to cycles of boom and slump, and a tendency to extend capitalist commodity production progressively into wider territories and more products. These are emergent effects that result from interactions of individuals and firms produced by the appropriative practices characteristic of capitalism.[5] If this is the case, then we must ask what mechanisms generate these tendencies, and precisely what relations do they depend upon? Different varieties of capitalism, characterised by the addition of further practices to the basic set that defines capitalism in general, may have different systemic consequences, and tracing the development of those practices may allow us to explain developments in the systemic effects of capitalism as it evolves through different mixes of these varieties over time.

The appropriative practices approach also enables us to consider what systemic effects might arise from the interaction of *different* economic forms. In practice, radical thinkers have been doing this for a long time, but they have always faced objections to any treatment that gives equal status to economic forms other than the mode of production considered dominant in the epoch concerned. Marx himself theorised the reproduction of labour power in the household, but only as a kind of auxiliary function of capitalist exploitation, yet the thrust of his argument is that the capitalist form is utterly dependent upon these other forms of production and appropriation (Marx, 1954, chapter 6).

---

[5] I should stress that there is no inconsistency in principle between practice-based explanations of such effects and structural explanations. Practices themselves have structural explanations, and they also form elements of the mechanisms that generate the causal powers of further structures. We cannot plausibly claim structural explanations, though, unless we can identify the structures and mechanisms concerned (Elder-Vass, 2010b).

More recent thinkers in the Marxist tradition, particularly under the influence of Althusser, have discussed the possibility that multiple modes of production might be articulated within a social formation (see Chapter 3). Imperialism, for example, has been interpreted 'as an "articulation" between capitalist and pre-capitalist modes' (Benton, 1984, p. 131). Similarly, John Harrison has argued 'that within a determinate social formation there may be subordinate modes distinct from the dominant, constitutive modes' (Harrison, 1973; Molyneux, 1979, p. 8). But for Harrison, and here he is representative of the vast majority of the Marxist tradition, if there can be such modes they must be either traces of past or future dominant modes, or 'client' modes of production performing functions delegated by the currently dominant mode (Molyneux, 1979, p. 8). Similarly, the French Regulation School theorists have argued that the capitalist economy has gone through a series of *regimes of accumulation* marked, amongst other things, by changing relations 'between capitalism and non-capitalist modes of production' (Brenner & Glick, 1991, p. 47). Thus, for example, Aglietta argues that in the United States in the nineteenth century capitalism benefitted from an environment in which its workers depended on non-commodity relations in the realm of domestic production to supply much of their consumption needs, as a result of remaining embedded in 'the extended family and neighbourhood community' (Aglietta, 2000, p. 80). This interaction of different complexes of appropriative practices benefitted early American capitalism by enabling it to pay lower wages than would otherwise have been required to sustain the workforce. But even the regulation theorists are deeply ambivalent about the status of these other economic forms. Only a few lines later, for example, Aglietta argues that 'there certainly is a universal extension of the capitalist mode of production in the social formations in which it is implanted' (Aglietta, 2000, p. 81). For him, it seems, dependence on other modes of production is no more than a transitional phenomenon. Perhaps these interactions sometimes are transitional phenomena, but the difficulty with the Marxist framework is that it *requires* non-capitalist complexes of appropriative practice to be framed as transitional or marginal, regardless of the empirical facts. By contrast, the framework proposed here avoids these assertions of primacy and examines the actual relations between appropriative practices without preconceptions about their relative significance.

Despite its many advantages, this framework is not without its challenges. Perhaps the most significant is that it may be difficult to tell where to start on theorising appropriative practices. Arguably, to apply the framework to a specific case we need coherent accounts of all of the practices and mechanisms involved in it, but to develop a coherent account of a practice and its associated mechanisms we would have to look at multiple specific cases of the practice in action. This may seem like a chicken and egg problem, but all empirical sciences face the same problem, which is the inevitable consequence of the need for both retroduction and retrodiction in causal explanations – the need to identify both mechanisms and their interactions (Elder-Vass, 2007a, 2010b, chapter 4). In practice, scientists address this problem by drawing on existing accounts of many causal mechanisms, which are provisionally taken as reliable, while focussing their attention on one or a few that seem to need re-theorising. If this book was proposing a model that rendered all previous work on the economy redundant this would be a massive obstacle: we would need to reinvent political economy from the ground up. But a great deal of previous work could be reframed and reused in the context of this model, to provide provisional accounts of practices and mechanisms that we can build on, revise and combine.

Readers of my earlier work may also suspect that this framework poses some challenges to the approach to social ontology I have advocated there. In particular, I have argued that social causes are powers of social entities, which in turn are composed ultimately of groups of people in particular types of relations to each other, and I have paid little attention here to reconciling my account of appropriative practices to that approach. On the whole, I am confident that such a reconciliation is possible, but to devote space to it here would be something of a distraction from the main argument. There is one respect, though, in which the work in this book has encouraged me to consider an extension to my earlier ontological work: it is becoming increasingly clear to me that many social entities with causal powers are composed of not *only* groups of people but *also* non-human material objects. Many structures in the digital economy, for example, have computers and communication networks as essential parts as well as people. While I intend to develop this argument more rigorously elsewhere, the reader will find traces of it in the second half of this book already.

Conclusion

This chapter has built up the concept of complexes of appropriative practices, illustrated it and argued that it provides a more flexible and more powerful understanding of economic forms and the relations between them than those available in competing traditions of political economy. Drawing on the critiques of those traditions presented in the previous two chapters, it has started to develop a framework – a political economy of practices – that is tailored to the economic diversity of modern societies, and sensitive to the ontological requirements of theorising phenomena in open systems.

The real test of such frameworks, however, comes in their application to concrete cases. The second half of this book is composed of a series of case studies, drawn from the contemporary digital economy. They constitute neither a complete test or proof of the framework nor a complete account of the appropriative practice structure of the digital economy itself. Rather, they examine a strategic selection of cases that is designed on the one hand to show the flexibility and power of the framework and on the other to highlight what I take to be the central political-economic tension within the digital economy today: the complex and diverse relations between the capitalist and gift-forms of digital economy.

PART III

Digital economies

6 | *Digital monopoly capitalism: Apple*

Introduction

Each of the next four chapters examines one particular economic model within the digital economy by focusing on a single case (two in Chapter 9). The cases covered are some of the most successful undertakings in the digital economy – Apple, Wikipedia, Google search, Facebook and YouTube. They are significant as individual cases because of the scale of their use and the scale of their influence on the digital economy, but they are also significant as examples of models that are or could be more widely adopted in the digital economy, and indeed to some extent beyond it. They are studies, ultimately, not of specific organisations or websites, but rather of complexes of appropriative practices. While these cases are unrepresentative, not least by virtue of all being large and successful, the purpose of these chapters is not to be representative but to illustrate some cases and briefly consider how widely they might generalise. In each case, I will seek to identify specific appropriative practices, how they are combined in the case concerned and others like it, and how these complexes lead to certain characteristic patterns of appropriation of economic benefits. Some of the appropriative practices theorised here may not have been described in a similar way before, but most have been discussed by other writers. What is novel in this book's approach is not the identification of new practices but the creation of a framework that allows us to explain economic outcomes by examining how these practices interact. This is not to say that no scholars have ever done so before,[1] but rather to argue that this, rather than an obsessive focus on the dubious concepts of surplus value or market equilibrium, is how to study the economy, and to demonstrate the kind of analysis that results.

---

[1] For example, Froud et al. identify some of the appropriative practices (without using that term) employed by Apple (Froud Johal Leaver & Williams, 2014).

The case examined in this particular chapter is thoroughly conventional in the sense that it is a large-scale capitalist business, indeed as of mid-2015 Apple is the largest company by market capitalisation in the world (Forbes, 2015). It is a strongly profit-oriented public company, and makes a significant share of its profits by selling manufactured goods. This sounds like the sort of enterprise that the established economic traditions ought to be good at explaining, yet even in this case the practices upon which it relies for its profits cannot be fully or adequately described in terms of either the Marxist model or the mainstream economic tradition. It is enormously profitable, not because it is more exploitative of wage labour than other companies (though it does depend on wage labour done for low wages in extremely alienating conditions) but because of its outstanding product innovation, design and marketing, and because, in contrast to neoclassical dreams of perfect competition, it is ruthlessly anti-competitive. Moving beyond the limitations imposed by monolithic ways of thinking about the economy, this chapter considers in turn seven different elements of the mix of appropriative practices that underpins Apple's profitability: entrepreneurial innovation, securing the preferential attachment of consumers to their products, the sale of immaterial goods that depend on the construction of intellectual property rights, exercising control over 'markets', supplier subordination, labour exploitation, and avoiding taxation.

Innovation and entrepreneurship

Most popular accounts attribute Apple's success to the genius of its late CEO Steve Jobs – his innovation, design philosophy, marketing and negotiation skills, and authoritarian single-minded pursuit of perfection. Lashinsky, for example, writes that 'After his death at age fifty-six on October 5, 2011, Steve Jobs was rightly celebrated for his extraordinary contributions to the reordering of multiple industries. He revolutionized no fewer than four: computers, music…, film…, and communications' (Lashinsky, 2012, p. 6). He featured on the cover of *Time* magazine no less than eight times, and even the most balanced of his biographers describe him as 'the master evangelist of the digital age' (Young & Simon, 2006, p. 322). Multiple biographies have eulogised his two spells at Apple, which he co-founded with Steve Wozniak in 1976 (Young & Simon, 2006, p. 34). In the following nine years, they developed the Apple I, II and Mac computers, with Jobs focussing on designing an exceptional experience for the end user. At one stage Apple was the largest manufacturer of personal computers in the world (Young & Simon, 2006, p. 59). Jobs lost the CEO role, however, after outside investors took financial control of the company and by 1985 Apple was in decline and Jobs was forced out (Young & Simon, 2006, chapter 4). After leading the computer-generated animation company Pixar to huge success, he returned to the still-faltering Apple in 1997, reinstating its emphasis on stylish user-oriented design, and dropping a wide range of product lines and development projects to focus the company on a small but growing range of innovations: the iPod, iTunes, the iPhone, and the iPad. These were the products that propelled Apple to its position as the most successful company in the world and Jobs to an extraordinary degree of adulation from the consumers of his products: after his death over a million messages were posted to the tribute page set up by Apple (www.apple.com/stevejobs/).

Jobs was clearly very different from the typical CEO – who idolises the CEO of the company that designed and marketed their hairdryer, their spectacles or their bicycle? Who even knows who they are? We can attribute the difference to two factors. First, the particularly emotional role played by these new products in their users' lives as a result of the new connections they enabled: to music, to the Internet, and to other users; and second, the particular role that Jobs played in creating and marketing these products. Internally, Jobs maintained total control over the design and quality of Apple's products, demanding both an elegant minimalism of style and revolutionary new features – the features that he himself would want in such a product (Lashinsky, 2012, pp. 54–5). Externally, he maintained total control over the image of its products that Apple presented to the world – the advertising, the packaging, and the information released to the press – and ensured that they were presented as both technologically cutting-edge and as the acme of cool personal style (Isaacson, 2011, p. 347; Lashinsky, 2012, pp. 19, 50, 115–6).

This book stresses the importance of generalizable appropriative practices in shaping economic outcomes, but this is entirely consistent with recognising that individual human agency – such as the entrepreneurship of Steve Jobs – also has a causal role. For critical realists, all events are the consequence of multiple kinds of interacting causal powers, including both individual agency and the normative forces that support appropriative practices, as well as many others.[2] Economic phenomena are not *only* the product of appropriative practices, but rather of the interaction of these practices with human agency and indeed with other social and material entities and their powers. Innovation and entrepreneurship are themselves practices, but like all practices they depend on individuals to enact them, and there is always the potential for creativity in the ways in which they do, and always the potential that the ways in which they are enacted might transform rather than simply reproducing the structural context. We need not doubt, then, that Jobs made a central contribution to Apple's success, or that Apple produced a series of remarkable, and remarkably successful, products under his direct influence, but we do need to put his contributions in a wider perspective and recognise the significance of the other factors with which they interacted.

However brilliant an innovator may be, innovation (as opposed to invention) is always a process of recombination of already-known or at least already-imagined possibilities (Schumpeter, 2000, p. 51). Novelty 'tends to involve rather mundane processes of piecing together existing components and ideas': components that come from 'the stock of existing technology' and ideas that mostly come from the stock of existing knowledge (C. Lawson, forthcoming, chapter 8). Jobs, like any other innovator, was utterly dependent on those existing stocks – the path-breaking graphical user interface on the Apple Mac, for example, was a development of work he had observed at Xerox's Palo Alto Research Centre (Young & Simon, 2006, pp. 60–1). One consequence was that his innovations were products that were only marginally or incrementally different, at many levels, than others that were either already available or were developed in parallel from the same existing stocks. Those existing components and ideas, then, play a causal role in innovation alongside the innovators themselves.

Jobs's particular talent was to imagine new versions of old types of product that met their users' needs more effectively, more usably and more elegantly than the existing versions, and to demand new combinations of components that made this possible. Jobs claimed,

---

[2] The recognition that *both* structure, or culture, and agency play complementary and interacting causal roles is a centrepiece of critical realist social ontology, as expressed in Roy Bhaskar's Transformational Model of Social Activity (Bhaskar, 1998, pp. 34–7), Margaret Archer's morphogenetic cycle (Archer, 1995) and my own work on structure and agency (Elder-Vass, 2010b).

for example, that Apple made the iPhone because its senior executives hated their existing smartphones – and he saw the potential to make something better (Lashinsky, 2012, p. 54). One of the challenges in creating new technology is to make new features easy to use with as little learning required as possible: to make it easy for the consumer to enrol the technology into their lives (C. Lawson, forthcoming, chapter 8). For Jobs, this was a central feature of design, which was not just about appearance but about designing the user's whole experience of the product: 'Some people think design means how it looks. But, of course, if you dig deeper, it's really how it *works*' (also see Isaacson, 2011, p. 343; Steve Jobs, quoted in Young & Simon, 2006, pp. 280–1). Design, in both senses, was absolutely central to Apple's product development process (Isaacson, 2011, p. 344; Lashinsky, 2012, p. 55). And design, in this sense, is an application of the multiple determination theory of causality to product design. What is to be designed is the user experience, and this proceeds from the recognition that this experience is a product of multiple interacting factors: not just the physical object but also the presentation of its facilities and the capacities of the user. Consistency in the interface, for example, produces a capacity in the user that can be reused from application to application – and therefore a sense that the product is 'intuitive' to use – whereas variation in user interfaces creates obstacles to the enrolment of the device in the user's life. As Jobs put it, 'It takes a lot of hard work to make something simple' (Steve Jobs, quoted in Isaacson, 2011, p. 343).

Innovation, then, is strongly influenced by the material possibilities, the existing stock of technical knowledge, and the culturally shaped needs and capacities of its users, but it is also a social practice in its own right, and one that is widely practiced in both capitalist and non-capitalist economic forms. It is largely synonymous with entrepreneurship – both are concerned with recombining existing technologies to produce new things, or to produce in new ways – and thus with the development of new forms of production.

While entrepreneurship too can be practiced outside the context of capitalism, it is nevertheless a practice that is fundamental to capitalism and its dynamism, as we learn from the heterodox economic theory of Joseph Schumpeter. Schumpeter saw that the neoclassical focus on the equilibrating tendencies of the economy ignored the equally important dynamic tendencies that generated change, growth, profit and progress. He argued that perfect competition as theorised by the neoclassical tradition would gradually eliminate all profit in a capitalist economy, and therefore the continuing existence of profit as a central feature of real capitalist economies meant that equilibrium theory was radically inadequate (Heilbroner, 2000, p. 294). It was innovation that generated profit: by introducing 'new or cheaper ways of making things, or ways of making wholly new things', entrepreneurs were able to undercut existing producers, or create distinctive new products that commanded a price premium and thus create profits – at least until equilibration caught up with them, as other capitalists copied their innovations and those who failed to do so went out of business (Heilbroner, 2000, p. 295).

Innovation, then, is not just an incidental disruption to the normal self-stabilising economy, but 'The fundamental impulse that sets and keeps the capitalist engine in motion' (Schumpeter, 1994, pp. 82–3). This is a process 'that incessantly revolutionizes the economic structure *from within*, incessantly destroying the old one, incessantly creating a new one. This process of Creative Destruction is the essential fact about capitalism' (Schumpeter, 1994, p. 83). Nor are innovators anything like the rational calculating optimisers with perfect information theorised by the neoclassical tradition. They do not even deal with uncertainty, in which the probabilities of different outcomes can be known, but step into conditions of risk, taking a leap into the unknown. The outcome of any individual innovation may be triumph or disaster for the innovator, but the *systemic* consequence of the practice of innovation under capitalism is creative destruction, with new businesses rising and old ones falling. One result is massive shifts in benefit allocation, towards the managers, the employees and above all the shareholders in the winning firms, and away from those in the losers. As Apple rises, IBM and Nokia for example decline. But innovation also creates new benefits for consumers: iPhones and iPads can improve the quality of their users' lives in ways that simply were not possible before them. Entrepreneurship, in other words, is an appropriative practice, a practice that has profound consequences for the question of *who benefits* from economic activity, and also a practice that transforms and reconfigures other appropriative practices.

Schumpeter sees profit as a *systemic* consequence of innovation. But for individual corporations like Apple innovation is directed entirely at increasing their *own* profit. Writers who focus on the personal contribution of Steve Jobs tend to obscure this. One theme that is common to his biographies is that Jobs didn't really care about money and the things it could buy at a personal level. He lived quite simply, given that he was a very rich man for many years. He is portrayed as being motivated by the idea of winning and by the satisfaction of making something great, rather than the company's bottom line. These are remarkably similar to the motivations Schumpeter ascribes to entrepreneurs: 'the will to found a private kingdom', 'the impulse to fight, to prove oneself superior to others, to succeed for the sake, not of the fruits of success, but of success itself' and 'the joy of creating, of getting things done, or simply of exercising one's energy and ingenuity' (Schumpeter, 2000, p. 70). But whatever Jobs's own personal goals, he owed his ability to pursue them to his structural position as CEO of Apple. From the moment that outside investors took majority control of Apple, and particularly once it was floated on the stock market, the position of the CEO was in the hands of the board and ultimately of the shareholders. Whatever manoeuvring Jobs might have done behind the scenes (Young & Simon, 2006, pp. 231–2), he ultimately became CEO again in 1997 because the board and major shareholders believed that he could deliver large and growing profits and stock values and he remained CEO only because he did deliver them. This is a systemic imperative which CEO's must follow or be fired. Like other capitalist businesses, Apple is a money making machine, driven to accumulate capital by the very structure of the stock market: by the logic of the system in which it is embedded. The drive to accumulation is the *definitive* appropriative practice of capitalism, imposed on the managers of public companies whether they like it or not.

Capitalism needs innovation to fuel its insatiable appetite for growth, and drives it forward relentlessly to support its drive to accumulate. Innovation, however, is only one of the appropriative practices that firms like Apple link together in their pursuit of accumulation. Another is the pursuit of power over the customer.

Preferential attachment

Economists tend to think of monopolies as relatively rare cases in which infrastructure investments, legal restrictions or natural resource limitations mean that one large company faces a situation in which it has no significant competitors: no rival suppliers of equivalent products. Their supposed rarity means that market economies can be theorised in terms of competitive markets in which sellers must compete on price with large numbers of other suppliers of equivalent products. But the reality is that most sellers (whether capitalist or not) are constantly seeking to differentiate their offerings from the competition, and to secure what I have called the *preferential attachment* of buyers to their offerings (Elder-Vass, 2009, and see Chapter 5). A buyer has preferential attachment to a seller when they have a disposition to buy from that seller rather than others. Such dispositions are not unshakeable, and on any particular occasion other factors may also influence buying decisions, but they do produce a tendency to buy from the seller concerned, and such tendencies may be developed even though the seller is charging a higher price than a competitor for an equivalent good. In the terms of mainstream economics, they are effectively monopolies. Such monopolies are not rare exceptions, but the *normal* situation in many and perhaps most markets.

Preferential attachments are non-price reasons why buyers prefer to purchase from one seller rather than another. For sellers, securing preferential attachment rests on differentiation of the seller's product or of some other aspect of their offer in a way that keys into an element of their buyer's motivations. For example, a shop may secure preferential attachments by developing personal relationships with customers that encourage a sense of loyalty. This may be a particularly important strategy for smaller businesses, and it is keyed into the value we place on such relationships, but also into our tendency to feel a sense of reciprocal obligation to people that we deal with: we may feel, for example, that we ought to buy from a shop where the staff are particularly helpful in identifying the most suitable product, even though that same product is available more cheaply elsewhere. This, incidentally, is another reason for breaking the gift/reciprocity identity criticised in Chapter 4: not only are many gifts *not* reciprocal, but reciprocity is also a feature of other forms of economy.

There is a vast range of techniques for securing preferential attachment from customers. For another example, an online grocery retailer may appeal to the desire of customers for routine buying to be as simple and quick as possible and secure their preferential attachment by providing a particularly user-friendly interface on its website, or one that enables the user to invest their time in activities that simplify future shopping, such as the creation of a reusable shopping list, which they can return to on this shopping site but not transfer to others. This is perhaps a special case of a more general desire of customers to reduce the costs associated with buying, and other preferential attachment strategies also appeal to the same desire. For example, when a purchase must be made physically, suppliers can make this easier by locating themselves conveniently – the only shop in a certain area, or the petrol/gas station located on a commuter's route to work. Or they may stay open late to be available after shoppers leave work. These different strategies can also be combined productively: a local convenience store that stays open late and has helpful staff, for example, may be able to compete effectively with an online supermarket selling the same products for less by securing the preferential attachment of local shoppers. Nor need preferential attachment strategies be keyed so directly into the provision of benefits for consumers. Other kinds of seller, for example, might exercise various forms of power to secure preferential attachment, such as pressing governments to place non-price obstacles in the way of other sellers, or bribing purchasing staff in buying organisations.

The implication, at the level of economic theory, is that we cannot theorise the relation between buyers and sellers of commodities in terms of price alone. As Schumpeter saw, innovation is frequently linked to non-price competition, and thus 'the price variable' must be 'ousted from its dominant position' in economic theory (Schumpeter, 1994, p. 84). In particular, the neoclassical model rests upon the belief that there is one and only one price for any given product at any time because anyone who prices the product higher will be unable to sell any, whereas the consequence of preferential attachment is that identical products can be priced quite differently by different sellers, who may all nevertheless be able to sell at their varying prices and sustain these price differentials indefinitely. In other words, buyers' motivations and sellers' preferential attachment practices combine in ways that generate quite different market mechanisms than those theorised by neoclassical economists: and this is not an exceptional state of affairs but rather the norm in capitalist economies.[3]

---

[3] This is related to Chamberlin's account of monopolistic competition (Chamberlin, 1956), although Chamberlin seeks to model this process using conventional mathematical models of supply and demand whereas I am not convinced that the dynamic interaction between sellers' practices and buyers' motivations upon which preferential attachment depends can be represented adequately in conventional demand curves.

Apple's preferential attachment strategy combines two deeply inter-woven elements. First, as we have already seen, it seeks to make its products more functional and more usable than the best available equivalents by careful attention to customer usability and the employ-ment of innovative technology. Second, it markets its products not just as premium quality, but also as 'cool': as embodying a kind of lifestyle choice that is ascribed high cultural status (without necessarily being correlated with high social position) in contemporary society.

Apple's marketing depends heavily on this cultural positioning of its products, and exemplifies what Jim McGuigan has called 'cool capitalism': 'the incorporation of disaffection into capitalism itself' (McGuigan, 2009, p. 1). McGuigan traces the origins of 'cool' from the African roots of Afro-American culture, through 'a kind of passive resistance to the work ethic through personal style' (Pountain & Robins, 2000, p. 41), and on to its contemporary cultural usages, in which it 'floats free, available for the articulation of both resistance and incorporation, and, over time, traversing from one to the other' (McGuigan, 2009, p. 5). Its contemporary development is linked to the counter-culture of the 1960s, which appropriated the concept and carried it with it on its journey from rebellion to the mainstream (McGuigan, 2009, p. 6).

Cool operates culturally for capitalism at two distinct though interconnected levels. At the macro-cultural level, it helps to provide legitimacy for capitalism itself, as an element of what Boltanski and Chiapello have called the 'new spirit of capitalism' (Boltanski & Chiapello, 2005). Capitalism, they argue, is an absurd system in which wage earners are condemned to subordination and capitalists 'find themselves yoked to an interminable, insatiable process': the endlessly expanding pursuit of profit (Boltanski & Chiapello, 2005, p. 7). Hence it always requires an ideology to justify our engagement in it, and since capitalism's own logic is so amoral it relies on drawing moral reasons from outside itself and reframing them as legitimations for its own system. Boltanski and Chiapello reinterpret Weber's 'Protestant ethic' argument as an account of the ways in which early capitalism was legitimised by the reframing of Calvinist religion. The Calvinists originally were strong critics of capital accumulation, yet in seven-teenth century England their theology was refashioned to support it, justifying the pursuit of profit as a religious duty. With the growth of industrial capitalism this first spirit became increasingly inadequate as socialist movements developed in opposition to its degradation of the working class. But again capitalism was able to refashion the arguments of its opponents, incorporating social democracy into the justification for capitalism in the twentieth century. A new social contract developed in which we accepted capitalism because it delivered security, and an element of justice and humanity, by generating the resources required to support the welfare state.

Most recently, they argue, with the welfare state itself under attack, a new spirit has been emerging, which draws not on the religious critique of capitalism refashioned in the first spirit nor on the political critique of capitalism reframed in the second, but instead on artisitic critique. The artistic critique attacks capitalism not for exploitation but for alienation: for the ways in which it suppresses authenticity, autonomy, creativity and personal relationships in our lives as producers and consumers. Here their story connects up with McGuigan's: the hippie counterculture of the 60s exemplifies this critique and cool capitalism is precisely the incorporation of a refashioned version of this critique into the justification for capitalism itself. The artistic critique is refashioned into the claim that revolutionary new consumer goods deliver the opportunities that capitalism was traditionally thought to suppress, and thus that capitalism is legitimate because rather than suppressing authenticity, autonomy, creativity and personal relationships it positively enriches and enables them.[4] Here we can also see the link with the second, micro level, at which 'cool' becomes a marketing tool for these specific products. The two levels are recursively connected: the macro-cultural shift is in part the product of the aggregation and interaction of the micro-marketing campaigns, and these campaigns themselves draw on the developing discursive macro-cultural tropes: the new spirit of capitalism.

Apple, born in California – the epicentre of 60s counterculture – and inspired by Steve Jobs, who embraced pot, LSD, Eastern mysticism and fruitarianism in his youth, dated Joan Baez, and retained a long-term

---

[4] Although Boltanski and Chiapello's argument is brilliantly constructed, they are perhaps too determined to insist that capitalism draws its legitimacy only from appropriating the arguments of its opponents. Capitalism also draws legitimacy from its ability to provide consumers with a wide range of affordable and appealing goods, and consumerism has arguably been at least as important as the welfare state in legitimising it over the last half century or so. Cool capitalism *hybridises* consumerism with the artistic critique.

attachment to Zen Buddhism, is the definitive embodiment of this spirit (Young & Simon, 2006, pp. 20–2, 31–2, 86). The Mac was marketed as the tool of artistic expression – for graphic designers and musicians in particular – and thus of creativity and authenticity. iTunes and the iPod deliver the autonomy to access any music, anytime, anywhere. And the iPhone and iPad are marketed as the ultimate cultural platforms and the ultimate communication devices, allowing us to be constantly connected to our friends, constantly engaged, constantly creative. Most remarkably of all, Apple has succeeded in its marketing campaigns in linking its products to a sense of rebelliousness[5] – from the 'Rip, Mix, Burn' marketing campaign for iTunes that seemed to many to be encouraging music piracy (Strangelove, 2005, p. 66; Young & Simon, 2006, p. 303), through the stress on youth in much of its advertising, to its carefully sustained design aesthetic. The same somewhat minimalist aesthetic style marks Apple hardware, software interfaces, and even its packaging and its stores, and it marks them as different from the commercial mainstream and yet also as sophisticated: this is *expensive* cool culture, with the design to match. The intention, and the outcome, is that Apple's products achieve a cultural status that derives from being read as symbols of rebellious individuality, while *actual* individuality can be dispensed with in favour of buying the image. What is on offer is 'the aesthetic of radicalism' rather than its substance (Wu, 2012, p. 274). The new deal that the third spirit offers is no longer work in exchange for security and humanity, but work in exchange for the opportunity to buy stuff that lets you look and feel cool. As Lashinsky puts it,

Apple storytelling initially is high concept, telling customers not what they want to buy but what kind of people they want to be. This is classic 'lifestyle' advertising, the selling of an image associated with the brand rather than the product itself. From Apple's iconic 'Think Different' campaign in 1997 featuring images of Gandhi and Einstein and Bob Dylan (and no Apple products) to its later silhouetted hipsters grooving to music on their iPods… Apple has excelled at selling a lifestyle (Lashinsky, 2012, p. 119).

Apple's strategy for preferential attachment, then, combines exceptional product functionality with highly attractive design, but there is

---

[5] Lashinsky points to the extraordinary 'fact that a company worth $360 billion is embraced as revolutionary and not derided as "the man" or "the establishment"' (2012, p. 196).

much more to it than that. It draws on the larger cultural context and uses it to position the brand as a signifier of cultural distinction, that consumers can acquire for themselves by acquiring Apple's products. The logic of cultural distinction is outlined brilliantly by Pierre Bourdieu, in his classic work *Distinction* (1984), but in Bourdieu's France cultural distinction was intimately connected to social position. The triumph of cool capitalism is that it has transformed cultural distinction – of some varieties, at least – into a commodity that is available to anyone with the funds to purchase it.

Constructing monopoly using intellectual property rights

Apple, then, has perfected the art of preferential attachment and used it to create a sense that its products provide greater benefits than the competition. By distinguishing its products in this way it creates a series of monopolies: if you must have an iPod, an iPhone or an iPad (and not just a music player, a smartphone or a tablet computer) then you can only buy one that comes from Apple. But according to Schumpeter's logic, Apple's innovations should attract a swarm of imitators who produce more or less identical products and compete away Apple's ability to charge more than the going rate (Heilbroner, 2000, p. 296). Perhaps if it innovated quickly enough, it could keep ahead of the swarm, but in some respects Apple is now *behind* its competitors. According to one industry commentator, for example, 'A lot of iOS 8 features were on Android first, and bigger iPhones are a validation of the direction Samsung and the other Android OEMs have been pushing things. Android copied Apple a lot in the early days, but now it seems like the pendulum is swinging in the other direction' (Ron Amadeo, quoted in Ramos, 2014).

There are, however, other practices and other resources that can be deployed to protect a monopoly position, and Apple is a master of them. We have already seen one of those practices: the use of marketing to create a cultural sense of product superiority that is independent, to some extent at least, of the actual functionality of the products themselves. But even this strategy is in principle vulnerable to imitation: competitors could simply produce products that looked exactly like the Apple versions, so that users could acquire the cultural status that derives from appearing to own an Apple product while actually using cheap copies. Indeed, there are many lookalike products available, but Apple makes aggressive use of intellectual property rights to suppress them wherever possible.

Intellectual property rights fall into three groups: trademarks, patents, and copyright, and Apple employs all three to protect its monopoly power. Trademark law is used to prevent use of the bitten apple logo and other Apple trademarks on non-Apple products. Apple brought a lawsuit against one 'New York teen' in 2011, for example, for importing and selling white iPhone 4 covers. These were actually replacement covers for Apple's own phones, but because they carried the Apple branding, including the bitten apple logo, and enabled users to have white iPhones in advance of Apple's own launch, Apple saw them as a threat to their revenues and sought to suppress their sale (Purcher, 2011). One fascinating aspect of the evidence presented in this case is that several major carriers refused to ship the covers from China on the grounds that they carried unlicensed Apple logos. It seems that there are plenty of agencies willing to do Apple's trademark enforcement for them. Still, though trademark law can be abused, for example when it is wielded against businesses that were genuinely using the mark before it was registered by another company, it is generally desirable: it prevents sellers deceiving customers about the origin of the goods they are selling.

Apple also uses patent law to try to prevent competing manufacturers creating products that have similar features to its own. It has launched a long series of lawsuits, in particular, against Samsung, currently the leading manufacturer of Android smartphones, alleging that their products employ technology patented by Apple, though Samsung have also launched a number of counter suits. As of August 2014, the two companies have agreed to drop most of these suits, but two cases in California in which Apple was originally awarded over $1 billion in damages are currently still under appeal (Bradshaw, 2014a; Vascellaro, 2012). The final objective of such cases, however, does not seem to be to secure damages but to preserve the uniqueness of Apple's products by warning off their competitors from copying too closely, and perhaps also to encourage consumers to believe that Apple is a technology leader as well as a cool brand. Again, Apple is employing legal means to protect its monopoly. Again, this form of intellectual property law isn't a bad thing in itself: it gives inventors the right to take advantage of their ideas without imitation by others and so encourages research. But patent periods should be short, and patents should only be awarded for inventions that are significantly new and significantly different from existing technologies, otherwise they unreasonably restrict other producers and cumulative innovation. Apple, for example, actually secured a US patent asserting the exclusive right to produce rectangular devices with rounded corners (Macari, 2012). Although in practice this particular patent seems unenforceable, Apple has repeatedly used patent law to protect monopolies on relatively trivial design features. The use of intellectual property law in this way is another appropriative practice, though once again we must recognise that other causal forces are also at work: these are practices that depend in turn upon the prior enactment of law and the power of the state to enforce it.

Apple doesn't just sell hardware, although the iPhone now accounts for over 60% of its profits (Yarow, n.d.). It also sells digital content, notably on iTunes and the Apple App Store, which provided almost $13 billion of revenue in the 2012 tax year (Elmer-DeWitt, 2013). But digital media files, unlike mobile phones, are remarkably easy to copy – even ordinary consumers can do it themselves – and most of the digital content that Apple sells is available to download for nothing from various sites on the Internet. Why do people pay for it at all? Once again, intellectual property law is a key factor, this time in the form of copyright: the right to prevent others from making copies of content that you control. Although it is constantly legitimised as a protection for content creators, and does provide them with some benefit, the primary beneficiaries of copyright in music are typically the large media companies, who have a long history of taking legal action against those who make or distribute what they call pirated copies. At the beginning of the twenty-first century, the music companies were unwilling to offer a digital alternative to buying music on CDs, but were also fighting a losing battle against internet file-sharing. As soon as they used their legal muscle to take down Napster, for example, a host of other file-sharing services sprung up in its place, structured differently to reduce their legal vulnerability (Goldsmith & Wu, 2006, chapter 7). By 2003 the leading file-sharing service was Kazaa, with hundreds of millions of users, but Kazaa was under legal attack from the music industry and also unable to control the quality of the files being shared, many of which weren't what they were claimed to be, sometimes carrying viruses, advertising or pornography (Goldsmith & Wu, 2006, pp. 109–17). Having difficulty closing down Kazaa, the music industry started prosecuting individuals who had downloaded pirated music (Goldsmith & Wu, 2006, p. 115).

It was in this context that Steve Jobs set up the iTunes Music Store. He persuaded the big music companies that they would be better off allowing him to sell their music in digital form rather than standing by while the same files were distributed freely by the filesharers – partly because the technical restrictions built into Apple's iPods and computers would prevent further sharing of iTunes purchases (Young & Simon, 2006, pp. 287–93). The result was that Apple secured a leading position in the legal distribution of digital music. The price, for the music companies, was that Apple would take 30% of the revenue, while consumers could purchase downloads at 99c per song. Jobs felt that many consumers would rather pay 99c for a quick easy download that they knew was legal and safe than take the risks associated with filesharing (Goldsmith & Wu, 2006, p. 120). iTunes quickly became the leading source of legal music downloads and started to outpace even the illegal filesharing services (Goldsmith & Wu, 2006, p. 121; Young & Simon, 2006, p. 293).

By 2013, iTunes was generating enough revenue that as a standalone business it would have been one of the top few hundred companies in the world (Elmer-DeWitt, 2013). This is a business that is utterly dependent on the use of intellectual property laws to turn a virtually costless digital download into a saleable commodity. But these laws are not a natural or exogenous factor. As Davies puts it, 'the categories of what can and should be owned are somewhat transient, and often controversial' (M. Davies, 2007, p. 81). From the very first introduction of copyright law, in England in 1710, copyright has been introduced and extended at the behest of businesses that sought to use it to create monopoly control for themselves over certain cultural content. While it is reasonable to allow the creators of original cultural content a period of exclusive ownership that enables them to obtain some reward for their creative work, media corporations frequently share only a small portion of their income with the original creators, and companies like Apple also take a much larger share than the original creators of the revenue created by the copyright system. Ironically, as Lawrence Lessig has explained in detail, 'Every important sector of "big media" today – film, records, radio, and cable TV – was born of a kind of piracy' – they all began by 'using the creative property of others without their permission' (Lessig, 2004, p. 53). Each of these industries appeared when new technology made it possible to do new things with cultural content that were not covered by existing copyright law. Still, despite their roots, the media corporations have consistently pushed for extensions of copyright law that have increased their control over the content they own rights over. Since copyright law was introduced into the United States in 1790, the period of time for which content is protected in the United States has increased from fourteen years from first publication, extendable to twenty-eight, to its current level of ninety-five years (Lessig, 2004, pp. 133–5). In 1790, copyright applied only to printed maps, charts and books; today it applies to a broad range of cultural content, but particularly to music and film/video, and the film and music industries have been in the forefront of pressing for these extensions. This is hardly suprising: the more that copyright is extended, the greater their monopoly power. We may therefore say that pushing to extend copyright provision, and finding ways to make it more effective, are themselves appropriative practices, practices which shift the allocation of benefit away from consumers of media content and towards the corporations that control that content.

Nor is such activity confined to lobbying for legal change; the effectiveness of law does not just depend on the state, but also on whether it has normative support, and indeed on whether it is enforceable in practice. The lobbyists, most prominently Jack Valenti of the Motion Picture Association of America, have not just sought to change the law but also to change the dominant discourses relating to the legitimacy of copying content (Gillespie, 2007, p. 108). Thus, for example 'sharing becomes stealing. Creative work becomes private property, Corporations become victims of piracy' (Halbert, quoted in Gillespie, 2007, p. 106). In particular, copying for personal use by consumers, which was largely tolerated prior to the appearance of the Internet, has become the target of new criticism, being branded as criminal piracy in an effort to generate both disapproval of the practice and fear of prosecution amongst those who are tempted to do it. These discursive pressures form one side of what Gillespie calls the 'square of regulation' (Gillespie, 2007, p. 17): the combination of legal, cultural, commercial and technical measures to suppress private copying.

Apple has certainly played a part in this discursive campaign, for example through the US TV ad it ran in collaboration with Pepsi during the 2004 Superbowl. In the ad teenagers who had been prosecuted for illegal music downloads advocated the use of iTunes instead.

The message was carefully crafted to conform with Apple's cool credentials: the downloads they advocated were free, given away with Pepsi purchases, and signed off with tag line 'and there's not a thing anyone can do about it' (the video can still be found online, e.g. at McNamara, 2014). While some commentators have seen this as encouraging piracy (Strangelove, 2005, p. 66) nothing could be further from the truth. The soundtrack was 'I fought the law and the law won' and the message was clear: even for young rebels, iTunes is the place to go for digital music.

Constructing monopoly using technology

Apple's most significant contribution to Gillespie's square of regulation, though, is arguably to the fourth, technological, side. MP3 tracks from filesharing sites can be copied easily from device to device without restrictions, but downloads from iTunes were restricted by Apple to the user's own devices. When you buy a track from iTunes, you only buy the right to play it on a restricted set of devices, and Apple's objective is to prevent you from playing it anywhere else. Copyright isn't just enforced by the law and by persuasion, but by the use of technology to create what Mark Stefik calls 'trusted systems' (Lessig, 2006, pp. 176–9). Systems, that is, that can be trusted by corporations to limit what we can do with what we buy from them. Having charmed its customers, Apple then entraps them: 'they, too, must abide by strict rules in exchange for interacting with Apple' (Lashinsky, 2012, p. 149).

But this is only the beginning of Apple's ambition to control the ecosystem built around their products. Unlike PC's and Android smartphones, which anyone with the relevant skills can write software for and tailor to their personal preferences, the software environment on Apple's products is strictly controlled by Apple itself. You may only download apps to an iPhone, for example, that Apple has approved for sale through their App Store, and they exclude apps for a variety of reasons (Gray, 2013). Steve Jobs banned Adobe's widely used Flash software, for example, along with a number of other programming environments by changing 'the terms and conditions of the licence that software developers must sign when writing code to run on Apple products' ('Apple boss explains ban on Flash', 2010). It has been speculated that one reason was that these tools might allow users to download other software without going through Apple's App Store, which like the iTunes store, skims off 30% of the user's payments for Apple: 'Allowing Flash – which is a development platform of its own – would just be too dangerous for Apple, a company that enjoys exerting total dominance over its hardware and the software that runs on it' (Chen, 2008).

Indeed at first Jobs would not allow third-party apps to run on the iPhone at all, and only agreed once he had established that 'they would have to meet strict standards, be tested and approved by Apple, and be sold only through the iTunes store' (Isaacson, 2011, p. 501). Apple's logic is the logic of what Jonathan Zittrain has called *appliancisation* (2008). Zittrain argues that technology can be delivered in two forms. *Generative* technology is open to modification and enhancement by its users, which allows the development of whole industries to extend its capability and take it into new areas. The Internet itself is just such a technology. By contrast, *appliances* are locked-down, with strictly limited functions and strictly limited opportunities for configuration by their users. Many technologies take the form of appliances – fridges, TVs and cars, for example – and appliances have significant advantages for their users: because there is only a limited number of ways to use them there is less learning needed to understand them, more possibility of thorough testing so that they go wrong less often, and more possibility of all the features being carefully integrated and operating consistently with each other. Jobs tended to make similar arguments in favour of Apple's control over the iPhone: 'He didn't want outsiders to create applications for the iPhone that could mess it up, infect it with viruses, or pollute its integrity' (Isaacson, 2011, p. 501) – not only its technical integrity but also the integrity of the user experience.

But the appliance model also has other benefits for Apple. In the world of generative systems, hardware manufacturers lose control over what happens on their products when they go out of the factory door. In the world of appliances, Apple can exert control over what happens on your iPod, your iPhone and your iPad for their entire useful life. In particular, they can, and do, ensure that you only buy music and software through their own online stores,[6] and because they have a monopoly over these purchases, they can insist on taking a substantial

[6] Apple has been accused in court, for example, of generating messages to users with non-iTunes music on their iPods prompting them to take action that would lead to the deletion of that music (Gibbs, 2014).

cut of the revenue this raises, since content providers have no other way to sell to users of these devices. Apple's innovation, it turns out, isn't all about improving the choices available to consumers; it's also about restricting and excluding alternative competing products and suppliers. This is what Lashinsky means by entrapping the customer, but Apple has also entrapped these third-party suppliers in an ecosystem that it squeezes for further revenue at every opportunity. This is a very directly appropriative practice – consumers pay more as a result, other firms earn less than they could in an open system, and benefit is transferred to Apple's shareholders as a consequence. Apple, it is clear, is thoroughly devoted to constructing and exploiting its monopoly position, both as a supplier of devices that are seen as uniquely capable and uniquely cool by its customers, and as the arbiter of every related revenue opportunity it can find a way to control.

This chapter so far has analysed the construction of Apple's monopoly as a configuration of appropriative practices, orchestrated to some extent by Apple itself, but drawing on a range of other resources, including a legal and discursive environment that has been strongly shaped by the media corporations with which Apple works. Mainstream economics has some useful things to say about the ways in which monopolists can exploit their position by charging higher prices, which are often known as rents,[7] but it has relatively little to say about how monopolies are created. This might be excusable if monopoly was a rare distortion in a world of fully competitive markets with prices equalised by the interaction of well-behaved demand and supply curves, as the political wing of mainstream economics seems to imply: an exception that could be ignored in assessing the merits of markets and capitalism. But monopolies and monopoly profits are not an aberration in capitalist systems (Schumpeter, 1994, pp. 81–2). On the contrary, a degree of monopoly is the normal state of capitalist markets, and it is the product of mechanisms that are just as

---

[7] Although we usually think of rent as a payment for the use of land or buildings, economists use the term more widely to refer to any excess of the price of a good over its cost of production, which is assumed to arise from its scarcity. The term has been used to criticise price rises that are sustained by artificially created scarcity, which is precisely what monopolists attempt to create for their own products (Sayer, 2015, pp. 52–3). Criticism of rent-seeking is important (e.g. Stiglitz, 2013, pp. 119–27), but on the whole I avoid the term as the theory of rent is closely tied to equilibrium price theory.

characteristic of capitalist production as the price equilibration mechanism upon which the mainstream is focussed. One of the merits of the approach to political economy proposed in this book is that it enables us to analyse those factors that do generate monopoly. Apple takes advantage of a very specific combination of practices, but other businesses also employ these practices, in different variations and in varying combinations with other practices, to achieve monopoly power of their own. A more general account of monopoly would need to examine a range of other cases and the similarities and differences between the cases, but this chapter seeks only to open the way to such thinking by examining a single case.

Exploiting workers and suppliers, and avoiding taxes

Apple, like other capitalist corporations, is necessarily oriented to making profit: to earning revenues that exceed its costs. So far this chapter has focussed on the factors that have enabled Apple to earn extraordinary revenues, but the profit equation also rests on controlling the costs of production, and here Apple is little different from other capitalist corporations. In particular, Apple has followed the widespread trend of outsourcing and offshoring its manufacturing operations to low-waged suppliers in developing economies. It is perhaps unusual in the degree of detailed control it exercises over these outsourced processes (Lashinsky, 2012, pp. 58, 143–4) but in other respects Apple's production strategy is thoroughly typical of the many capitalist businesses that have taken advantage of (and indeed driven) the globalisation of the world economy in recent decades.

Apple has outsourced the manufacturing of its most successful hardware products to factories in mainland China, including several operated by the Taiwanese company Hon Hai, widely known as Foxconn. In late 2013, Foxconn employed over a million workers in China, including 300,000 at its plant in Zhengzhou, which at that time was dedicated to producing Apple's iPhone 5S, and it makes around 40% of its revenue from manufacturing products for Apple (Luk, 2013). Although Hon Hai is 'the world's largest electronic component manufacturer' with a turnover that rose above $10 billion per annum in the mid-2000s, and thus an enormous company in its own right, it is nevertheless in a 'dependent relationship' with Apple, which is able to use its control of the downstream market to dictate terms to its suppliers that squeeze their margins to the limit (Froud Johal Leaver & Williams, 2014, p. 52). One consequence is that, during the period in which Apple ascended to become the most highly valued company in the world, Foxconn's rate of profit has been rapidly shrinking (Froud et al., 2014, p. 52). Apple, in other words, exercises power not only over its customers but also over its suppliers, and uses that power, once again, to increase its profits at others' expense.

Those profits also come at the expense of Foxconn's workers. Apple and Foxconn have been widely criticised for the treatment of the workers in Foxconn's factories, following investigations by the Fair Labor Association (which is funded by corporations like Apple) and the independent Hong-Kong based Students and Scholars Against Corporate Misbehavior (SACOM). Many of the workers at these plants are young rural migrants, who live in company dormitories cut off from social contact (Ngai & Chan, 2012, pp. 402–3) and are paid wages well below the minimum required for a decent standard of living (though more than the legal minimum wage). They are often obliged to work many hours of overtime (sometimes unpaid), and subjected to petty and humiliating management (Fuchs, 2014, pp. 186–8, 193; J. Johnson, 2011; Ngai & Chan, 2012, pp. 397–8; Shah, 2012). They are subjected to 'gruelling workloads, humiliating punishments and battery-farm living conditions' (Garside, 2012). Many are obliged to stand at their work stations for their entire shift (Garside, 2012), which one eyewitness describes as 'repetitive, exhaust-ing, [and] alienating' (J. Johnson, 2011, p. 105; also see Ngai & Chan, 2012, pp. 399–401). Many of the workers come to the city under the impression that wages and conditions will be far better than the reality: Foxconn's Shenzen plant (their largest) paid a basic wage equivalent to £120 (British pounds) per month in 2010 (Fuchs, 2014, pp. 187–8). They are deprived of effective representation by being 'ordered to sign up for the company-controlled union without knowing the functions of the unions' (SACOM, 2012). It is hardly surprising that Foxconn's labour turnover rate is 30–40% per annum ('Light and death', 2010).

While Foxconn's wages and employment conditions may not be any worse – and are perhaps better – than those of other manufacturers in China, there can be no doubt that their workers are subject to high levels of alienation, and that they are severely exploited by the stand-ards of most of those who purchase Apple's products. Given the extent to which it micromanages its suppliers, Apple cannot escape responsibility for these conditions, and indeed it has repeatedly argued that 'We care about every worker in our worldwide supply chain' (Apple spokesperson, quoted in Garside, 2012). As Kieran Healy has pointed out, Apple's public focus on 'love and attention to creativity is severed from the manufacturing process': the 'intimate quality' of objects like iPhones contrast starkly with the treatment of Foxconn's workers as impersonal machines (Kieran Healy, 2011). Apple insists that it is trying to reduce the problems, but it is hard to avoid the conclusion that it is doing only what is necessary to manage the public relations damage these revelations have caused. Low-cost manufacturing is one of the planks upon which Apple's profitability is built, and low wages are the primary contributor to those low costs.[8]

On what grounds, though, could we describe this as exploitation? The dominant understanding of the concept of exploitation in political economy is based on Marx, and as we saw in Chapter 3, for Marx a worker is exploited whenever she is paid less than the value of the product that her labour produces – and only labour is taken to contribute to the value of the product (Marx, 1954, pp. 208–9). This supposedly technical definition of exploitation is frequently seen by writers in the Marxist tradition as justifying an ethical critique of capitalism, on the grounds that capitalism necessarily exploits workers in this sense. But any ethical critique of a state of affairs implicitly compares it with some other imagined alternative and judges it inferior, and such critiques rest on the genuine possibility of a superior alternative. Marx's theory of exploitation implicitly compares real appropriations with an alternative in which all the product of labour is appropriated by the workers, and judges capitalism ethically inferior to it. But this is an alternative that is neither economically feasible nor ethically desirable: it would, for example, deprive not only capitalists and entrepreneurs of a share in production but also children, the unemployed and the retired.

While we could consider a multitude of other alternative systems for use as comparators, it seems unlikely that we would find one that was both widely accepted as fair and *also* provided us with a clear standard against which to judge existing appropriations. Does this mean we must abandon the concept of exploitation altogether? I don't believe so, but it does mean that we must be more circumspect and more

---

[8] See the cost breakdown for the iPhone 4 in Froud et al (2014, p. 55).

contextually specific about how we use it. The biggest problem with Marx's concept of exploitation may be that it encourages us to believe that there could be a single well-defined standard of just appropriations, and the most appropriate reaction to this may not be to look for an alternative standard but rather to re-localise our understanding of exploitation. We use the term *exploitation*, in other words, to express the judgement that a social actor is receiving less than their contribution deserves, given the legitimate demands of other parties, according to our ethical standards, and indeed that some other actor is receiving *more* than they deserve, at the expense of the first one. Ultimately we ought to be prepared to offer grounds for these judgements, but these will be contextually specific, balancing multiple claims, rather than mechanical applications of a universal principle.

From this perspective, we may still say that Apple exploits the workers who produce its products in Chinese factories, but rather than a trivial application of the questionable principle that all wage labour is necessarily exploited under capitalism, this becomes a more specific, and as a consequence a more powerful and more damning, ethical judgement: that it is wrong for Apple, through Foxconn and its other manufacturing suppliers, to pay so little to production workers and subject them to such alienating work processes, given the enormous profits it earns from these products.

Marxist discussions of exploitation also restrict the scope of ethical evaluations of appropriations by confining their attention to only two classes of beneficiary and only two classes of contribution to the process of production. I have already mentioned others who have needs that production ought to meet, and must meet if social life is to be adequately preserved: the young, the old and the unemployed. Similarly, production itself, as well as social life more generally, depends on the contributions of education, health services, law and shared infrastructure such as roads and water supplies. Economic production in general must generate the resources required to support all of these demands, and in contemporary societies much of this is delivered by the state and therefore must be funded through taxation. Taxation itself is therefore an appropriative practice, which appropriates resources to support state provision of all of these services, and state service provision is another, since it employs these resources to deliver benefits to a broad range of service users, including capitalist businesses themselves.

All modern states have taxation systems designed to raise the revenue required to provide these services, and all those who earn significant incomes are both legally and ethically obliged to contribute through the payment of an appropriate level of taxation. Apple, for example, raises huge revenues in many countries of the world, and in doing so depends on the provision of state services, and thus has an ethical obligation to pay tax according to the local rates in each of these countries. Apple, however, is a notorious tax avoider. While its headquarters are in Cupertino, California, it channels substantial amounts of revenue through a tiny office in Reno, Nevada in order to avoid state taxes in California – having previously lobbied California to reduce business taxes to help corporations based there but also operating in other states (Duhigg & Kocieniewski, 2012). When it sells content on iTunes in Europe, Africa or the Middle East it routes the sale through the tax haven of Luxemburg, avoiding tax payments in both the country where the sale is made and in the United States, covering an estimated 20% of iTunes worldwide sales (Duhigg & Kocieniewski, 2012). When it sells other products in the United Kingdom, much of the revenue is booked in Ireland, and routed to tax havens in the Caribbean, reducing its annual tax bill by an estimated £570 million in 2011 (Duke & Gadher, 2012). US analysts estimate it used creative tax schemes to reduce its federal tax bill in the United States by $2.4 billion in the same year (Duhigg & Kocieniewski, 2012). Overall worldwide in 2011 it paid a tax rate of 9.8 percent on profits of $34.2 billion, when Walmart, a more traditional US business, paid a rate of 24 percent on its profits of $24.2 billion (Duhigg & Kocieniewski, 2012). Here is another respect in which Apple's innovation is less than beneficial to society as a whole: it has been in the forefront of developing corporate tax avoidance strategies. For example, it 'was among the first tech companies to designate overseas salespeople in high-tax countries in a manner that allowed them to sell on behalf of low-tax subsidiaries on other continents, sidestepping income taxes' (Duhigg & Kocieniewski, 2012). No doubt all of these schemes are legal, but Apple's claim that it 'has conducted all of its business with the highest of ethical standards' is farcical (Apple statement, quoted in Duhigg & Kocieniewski, 2012). On the contrary, 'it's clear that they don't pay tax where they are really earning their profits – and that's deliberate' (Richard Murphy, quoted in Duke & Gadher, 2012).

Apple, in other words, benefits enormously from the appropriative practice of tax avoidance. Its capacity to do so is closely linked to the nature of the contemporary global economy, in which multinational companies can both relocate their business processes and in other cases manipulate them to create the legal fiction that they have been relocated, in order to take advantage of a global regulatory context that provides opportunities to shift business to low tax states. The digital format of some of their products makes this particularly easy, but Apple is a master of the game whatever the form of the product. Of course Apple is only one of many multinational corporations that avoid taxes creatively, but there can be no doubt that these practices deprive governments of huge amounts of revenue, not only appropriating funds that should be going to the benefit of the populations of the states concerned but also contributing to the fiscal crises of recent years. Governments should take action to eliminate tax havens entirely and force corporations to pay tax on a basis that genuinely reflects where they produce and sell their goods.

Conclusion

Apple is the largest company by market capitalisation in the world because it derives enormous profits from a carefully designed complex of appropriative practices: outstanding product innovation and design, marketing campaigns that construct its products as markers of cultural distinction, intellectual property laws that help it to secure continuing monopolies on its products, a strategy of controlling the entire commercial ecosystem on Apple hardware even after the consumer has purchased a device, the subordination of its manufacturing suppliers, exploiting low-waged production workers, and avoiding taxation to the maximum extent that is legally viable. In an ethical economy Apple would be enormously less profitable because it would be less able to protect its monopoly using patent and copyright laws, it would be less able to exclude other suppliers from selling to Apple users and it would pay higher wages and more taxes. But that doesn't necessarily mean that in an ethical economy there would be no Apple, no iPhones and no iPads. There are places for capitalist business in a diverse mixed economy, and the development of innovative new consumer products may well be one of them, but the example of Apple demonstrates that we must nevertheless regulate such businesses in order to maximise the social benefits that arise from their products.

There are many other monopolistic capitalist businesses, some of them in the digital economy. None of them is exactly like Apple, but many of them employ similar mixes of appropriative practices and to the extent that they do, we may judge them similarly. But many capitalist businesses employ other practices, and have other sorts of social effects, that we may want to judge differently. Not all capitalist businesses are the same, and in assessing their role in a diverse mixed economy we must be prepared to recognise their differences as well as their similarities.

7 | Co-operative peer production: Wikipedia

Introduction

Like the iPhone, Wikipedia is ubiquitous. In October 2014, the English-language version was viewed over 8.5 million times per hour, and the other 286 language versions collectively were viewed over 9 million times per hour – a total of over twelve billion views per month (Wikimedia, 2014b). With over 4.7 million articles, English Wikipedia is not only the most heavily used but also the largest encyclopaedia the world has ever seen (Dalby, 2009, p. 42). Unlike Apple, however, Wikipedia makes no profit and is worth nothing on the stock market. Although it now pays salaries to over 100 staff at the Wikimedia Foundation (Orlowski, 2012), other than this Wikipedia is a particularly pure case of the gift economy in action. It is created entirely by unpaid volunteers, and indeed anyone can edit (almost) any Wikipedia page. It is run with minimum levels of formal hierarchy, with disputes being resolved largely by the achievement of consensus under the guidance of a well-developed set of normative standards, and only rarely by the intervention of administrators, who are themselves volunteers selected on the basis of their previous contributions to the project (Forte Larco & Bruckman, 2009). Its product is freely available to anyone who chooses to make use of it. At the time of writing it is the seventh most visited site on the Web (Alexa.com, 2015) but its running costs are remarkably low given the enormous levels of usage and are met entirely by soliciting voluntary donations, indeed the site does not even accept advertising. This is a spectacularly different economic model than monopoly capitalism, and yet it coexists quite stably alongside it.

In the last chapter, we fell easily into some conventional assumptions about what sorts of benefits and harms a political economy should explain and evaluate. Apple and other companies make profits; consumers enjoy useful products; workers receive wages and suffer alienating workloads. All of these are grist to the mill of the old political economies, though they differ in how much attention they pay to each and in how they account for them. But different complexes of appropriative practices generate different kinds of benefits and harms, requiring different kinds of explanations and evaluations, and here we are on ground that is much less familiar to the old political economies. Wikipedia produces no profits, no wages, no alienation, no shiny boxes of electronics, and the old political economies have no tools – not even broken ones – with which to fashion an analysis of what it *does* produce: freely shared information and satisfying work conducted outside traditional hierarchical structures of organisation. This very different set of outcomes can only be explained by reference to a very different set of mechanisms, but it *can* still be explained within the terms of the appropriative practices model, as this chapter will seek to demonstrate.

However, this chapter also goes beyond the focus on appropriative practices that is the central theme of this book by touching on the contribution of *technology* to Wikipedia. Both Wikipedia and the digital gift economy more generally have been premised on the development of new social practices and the construction and maintenance of normative communities to support them, but these practices have been made possible by technological developments. To understand the digital economy, then, we must recognise that social and technological factors interact in mutually dependent complexes, sociomaterial structures of appropriation with emergent causal powers that depend on both social and technological elements as well as the interactions between them.[1]

The chapter begins by considering the appropriative practices relating to the transfer of Wikipedia's product to its users, the funding of its operations and the labour processes that generate its product then moves on to consider some of the practices that sustain the quality of its product and the commitment of its contributors: its normative environment, its use of technology and its governance processes.

---

[1] By contrast with the view advanced by actor-network and similar theorists, these structures are not just fleeting networks of associations but persistent entities and relations that combine to produce continuing structures of appropriation that fall into recognisable types with consistent causal influences (Elder-Vass, 2015a).

Encyclopaedic knowledge as a digital gift

The most striking difference between Wikipedia and the typical capitalist business is that its products are given away freely to anyone who wishes to use them: they are digital gifts, the first appropriative practice we will consider in this chapter. Digital gifts have become ubiquitous on the Internet, and indeed the Web is based on digital gifts: this technology was explicitly designed to make it easy to access information that is freely available on web servers. Almost every web page we load into our browsers is a complex text offered for downloading without any requirement for, or expectation of, any return to be made in exchange for viewing the content concerned (Barbrook 2005 [1998]; Berry 2008: 12). Blog posts, videos on YouTube, photographs, advice offered in a vast range of forums and status updates on Facebook, for example, are products of labour that are given freely by their creators, and although sites like Facebook allow creators to restrict who may access their creations, much of this material is freely available to anyone.

This is not charity: there is no sense that those strangers to whom we give digital gifts are necessarily worse off than ourselves and there is no stigma associated with accepting such gifts. When we give such digital gifts we are giving to strangers as equals, not only without any obligation to pay but also without any expectation of subsequent reciprocation of the gift. There is no sense of dishonour arising from failure to reciprocate such gifts, ultimately because digital giving is giving without sacrifice: when we give a digital product we give without giving up, without losing the thing that we are giving away. In economies of scarcity, we give up what we give, and there is therefore a limit to how much we can give. We must therefore limit our giving, and ensure that our gifts reap rewards – whether in terms of reciprocity, social relationships, a sense of satisfaction in caring for our family or standing in the community – that justify the personal costs of giving. In economies of abundance, like the digital information economy, there is no longer a need for every receipt of a gift to generate a benefit for the giver, as long as a few of them generate enough benefit in total for the practice to be sustainable. Reciprocity, at the level of the individual recipient, is essentially obsolete in such economies, and the meanings of giving practices have developed accordingly. In the digital economy, I suggest, our recognition of abundance, of the trivial marginal cost of the digital gift, has eliminated any sense of dishonour in accepting it without reciprocation.

Digital goods are *nonrival* – their use by one person does not prevent others from using them too – and Wikipedia's product, information or knowledge, is the classic nonrival product. To some extent this was true already for scientific knowledge, and indeed this too is now a digital product, but before the Internet, giving away copies of scientific knowledge was not a cost-free activity: paper had to be produced and distributed, introducing costs into the process, the need for a funding model to finance those costs and often the intrusion of commercial activities that monetised the distribution of such knowledge. The Internet has transformed this situation (though not yet, ironically, for scientific publishing). The original *creation* of a digital good may involve substantial investments of personal time, and perhaps even the purchase of equipment, but once a digital good has been created, the cost of replication and thus the marginal cost of giving away more copies of the same material is effectively zero.

Once created, Wikipedia articles become part of the new *digital commons*: digital public goods, available for all to share without charge (Clippinger & Bollier, 2006; Stalder, 2010). The concept of the commons originally referred to common land that was available to all the inhabitants of a village to graze their animals, although it has also been extended to discuss a variety of other shared resources such as groundwater and fishing stocks (Ostrom, 1990). The digital commons differs from the old commons, however, in at least two respects. First, digital information is, at least potentially, available to *everyone*, and not just to a specific local community; access to Wikipedia, for example, requires only a device with a browser. This might at first sight amplify the dangers of the so-called tragedy of the commons, in which users over-exploit common resources with the result that the resource is degraded or even destroyed for everyone (Hardin, 1968), but this brings us to the second major difference. Because information is a nonrival good, the digital commons is not degraded by use, and therefore is not vulnerable to Hardin's tragedy. Because one person's use of it does not reduce its availability for others, free riders are now much less of an issue. If a million people consume a digital product and only a tiny fraction of them contribute to its further development this may be enough to sustain a vibrant information economy. Communities generating information goods can survive when only a small proportion of members contribute, and those few that do can have the satisfaction of knowing that their work has helped an enormous number of other people. And often it is largely because a product is free that it has such enormous social benefits: to demand payment for an encyclopedia would massively restrict the number of people who could make use of it.

Wikipedia vs. *Encyclopaedia Britannica*

This, of course, was exactly the situation before the rise of the digital economy. Encyclopaedias were physical books, available only as commercial products – as commodities. The role of an encyclopaedia is to provide a wide-ranging set of well-informed but usually quite brief introductory articles, each distilling the most important things the typical reader might wish to know about a topic. They are rarely regarded as fully authoritative sources by academic experts in the relevant fields, but for other people they may be seen as reliable sources of the kind of knowledge that they need. Some encyclopaedias have traditionally had higher reputations than others. In the English-speaking countries, the gold standard for many years was the *Encyclopaedia Britannica*. According to Wikipedia, 'Since the 3rd edition, the Britannica has enjoyed a popular and critical reputation for general excellence' (Wikipedia, 2014b). In most non-academic contexts a claim would be accepted as knowledge if it had been obtained from a reputable encyclopaedia like the Britannica.

There have been a number of comparisons between Wikipedia and the Encyclopaedia Britannica, most famously one reported in *Nature* in 2005 when Wikipedia was only four years old. In this study experts were asked to review 42 pairs of corresponding articles in the two encyclopaedias (Reagle, 2010, p. 7) and concluded that 'the average science entry in Wikipedia contained around four inaccuracies; Britannica, about three' (Giles, 2005). While this suggests that Britannica was, in fact, a little more reliable, the study was widely reported as evidence that Wikipedia was as accurate as Britannica (Dalby, 2009, p. 56), and subsequent studies have found relatively little difference in overall quality (Reagle, 2010, p. 7). Wikipedia has grown substantially since then and is now vastly larger than Britannica,[2] hence the reader is

---

[2] 'The English Wikipedia alone has over 2.6 billion words, over 100 times as many as the next largest English-language encyclopedia, Encyclopædia Britannica' (Wikipedia, 2014g).

more likely to find an answer to their question on Wikipedia. For example, as of 1 Jan 2015, the Britannica entry on Pierre Bourdieu consists of a single paragraph of mostly biographical information, whereas the Wikipedia entry runs to 16 screens of information including detailed explanations of many of his theoretical ideas. Furthermore, as a result of its editing process Wikipedia is likely to be more up to date. On the other hand, because it is open to editing by anyone, there are many occasions on which unqualified editors introduce errors, or indeed downright vandalism, and although most of these are quickly corrected (as we shall see later), some are not, hence it is impossible for the typical reader to know whether any specific claim in Wikipedia is reliable. While Britannica also has errors, because it is written by experts on the topic concerned these are likely to be less glaring than errors introduced by unqualified editors on Wikipedia (though not *all* Wikipedia editors are unqualified). We could perhaps sum up by saying that there is little to choose between them in terms of the likelihood that any given claim is accurate, but a higher risk of being *badly* wrong when relying on Wikipedia.

For this reason, Wikipedia is still not usually regarded as reliable for academic purposes. For example, it is currently regarded as unacceptable for students in British universities to cite Wikipedia as a source in their written work: claims that are supported purely by reference to Wikipedia are not accorded the status of knowledge in this context (though to be fair, other encyclopaedias including *Brittanica* are also unacceptable sources in many of these situations).[3] But in many other contexts, and for many other purposes, a claim would be accepted as knowledge, as justified belief, if it had been obtained from Wikipedia (indeed I will cite Wikipedia frequently in this chapter: it is by far the most authoritative source on how Wikipedia itself works). The wide reporting of the studies comparing Wikipedia to Britannica has been partly responsible for this, but there are many other factors. One of the most striking is the frequency with which Wikipedia entries appear at or near the top of Google search results (Dalby, 2009, pp. 82–3). These

---

[3] Aleksi Aaltonen has pointed out to me that 'the value of Wikipedia as a reference is partly due to the fact that people are more aware than usual that it may be unreliable' (personal communication). In a sense this is a more sophisticated attitude to knowledge than we are accustomed to, one that indexes 'knowledge' according to the quality of its sources, and the controversy over Wikipedia's reliability may have done us a service by encouraging such an attitude.

rankings drive an enormous amount of traffic to Wikipedia, (while Wikipedia also provides a reciprocal benefit to Google by creating relatively reliable and impartial sources for it to rank near the top of its search results)[4] and contribute to the confidence of users in the quality of Wikipedia's content. Every time a writer cites Wikipedia as a source, this also adds to Wikipedia's epistemic authority, and although academics generally still shun references to it, the news media do acknowledge it from time to time (Dalby, 2009, pp. 86–93). The consequence is that for many purposes, Wikipedia *does* provide us with content that has the status of knowledge because it is widely accepted as such.[5]

Wikipedia's success in establishing itself as a well-regarded source of useful information has made a major contribution to the transformation of the commercial encyclopaedia industry, replacing one complex of appropriative practices with another. Britannica's business model for over two hundred years was to print its encyclopaedia in enormous sets of leather-bound volumes, reaching a 32-volume set by the 15th edition, with the final version (published in 2009) retailing for over $1,000 (Silverman, 2012).[6] At its peak in 1990, Britannica sold over 100,000 sets in a year, earning revenue of $650 million (Channick, 2014). Even before the rise of the Web, however, Britannica's business was hit hard by digitised encyclopaedias on CD-ROM and in particular by Microsoft's bundling of free copies of Encarta on CD-ROM with the Windows operating system from 1994 – at a time when Britannica was launching its own CD-ROM, again priced at over $1,000 (Cauz, 2013, p. 40). The last edition of the printed version was published in 2009 – well into the age of Wikipedia – but had sold only 8,000 copies by the time that Britannica announced in 2012 that there would be no further print editions (Silverman, 2012). Britannica has survived, but only by radically transforming its business model. By 2012 it was obtaining 85% of its revenue by selling curriculum-oriented products to schools and colleges, and most of the rest by selling subscriptions for online access to its encyclopaedia to the general public, at $70 a year, or $1.99 a month for a smartphone app (Frenkel, 2012; Silverman, 2012).

---

[4] Another point I owe to Aleksi Aaltonen.

[5] In other words, there are epistemological norms, supported by widespread norm circles, that confer the status of knowledge on information provided by Wikipedia (Elder-Vass, 2012, chapter 11).

[6] For a brief history of *Britannica* see Dalby (2009, pp. 27–31).

In order to sustain the subscription model, 80% of Britannica's content was only accessible to subscribers (Channick, 2014). By 2014, however, with the encyclopaedia arm of the business 'barely breaking even' it had opened up over half of its content, and started to shift towards an advertising-based model to earn revenue from free access, while offering ad-free access to paid subscribers (Channick, 2014).

Although Britannica's print sales 'fell off a cliff' (Cauz, 2013, p. 40) well before Wikipedia became a significant competitor, Wikipedia's presence online has become the major obstacle to selling encyclopaedic content as a digital commodity. Britannica's response has been to attack the quality of Wikipedia's information. According to Britannica's president,

> we focused on editorial quality with Britannica Online and used Wikipedia's quantity-over-quality approach and its chronic unreliability as differentiators in our favor. We knew that Britannica's long-standing mission to bring expert, fact based knowledge to the general public met an enduring need for society. This resonated deeply in the education market (it's now standard practice for teachers to instruct students not to rely on Wikipedia as a reference source), and it helped boost sales there (Cauz, 2013).

This statement itself, in branding Wikipedia chronically unreliable, was part of the strategy it describes. Britannica also issued a spirited response to the *Nature* article comparing its quality with Wikipedia (Encyclopædia Britannica, 2006) (though Nature's responses are rather more persuasive: see Nature, 2006). This is in line with Britannica's long-term strategy (and appropriative practice) of securing the preferential attachment of customers by presenting itself as more authoritative and more reliable than its competitors. Before the digital era, this – and the sheer size of its product – was used to secure a price premium over its equally commodity-oriented competitors. More recently it has been used – and counterposed to size – to secure a price premium over 'free'. Although access to much of Britannica's content is also now free, preferential attachment remains a vital target of its marketing practice, since in addition to justifying the pricing of its educational products it must also attract growing traffic to its free pages to grow its advertising revenue. Whether or not its content is actually more reliable, it has been crucial to Britannica's commercial strategy to manipulate the discursive environment in the education sector to sustain preferential attachment to its products.

Funding the gift model

One part of Britannica's difficulty, which it shares with all sellers of digital commodities, is that giving is in many respects a far more efficient practice for the transfer of digital product than selling. Commodity producers must spend money on providing highly secure sales-processing systems, they must keep records of sales and customers, they must pay charges to payment-processing companies and they must put systems in place to handle complaints and returns, and to persuade customers to buy they must usually spend money on marketing their products. Selling, in other words, entails significant transaction and marketing costs and for digital products, where other marginal costs are close to zero, giving is a significantly cheaper method of distribution.[7] Giving thus eliminates activities that are only necessary because of the commodity form of transfer, many of which from a social point of view are essentially a waste of resources (cf. Clippinger & Bollier, 2006, pp. 276–7).

Wikipedia's product, encyclopaedic articles, is an excellent example of a nonrival good with a trivial marginal cost of provision. If one person accesses an article, this does not reduce the availability of the article to others, so this is not an economy of scarcity but one of abundance, and the cost of transmitting a page of information across the Internet to one more user is tiny. However, there is a difference between tiny and zero, and that difference starts to matter when a site has to deliver 12 billion pages a month: the *total* cost incurred is far from trivial. While many of Wikipedia's costs are very low relative to the scale of its operation (O'Sullivan, 2009, p. 105), it still needs to provide enough servers and bandwidth to enable its users to collect whichever of its products they want. In 2014, for example, the Wikimedia Foundation, the non-profit organisation that is legally responsible for Wikipedia, owned $10.6 million of computing equipment and spent $2.5 million on Internet hosting services. The Wikimedia Foundation also employs significant numbers of staff to perform non-editing duties, at a cost of $20 million in 2013–14, and incurs other operating

---

[7] There is a faint echo here of the work of Ronald Coase, who explained the existence of firms on the grounds that they eliminate transaction costs in relations within the firm, by contrast with market relations (Coase, 1937).

expenses, with a total expense budget of $46 million in the same year (Wikimedia Foundation & KPMG, 2014, pp. 3, 11).

In the absence of commodity sales, Wikipedia has employed an alternative appropriative practice to raise the revenue required to cover these costs. Here we come to the second sense in which Wikipedia exemplifies the gift economy: its running costs are funded more or less entirely by donations. In 2013–14, for example, $51.2 million of its total revenue of $52.8 million was provided by donations (Wikimedia Foundation & KPMG, 2014, p. 3).[8] While around $7 million of this came in the form of large grants from individuals and charitable foundations, the rest was raised through online campaigns in which ordinary users of Wikipedia were asked, via banner ads on Wikipedia pages and by email, to donate to its ongoing running costs (Wikimedia Foundation, 2014).[9] These donors are predominantly regular users of Wikipedia, who strongly approve of its non-commercial ethos. In a survey of donors conducted by Wikimedia Germany, the strongest motivation for giving was 'in order to give something back, since I use Wikipedia so frequently', closely followed by a desire to keep Wikipedia free and to protect it from being 'influenced and manipulated', with a desire to avoid advertising on Wikipedia also receiving substantial support (Wikimedia Foundation, 2011, p. 7).

The first of these motivations echoes theories of giving as a form of reciprocity, though this is rather a different sense of reciprocity than that described by Mauss (see Chapter 4). For Mauss, reciprocity was an obligation, a return that must be made in response to a gift, but most users of Wikipedia do not donate at all. Those who do are under no obligation, but seem to do it because they feel it is good or fair to give something back when you have received valuable benefits. It may be that they are also influenced by their ability to pay. The German survey includes some information about donor incomes, but this is difficult to interpret as there is no data about comparative reference groups. It does show that the donors are overwhelmingly male, that 65% have a university degree or higher qualification and that 72% are over 40 (Wikimedia Foundation, 2011, pp. 10–12), all of which suggests that these donors are more prosperous than average. While this

---

[8] The figure for donations includes $1.6 million shown as 'Release of restrictions on temporarily restricted net assets'.

[9] Some of the data used here is from the associated talk page.

evidence is rather circumstantial, it does suggest an interesting conclusion: that this may be a *fairer* way of funding a resource like Wikipedia than a commodity model. On the one hand, unlike the commodity model, anyone can access Wikipedia pages, while on the other, those who are able to afford it carry the cost of funding them in proportion to their sense of the benefit they obtain from them.

The second motivation revealed in the survey – the desire to keep Wikipedia free – reveals substantial support for the concept of a gift-based approach to providing information on the Web. The third and fourth reflect a continuing concern amongst Wikipedia users and editors about the potential role of advertising. It is clear, given its massive number of visitors, that Wikipedia could easily fund itself by selling advertising on its pages (O'Sullivan, 2009, p. 106). However, it has consistently refused to do so since 2002, when the contributors to the Spanish language version 'forked' it – created a new version independent of Wikipedia itself and started to develop their version instead of the official one – in protest against the suggestion that Wikipedia might carry ads (Tkacz, 2011).[10] While the details of the decision making process are disputed, Larry Sanger, who co-founded Wikipedia with Jimmy Wales, has suggested that 'the fork of the Spanish Wikipedia might well have been the straw that finally tipped the scales in favour of a 100% ad-free Wikipedia' (quoted in Tkacz, 2011). One major reason for contributors' support of this policy has been a concern to ensure that the content of Wikipedia should not be influenced by commercial considerations such as the desire to avoid offending advertisers. There is a clear conflict here between the appropriative practice of funding through donation and that of raising revenue by commodity sales.

Why do people edit Wikipedia?

While donors could in one sense be replaced quite easily by advertisers, one reason this has not happened is that doing so might compromise the third appropriative practice through which Wikipedia belongs to the gift economy: its content is produced and maintained entirely through freely given gifts of labour by the many thousands of volunteers who

---

[10] Although it has accepted at least one donation of $2 million from Google (B. Johnson, 2010).

edit it. The labour practices of Wikipedia are an important example of what Yochai Benkler calls 'commons-based peer production' (Benkler, 2002, p. 375) in which large numbers of individuals collaborate voluntarily to produce benefits that are then given away. In addition to being voluntary, such production is marked by a decentralised collaborative form of organisation in which we find 'very large aggregations of individuals independently scouring their information environment in search of opportunities to be creative in small or large increments. These individuals then self-identify for tasks and perform them for a variety of motivational reasons' (Benkler, 2002, p. 376). Benkler argues that this form of production has played a major part 'in the construction of the networked environment, networked culture, and the networked social order' (Benkler, 2013, p. 214). It accounts for much of the standard-setting activity that has shaped the design of the Internet itself, for the 'development of some of the core software utilities that run the Web' (Benkler, 2013, p. 214) and indeed for a great deal of other widely used software through the open-source movement (Elder-Vass, 2014).

It is hard to see how mainstream economics could ever make sense of commons-based peer production as it is practiced in Wikipedia. This is a continuing enterprise in which hundreds of thousands of people give their time for no financial reward in order to create an asset that is of value to billions yet is made available to them for nothing. There is no market here, no exchange, no commodities, and from the mainstream perspective therefore, no economy. Yet we all need and benefit from good quality information – from knowledge – and it is something that the commodity economy has often succeeded in selling to us, so from the provisioning perspective Wikipedia is very much an economic enterprise, an enterprise in which people work to produce benefit for others. Anyone can edit a page,[11] simply by clicking 'edit', and any registered user can create a new page on a previously uncovered topic. Wikipedia's editors are, collectively, its creators. Some only contribute one or a few edits, while others may continue as editors for years – the three most productive human editors have each contributed over a million edits (Wikipedia, 2014a).

Why do they do it? Productive work is usually seen as a harm to the worker in both the mainstream and Marxist traditions, and therefore

---

[11] However, new and inexperienced editors are now prevented from editing a relatively small number of controversial pages (Wikipedia, 2015c).

someone that no-one would do without financial reward, but the English language Wikipedia was edited – for nothing – over 400 million times up to October 2014.[12] Some editors contribute partly for reasons of personal satisfaction, as Clay Shirky has stressed in a fascinating account of his reasons (as far as he can tell by introspection) for making his first Wikipedia edit. His first reason – 'a chance to exercise some unused mental capacities' (Shirky, 2009, p. 132) – is reminiscent of unalienated labour: work that is done for the sheer pleasure of exercising our creative powers (also see Benkler, 2002, p. 424). His second, he describes at first as 'vanity' but then as the desire to 'make a meaningful contribution' to changing the world (Shirky, 2009, p. 132) – another aspect of unalienated labour: work in which we can exercise our creativity by determining for ourselves what the product of our work will be and how it will impact on the world. And his third, which he considers 'both the most surprising and the most obvious' was 'the desire to do a good thing' (Shirky, 2009, p. 133): to do something for the benefit of humanity at large. Indeed all Shirky's reasons reflect the pleasure of unalienated labour, in which the worker chooses her task, controls her own labour process and product, interacts with other producers as a free and equal individual and can exercise her creativity for the wider benefit of humanity, by contrast with alienated labour as described by Marx (1978a, pp. 74–6).

O'Sullivan suggests that although these motivations may indeed be significant, for many contributors to Wikipedia there are also others that Shirky misses, notably 'the attractions of belonging to a community, and of being recognized and valued by that community, especially one which offers a non-hierarchical and collaborative form of organization. Membership gives participants a sense of belonging, a common purpose, and offers mutual support in achieving the aims of the group' (O'Sullivan, 2009, p. 87). The *users* of Wikipedia hardly form a community: their relationship with the pages it provides is essentially instrumental and they do not interact with other users on the site. But the contributors to Wikipedia are a different matter. Although some editors, particularly those who only make a few edits, do not interact

---

[12] 4.7 million articles, edited on average 87.8 times each (Wikimedia, 2014c). Note that around 5% of these edits would have been performed by software bots (the percentage is substantially higher on Wikipedias in some other language) (Kurzweil AI, 2014).

much with others, many do. Their sense of participation in a community comes not only from the feeling of having made a contribution to a common endeavour, but also from participation in processes of interaction with other contributors (Lessig, 2008, pp. 159–60). These processes are highly public, though unseen by most Wikipedia users, and anyone can obtain a flavour of them by simply clicking on the 'Talk' tab of any Wikipedia page. Wikipedia editors contribute under pseudonyms, with real names actively discouraged in order to encourage decisions to be made on the basis of the quality of an argument rather than the standing of the arguer, and in order to encourage unqualified editors who might otherwise feel intimidated (O'Sullivan, 2009, p. 88). This severely limits connections between users that extend beyond Wikipedia itself. Yet editors can interact with other editors through the Talk tabs and build up significant prestige within the Wikipedia community under their pseudonyms, for example by being awarded *barnstars* by other users in recognition of valuable contributions (Reagle, 2010, p. 10), and they can also take on more responsible roles as a result of community recognition (Forte et al., 2009).[13]

Perhaps the most prominent of these more responsible roles is the role of an administrator, or admin. In the Wikipedia community, an admin is a user with greater authority over the editing process than ordinary users, which is generally used to resolve disputes between editors, for example by blocking vandals from editing, by (rarely) protecting frequently vandalised pages against further editing, or by deleting pages that cover topics that are not deemed noteworthy enough for inclusion in an encyclopaedia (Reagle, 2010, p. 125).[14] A survey of 115 administrators found that their motivations for contributing to Wikipedia were quite similar to those identified earlier: the primary motivations included the desire to create something of public value, the pleasure of creative work and commitment to the Wikipedia community (Baytiyeh & Pfaffman, 2010, pp. 135–6). But the greatest motivation of all was the desire to learn, both from reading Wikipedia's own content and from doing research beyond Wikipedia to support editing activity (Baytiyeh & Pfaffman, 2010, p. 135).

---

[13] Wikipedia editors, then, are not so much anonymous as alternonymous: they develop an identity and accumulate prestige within Wikipedia under a Wikipedia-specific name.

[14] The admin role is discussed further in the next section.

The work of constructing Wikipedia, then, can be highly satisfying for the worker, producing both short-term pleasures and longer term personal growth. This is labour freed from the tyranny of the market, a kind of labour that is sometimes denigrated as a mere hobby, and yet a kind of labour that is potentially productive of the flourishing that our economies so often fail to generate. This is a model of economic production with overtones of Marx's vision of communism and Kropotkin's anarchistic view of societies based on mutual aid (Kropotkin, 2006). More generally we may say that voluntary work in the gift economy is an appropriative practice that can create benefits for *both* the producer and the users of the product, though not every Wikipedia editor finds the experience satisfying: some are alienated by reversion of their work and disagreements on the Talk pages (J. T. Morgan Bouterse Walls & Stierch, 2013; O'Sullivan, 2009, pp. 107–8).

There is a striking contrast between this model of labour and wage labour in industrial capitalism. Production line workers in factories like those run by Foxconn endure exhausting, stressful, soul-destroying and sometimes demeaning labour because they desperately need the pay that they receive in return. This dependence on wages provides the employing firm with a source of power over the workers that enables it to overcome their resistance to unrewarding work, to impose hierarchical and directive forms of authority and to enforce strict disciplinary control over the work process. This kind of labour is a very different form of appropriative practice than the labour of editing Wikipedia. It is a practice in which the product of the labour is appropriated by the employer, while the labour process creates substantial dis-benefits for the worker, which is sustainable only because of the worker's need for the compensating benefit of a wage.

By contrast, because Wikipedia's editors are volunteers, who can exit quite easily at any time, the power relations at work are very different, and Wikipedia as a consequence must be much more sensitive to the needs of its editors. The maintenance of Wikipedia's editing community depends on the site not only providing a rewarding experience to its editors, but also on it remaining a legitimate user of their work, in the eyes of those contributors. Here we see a different balance of need between worker and organisation: when a capitalist firm can easily replace workers and workers cannot easily find a new job that pays equally well, the balance of power is strongly in the employer's favour. On Wikipedia, editors can easily leave and when they do the result is a net reduction in the labour provided to the site, so the balance of power is very different.

Regulating quality: norms

One of the central challenges faced by Wikipedia is how to maintain the quality of the information contained in its articles – and thus their value to users, and the attachment of users to the site – in this context where there is very little hierarchical and directive power available to manage the contributions of its editors. That challenge arises because its articles can be edited by anyone, and many of those who edit them are quite poorly qualified by the standards we might expect of contributors to reference works. Even in a sample of administrators, 45% had educational qualifications less than an undergraduate degree (though many of them were presumably studying towards one: 38% were full-time students) and only 36% had a postgraduate qualification (Baytiyeh & Pfaffman, 2010, pp. 132–3). Furthermore, some editors have little interest in sustaining the reliability of Wikipedia – some vandalise it for no obvious reason, some seek to bias it for political reasons,[15] and others do so for commercial reasons. In these circumstances, how can Wikipedia be prevented from degenerating into a random collection of opinionated and unreliable claims?

There is a risk, perhaps, of a different kind of tragedy of the commons – degradation not by over-use but by over-editing. But the old commons weren't quite as vulnerable to tragedies as some scholars suggest. As Elinor Ostrom has shown, communities can often find ways to manage the commons without intervention from the state or privatisation of the resource and recourse to the market. They have often developed 'a self-governed common-property arrangement in which the rules have been devised and modified by the participants themselves and also are monitored and enforced by them' (Ostrom, 1990, p. 20) and something similar has occurred in Wikipedia. These are issues that Wikipedians – the committed editors of Wikipedia – have debated deeply and carefully, and an interlocking range of norms, processes, roles and technologies have evolved to meet this challenge.[16]

---

[15] See, for example, the discussion of changes to the page on the Armenian genocide in Hansen et al (2009, pp. 44–5).

[16] As Aaltonen and Lanzara have shown, Wikipedia's norms have changed in response to changing needs and circumstances (2015).

These are thoroughly but accessibly documented in a special section or *namespace* of Wikipedia that is devoted to Wikipedia itself. As a set of Wikipedia articles, these pages are editable in just the same way as any other, but given their importance to the project, they are monitored by many experienced users and changes that have not been established consensually by discussion on the related Talk pages are likely to be reverted quickly (Forte et al., 2009, pp. 57–8). Even the most strongly enforced Wikipedia *policies*, as well as the less strict *guidelines*, exist only as community-edited pages.

One focus of Wikipedia's norms, guidelines and policies is on civility towards other editors, even under provocation, while focusing one's contributions on coming to a constructive agreement rather than 'winning' an argument (for an introductory summary, see Wikipedia, 2014c). Indeed, the requirement that editors should 'treat each other with respect and civility' is one of the 'five pillars' that are the 'fundamental principles of Wikipedia' (Wikipedia, 2014e). Given that anonymous Internet users on other sites can be extremely uncivil and disruptive, the relatively low level of emotive conflict on Wikipedia's talk pages is extraordinary, and seems to flow largely from the widespread adoption and advocacy of these norms by experienced editors.

The second major focus of Wikipedia's norms and policies is the sort of content that is considered desirable or acceptable on Wikipedia pages, expressed in the first of the five pillars, that 'Wikipedia is an encyclopedia' (Wikipedia, 2014e). Because Wikipedia is an encyclopaedia it should contain certain sorts of material and not others: it is not, for example, 'a dictionary... a publisher of original thought... a soapbox... a blog... a guidebook... a scientific journal... a newspaper... or an indiscriminate collection of information' (Wikipedia, 2014f). Rather, it should include neutral, verifiable, factual overviews about subjects worthy of public note. These principles are widely used by editors to justify amending articles and reverting changes that do not conform to them. The principle of neutrality is so central, and perhaps so unfamiliar to some new editors, that it is also accorded the status of a pillar in its own right, the principle that 'Wikipedia is written from a neutral point of view', frequently abbreviated to NPOV:

We strive for articles that document and explain the major points of view, giving due weight with respect to their prominence in an impartial tone. We avoid advocacy and we characterize information and issues rather than debate them... Editors' personal experiences, interpretations, or opinions do not belong (Wikipedia, 2014e).

Norms, however, are only effective if they are endorsed and enforced in such a way that the people they are meant to apply to are conscious that they face pressures to conform to them (Elder-Vass, 2010b, chapter 6). This is achieved on Wikipedia through two primary mechanisms: by reverting changes that do not conform with norms, and through discussions on the Talk page associated with every page of content (accessible via a tab at the top left of the page).[17] Disagreements between editors that cannot be resolved this way may be escalated to administrators, who are able to take more radical action such as blocking disruptive editors, which is the most extreme sanction available for enforcing policies and norms (though there are further levels of dispute escalation) (Reagle, 2010, pp. 125–33). To counteract the tendency for normative messages to be critical, the community has also developed positive forms of feedback – both simple praise for good contributions, but also the slightly more formal idea that any editor may award a *barnstar* to an editor who makes a particularly valuable contribution, which is then displayed on the editor's own user page (O'Sullivan, 2009, p. 89).

It is tempting to think of Wikipedia's policies and guidelines as regulative rather than appropriative, in that their focus is not so much the allocation of benefits from Wikipedia as the regulation of what is produced within Wikipedia. Wikipedia clearly has a distinctive set of regulative practices, but do these affect appropriation? There are at least two senses in which they do. First, they have a substantial impact on the content of Wikipedia articles, and by maintaining a clear sense of what should be included in a Wikipedia article and how it should be presented, they contribute to maintaining the benefits obtained from Wikipedia by its users. Second, they affect the quality of the editorial experience, and hence the extent to which the *editors* receive benefits from their work on Wikipedia. On the one hand, the benefits experienced by those editors who dip their toes in the water and feel excluded by the regulative processes are sharply reduced, in particular their

---

[17] One nice example is the section 'Removing POV sentence from language section' in the Talk page for the Wikipedia article on Pierre Bourdieu, in which editors disagree on how to introduce some criticism of Bourdieu's prose style into the article, citing various Wikipedia norms (Wikipedia, 2014d).

sense of making a useful contribution to the greater good; on the other, the benefits to those who have understood and bought into the regulative process are presumably increased as they feel greater confidence that the enterprise to which they are contributing is a worthwhile one. Regulative practices in productive organisations are thus relevant to appropriation; perhaps we might call them secondary appropriative practices, in that they are not directly concerned with the allocation of benefit but affect it nevertheless.

Regulating quality using technology

In speaking of *practices*, however, I am focusing on the actions of and the interactions between human beings, and although this is crucial to Wikipedia and most other producing organisations, it also omits a set of causal factors that is equally crucial to the digital and indeed the conventional economy: the causal role played by non-human material objects and in particular by technological objects. Let me begin to explore this by looking at the role of vandal hunters in Wikipedia. We have already come across vandalism on Wikipedia pages: changes that are deliberately intended to reduce the quality of information they contain, for example by deleting useful material, adding false material or inserting abuse or nonsense. Vandalism is easy on Wikipedia, indeed it is made easy by the very technological processes that allow Wikipedia to be usefully updated by anyone who chooses to do so – the editable nature of wiki-based websites. One might think that it could easily overwhelm and destroy the much more difficult changes required to produce good quality content. Normative pressures help to ensure that editors with good intent are channelled into making productive rather than disruptive changes, but they are not much help against those outside the community who engage with the site only to disrupt it or pursue a sectional interest.

But the defenders of Wikipedia are assisted by a further range of technological tools that ultimately make it easier to remove vandalism than to perpetrate it. The very existence of Talk pages, and thus the communication between editors that enables both normative pressures and the coordination of defensive responses, is itself a feature of the wiki technology, but there is also a range of other features built into Wikipedia's technology that assist with resisting vandalism. Editors with an interest in a particular article can add it to a *watchlist* so that they are automatically informed of any changes to it. All changes to a page are recorded in the edit history of the page, accessible using a tab at the top right of the page, and this has a compare feature which makes it very easy to see what an editor has changed. Against each change there is an 'undo' link which allows any editor to revert it, and every change also shows the Wikipedia user name of the editor who made it or their IP (Internet network) address if they are unregistered. This makes it easy to find other edits made by the same user, so that if a vandal hunter finds that one edit a user has made is disruptive, they can quickly check whether they have vandalised other articles and revert those changes too. One administrator explains 'it takes about ten total clicks to check that editor has vandalized other articles and made no positive contributions, block the IP address or user name, and rollback all of the vandalism by that user' (slashdot user taxman415a, quoted in Rosenzweig, 2006, p. 133). One well-known case of vandalism reversion was prompted by an experiment by Alexander Halavais in 2005. As a test of Wikipedia, he introduced thirteen deliberate errors into different articles. All were corrected less than three hours later (O'Sullivan, 2009, p. 108). It seems likely that one of the editors who first found one of these edits followed the chain to the rest and corrected them.

Over time, the power of the technology available to vandal hunters has steadily increased. Assisted editing programs like Huggle analyse edits on groups of pages that the user has an interest in and identify suspicious ones automatically, present a list of them to the vandal hunter and can revert a change at the click of a button (Geiger & Ribes, 2010, pp. 121–2).[18] There are even fully automated programs known as *bots* which patrol Wikipedia pages and automatically revert certain sorts of edits, such as the addition of links to known spam sites (Wikipedia, 2011).[19] Certain sorts of misleading edits remain more difficult to detect, and some have survived for a remarkably long time before being identified – most notoriously in the Seigenthaler case (Dalby, 2009, chapter 7; O'Sullivan, 2009, pp. 108–10). Nevertheless it seems that the vast majority of vandalism is fixed rapidly.

[18] Geiger and Ribes describe a fascinating case in which several vandal hunters using these tools cooperated to block an editor who committed a series of disruptive edits over a short period of time (2010).

[19] Bots are also used for constructive but relatively routine edits, e.g. adding links between related pages (Niederer & van Dijck, 2010).

While we could attribute these regulative actions to the practices discussed previously, it is clear that this would be radically incomplete as a causal explanation: vandal hunting is not just a practice carried out by people under a certain set of normative influences, but a practice that is thoroughly dependent on the employment of a number of technical tools – and was so even before the introduction of tools like Huggle and editing bots. The success of vandal hunting on Wikipedia can only be explained as the outcome of a causal complex in which certain users, tools and practices are combined in a *sociomaterial structure* (cf Niederer & van Dijck, 2010). Such systems have emergent properties, in that the combination of different elements generates a causal capability that none of them would possess outside such a complex. Wikipedia's system for protecting the quality of its content and thus the benefits it provides to its users is thus sustained by a combination in which both appropriative practices and particular technological components make essential and complementary contributions. This is not a unique feature of Wikipedia: technology makes an essential contribution to every aspect of the digital economy, and indeed to the vast majority of economic activity, and this interdependence of social structures and technological objects is a burning issue for social theory in general.

Governance, legitimacy and participation

Although Wikipedia's success depends on maintaining a high level of quality in its articles, and policy enforcement actions make an important contribution to this, there is a tension between this and another necessity: Wikipedia needs a large and diverse population of editors and a continuing sense of commitment amongst them to Wikipedia's goals. Even editing bots, at the moment, remain tools that are deployed by human editors. For the foreseeable future, even if the role of automation tools increases, the development and maintenance of Wikipedia will depend on sustaining an effective population of editors.

In the early days of Wikipedia's growth, the number of editors rose very rapidly, growing from zero in 2001 to over 51,000 active editors on the English language version at its peak in 2007 (J. T. Morgan et al., 2013, p. 839; Wikimedia, 2014a). While the editing population on many other language versions is still growing, the English version has seen a retreat from that peak, gradually declining to around 30,000 by mid-2014 (Wikimedia, 2014a). The number of new articles has followed a similar trajectory, presumably influenced by the number of active editors. Some decline in both may be sustainable, and may even be symptomatic of an approach to maturity in Wikipedia's content – inevitably as the number of articles rises, the need for further articles declines, and there are less gaps in content to inspire editing activity. Still, the need for other activities continues, including improving the quality of existing articles and protecting the encyclopaedia against vandals, so the editing community does need to be sustained at some level.

Freely given labour, even if it is enjoyable, will only continue to be given if the labour process is not linked with other dissatisfiers that outweigh the benefits to be had from the labour itself. Wikipedia's norms make a significant contribution to maintaining a relatively pleasant social environment for its editors, notably the 'civility' policy – one of the five pillars – which requires editors to 'participate in a respectful and considerate way' and avoid offending others (Wikipedia, 2014h). But another key contributor to continued participation is the worker's sense of the value of the larger enterprise to which they are contributing. To put it differently, those who give their labour freely will only do so if they believe in the *legitimacy* of the project and the organisation. Two factors in particular are significant here: the governance of the project, and the pattern of benefits that others are receiving from it.

Wikipedia is a fascinating experiment in governance. While it began as an offshoot of a commercial business owned by Jimmy Wales, it has evolved into a non-profit enterprise with a unique governance process. This is divided between the Wikimedia Foundation and the Wikipedia editors themselves. The Wikimedia Foundation acts as a kind of resource provider for Wikipedia, collecting donations and using them to fund servers, bandwidth, non-editing staff and operational costs. It is the Wikipedia editors, however, that take decisions related to the content of Wikipedia and the processes of editing it. We have seen how those decisions work as far as day-to-day editing is concerned. What is remarkable is that policy making follows much the same model. As we have seen, all Wikipedia policies and guidelines are recorded as pages in the Wikipedia namespace, and are open to editing and discussion on the same basis as other Wikipedia pages. This means that Wikipedia's governance process has some interesting resemblances to Habermas's model of discursive democracy, in which all voices have a chance to be heard and discussion proceeds until a (necessarily provisional) consensus can be reached, guided by the force of the argument rather than by the relative power of the participants (Elder-Vass, 2010a, p. 50; Habermas, 1990, 1993; Hansen Berente & Lyytinen, 2009). This is very different from the majoritarian form usually implicit in contemporary notions of democracy. Indeed Wikipedia itself, with this form in mind, insists that it is not a democracy: 'Its primary (though not exclusive) means of decision making and conflict resolution is editing and discussion leading to consensus—not voting' (Wikipedia, 2014f). The intention is that majorities cannot simply suppress minorities but must come to agreements that reflect the interests of both. This is a challenging task in any context, but when participants accept Wikipedia's 'neutral point of view' policy this removes some major obstacles to securing agreement between those with different views and interests: the task is simply to agree how to describe the varying points of view, not to agree which one to endorse, since Wikipedia's articles should not endorse any of them.

This governance process is a significant contributor to Wikipedia's legitimacy with its contributors, since in principle it makes the exercise of power relatively marginal to a process that is open to all and designed to be inclusive. This is not to say that there is *no* power exercised within Wikipedia. The most visible power, for most editors, is that of other editors, who may revert or amend their posts. Although in principle all editors are equal, those with more time, more determination, more contacts with other editors prepared to support their point of view, and sometimes just more arrogance and inflexibility, are more likely to win out in edit wars, and in the process demotivate other contributors (see the comments on Schofield, n.d.). Next in line come the admins (1,373 of them on English Wikipedia as of January 2015: Wikipedia, 2015a), who in principle have no extra editorial powers and are simply charged with executing the community's policies in cases of dispute (Reagle, 2010, pp. 125–6). While they too are supposed to seek consensus, there are occasions when editors feel they have been the victims of administrator bias. There are also further structures, notably the Arbitration Committee which resolves disputes between administrators and handles appeals against their decisions, but also 'appears to often serve as a more general decision-making body for the English-language site' (Forte et al., 2009, p. 56).

Finally, there is Jimmy Wales, the co-founder and original funder of Wikipedia, who retains considerable power in his role as an officer of the Wikimedia Foundation, which ultimately 'has legal control over, and liability for, Wikipedia' (Wikipedia, 2015b) but has progressively reduced his use of it. Generally Wales steps in only when he sees it as strictly necessary for the defence of the larger project – to head off legal threats, for example (Reagle, 2010, chapter 6). Joseph Reagle has described Wales's role as 'authorial leadership', a model that is shared with the open-source community, in which individuals who have played a leading role in establishing and sustaining a project are respected by the related community for their contribution, and this legitimises their occasional use of autocratic power as long as it is clear they are acting in the larger interests of the project itself (Reagle, 2010, pp. 118–9). Wales's style is very light touch – according to one leading administrator it is 'essentially supportive. Very low direction but very high support' (Anthere, quoted in Reagle, 2010, p. 131), and at the time of writing, some 14 years after Wikipedia's founding, he clearly still retains the support of the Wikipedia community. His leadership style is another contributor to Wikipedia's legitimacy with its contributors, but in the longer term – and particularly when Wales's tenure ends – that legitimacy might be better served by a more democratic leadership structure, one in which the Wikipedia community controls the office of the Wikimedia Foundation rather than the other way round.

The second major legitimacy issue is the question of who benefits from Wikipedia. One of the reasons that editors are willing to donate their labour to the project is the belief that other people are not making money on the basis of their freely given work. They are happy to create content for the benefit of a host of anonymous users, but as the case of Spanish Wikipedia discussed earlier suggests, at least some of them would not be happy if their work was also entangled with commercial business by the presence of advertising on the site. The editor RodW, for example, told the *New Statesman* that he would not have contributed in those circumstances: 'It changes the trust mechanisms' (Bernstein, 2011, p. 36). Although he was initially open to the possibility of advertising, Wales himself now recognises that adverts would damage the 'DNA of the organisation' by leading to pressures to orient its content to the needs of advertisers (Bernstein, 2011, p. 36). It is not only the corruption of content that concerns editors, though, but the ideal of a non-commercial, non-profit project (O'Sullivan, 2009,

p. 107). Neither the idea that advertisers might benefit by linking their products to Wikipedia pages nor the idea that Wikipedia itself might be run as a profit-making business is attractive to editors motivated by these considerations.

The editing community, then, is sustained by a mix of practices that are sensitive to the needs and motivations of these volunteers. Normative policies and guidelines are used to regulate interaction practices between editors, with the intention of avoiding unnecessary conflict and conducting debates over editing in a respectful and inclusive way. Decision-making practices are designed to be inclusive and consensual, as far as possible, and commercial practices are consciously excluded in order to maintain the legitimacy of the project with its editors. All of these practices affect the benefits that editors obtain from editing the site, supporting their sense of contributing to a worthwhile enterprise and minimising the disbenefits arising from conflict. Actual behaviour on the site does not always conform to these normative standards, and this seems to be a significant contributor to the recent decline in the editing population (J. T. Morgan et al., 2013; Wikimedia, 2014a), but we must also recognise that some editors do not make useful contributions and an element of conflict with such editors is more or less inevitable. Striking a balance between preserving quality against poor editing while encouraging new editors will never be easy, and it may be that some aspects of Wikipedia's model will eventually need to change if this problem is to be controlled – perhaps more mature pages will have to be protected against uninformed editing, for example. Whatever the future may hold, so far Wikipedia has done a remarkable job of building governance practices that can sustain not only an encyclopaedia but also a community of editors.

Conclusion

Like Apple, Wikipedia is impressively successful, and like Apple, that success is built in part on the substantial benefits it delivers to the users of its products. Like Apple, Wikipedia is the site of a carefully designed, though evolving, complex of interlocking appropriative practices, but here the similarity ends. Rather than being oriented to maximising the profit that it can extract from its ecosystem, Wikipedia's practices are oriented to providing the best possible online encyclopaedia to its users while sustaining and motivating a community of voluntary editors – and thus itself. Wikipedia has no need for marketing spin, for exploiting workers and contractors, for enforcing rigid controls on the users of its products or for avoiding tax to the maximum extent legally possible. Instead, it can focus its energies on its product and its producers. In doing so, it provides ample proof of the possibility of providing high-quality benefits as gifts and running an effective organisation on the basis of decentralised and discursively organised collaboration. The primary appropriative practices here are the transfer of product as a gift, funding operational costs through donations, production by freely donated labour, co-ordination of production through self-selection of tasks and respectful and inclusive discourse between contributors and the minimisation of hierarchical and directive authority. Though it is far from perfect, on balance Wikipedia provides an inspiring model of the digital gift economy in action – and one that is virtually unthinkable in terms of the narrow economic categories of either mainstream economics or Marxist political economy.

This does not mean that Wikipedia's model could be replicated widely as it stands. That model has evolved through engagement with a very specific set of technologies, particularly the wiki technology that allows public editing of web pages and provides associated discussion spaces, to produce a very specific kind of product. The co-ordination process is tightly integrated with the technology required to deliver the product itself, and inevitably a project producing a different kind of product would need to be co-ordinated differently, though preferably in keeping with the discursive democratic spirit of Wikipedia's co-ordination processes. Impressive as it is, Wikipedia represents only one possible way of organising a gift-based model of economic production, and for a wider understanding of the potential of the gift economy we would also need to examine the broad range of other possible models.

The dependence of Wikipedia's form on its technology also reinforces the argument developed in this chapter that although social practices are vital to economic forms, they are always interdependent with material technologies. Wikipedia is a socio-technical system that requires *both* its social practices *and* its technological infrastructure. That infrastructure has mostly been purposefully developed to meet Wikipedia's needs, and indeed the underlying wiki technology itself was purposefully developed to make public editing possible (Reagle,

2010, p. 5) so the technology is not entirely independent of the social process. On the other hand it has created possibilities for social interaction and possibilities for new kinds of work that would not exist without the technology, so it has played an essential causal role in enabling Wikipedia's success, and in creating new opportunities for unalienated work.

More broadly, we may say that the development of the Web and of wiki technology has made it far easier and far more economically viable to provide information goods as a gift, and this has had substantial consequences for the existing information economy. By making it difficult to sell comparable information sources as a commodity, the digital information gift economy has squeezed capitalist businesses operating in this 'marketplace'. Wikipedia itself has succeeded in resisting significant entanglement with capitalist business, despite the fact that its co-founder and benevolent dictator continues to run a closely related capitalist business. No doubt it does benefit some commercial companies indirectly, including the network companies that all websites drive traffic to, and commercial sites that gain traffic from links to them on Wikipedia, but in deference to its contributors, direct entanglements have been carefully avoided. The consequence is that Wikipedia is as pure an example of the digital gift economy as we could plausibly expect in our current economic environment.

8 | *Does Google give gifts?*

Introduction

While the gift and capitalist economies might seem radically different, in practice capitalist entrepreneurs have found numerous opportunities to put gifts to work for profit. This chapter and the next one consider two of the resulting hybrid forms of economy that have developed in the digital space. While the forms overlap in practice, the next chapter looks at practices in which businesses take advantage of gifts *from* ordinary users, and this one examines the use of gifts – or something like gifts – by a company *to* its users. It focuses on Google's enormously profitable linkage of free services with targeted advertising – a linkage that depends on using those free services to acquire data about users. Business models like this, in which wage labour plays a marginal role because the core processes are operated largely by automated technology, illustrate the obsolescence of traditional Marxist analyses of capitalism. But Google's model also exposes the limits of mainstream economics: what is the relevance of price competition in a 'market' where the product is free? Neither of the established political economies is equipped to make sense of this kind of economic activity, but we *can* explain it in terms of interacting appropriative practices, as this chapter will show.

The chapter opens by introducing Google's web search service, then relates it to the concept of *inducement gifts*: a form of gifts designed to induce the recipient to take actions that generate benefits for the giver. Google has mastered the art of making web advertising highly effective by developing a series of strategies to secure user attachment to its search service, while seeking to minimise the dissatisfiers that advertising often produces: two goals that are often in tension. After examining these tensions, the chapter considers the issues of personalisation and privacy raised by Google's techniques. Finally, it puts together the pieces to summarise the complex of appropriative practices that produces both Google's profits and the search services that a huge proportion of Internet users rely on.

Web search and advertising

Although its enormous profits have allowed it to branch out into many other areas, Google's web search service is the primary source of its wealth and still the core of its business model. Google uses automated programs known as *web crawlers* or *spiders* to scan pages from the Web, following links from page to page and gathering information about these pages as they go. Then the information collected by the crawlers is used to construct an index with entries for every word showing all the pages where those words are found. Users may then invoke the search engine by typing a word or phrase into a box on the search provider's web page, and the search engine uses the index to build a list of web pages that include the word or phrase concerned (for more detail, see Battelle, 2005, pp. 19–24).

Perhaps the most important differentiator between different search providers is their page ranking algorithms: this is the part of the search engine that determines the order in which results are presented to the user. Google's explosive growth arose largely because its founders Sergey Brin and Larry Page devised an innovative and powerful page ranking algorithm (Battelle, 2005, pp. 74–7). Their algorithm, known as PageRank, ordered results depending on how many links each page had from other pages (though there has been a steady stream of embellishments to the central principle). This technique was derived from the academic practice of counting the citations that papers receive from other scholars as a way of deciding which papers are most important. On the web, Page and Brin assumed, the best pages are the ones that many other pages provide links to, so these were the sites that Google placed at the top of its search results. The underlying principle is only a rough rule of thumb thus the top result is not *necessarily* the most useful one but on the whole Google's early users found it much more useful than sites using other algorithms.

Although many other search services now imitate Google's page ranking algorithm, its early command of the technology helped it to establish a reputation as the most useful search provider on the Web. From experimental beginnings as a student project in 1996, Google was incorporated as a company in 1998, started earning revenue in

2000 and was already profitable, at a rapidly accelerating rate, by 2001 (Levy, 2011, pp. 18, 34, 69–70). Today, it has a dominant share of search activity in most of the countries of the world. As of 2013, one report showed Google as the most popular search provider in 27 of 31 significant countries, with 88% or more of the search 'market' in 24 of them (Return On Now, 2013).[1] Only in China, Russia and South Korea was a non-Google service the most popular.

In the early years of commercial activity on the Web, it was widely expected that companies that attracted large numbers of visitors to their sites would be able to make money from them, to the extent that loss-making businesses with many visitors were able to raise vast amounts of funding from venture capitalists and even on the stock market.[2] But many of those businesses struggled to find a way to earn revenue. Many sought to profit from their visitor numbers by selling advertising space on their pages, but early web advertising was a commercial disaster. Advertisers were not persuaded that using the Web was cost effective as web ads didn't generate enough leads to be worthwhile. This in turn was a consequence of the failure to make advertising relevant to the users it was presented to. Sites sought to compensate by making advertising increasingly intrusive – pop-up windows, banner ads that took up a large part of the screen and animated banners, for example – but this often antagonised users, who sometimes even switched to using other sites to avoid the ads.

This was the context in which, in 2000, Google introduced advertising to its search pages, but it delivered advertising rather differently from most of its competitors (Battelle, 2005, pp. 123–6). Google distinguished itself by striving to make its adverts both less intrusive and more useful. The paid ads on its search results page are similar in style and size to the organic search results, and both are in a simple, text-based format (though in the last few years some ads and a few organic search results have also featured very small pictures). Such ads are certainly unobtrusive but they can easily be confused with the organic results, and some search providers have been criticised for

---

[1] It was also the engine behind the most popular provider in one of the other four.
[2] A prime example was Priceline.com, an online travel agency that floated in 1999 at the height of the US dotcom boom. By the end of its first day of trading on the stock exchange, the company was valued at $10 billion, despite running an operating loss on turnover of a mere $35 million (Cassidy, 2002, pp. 2–6, 214–7).

mixing paid results with organic search results with no indication of the difference between them, thus potentially misleading users (e.g. in the case of GoTo: Levy, 2011, p. 87). Google has avoided this, with paid ads clearly but simply distinguished from organic results by being positioned distinctively on the page and coloured or marked subtly differently. Google's model also tends to provide ads that users might regard as positively useful rather than irritating distractions. A later section will discuss these questions in more depth; what is relevant here is that Google has found a formula for web advertising that does not antagonise users and can even seem like a useful part of the search service itself.

Google also found ways to make its service increasingly attractive to advertisers. Following a model that had been pioneered by GoTo.com, in 2002 it started to charge advertisers per click rather than per impression: advertisers did not have to pay every time their ad was displayed but only when a user actually clicked through from the ad to the advertiser's website (Battelle, 2005, pp. 109, 142; Levy, 2011, pp. 87–91). This immediately provides much greater confidence to the advertiser that their money is being well spent, but it also provides the original site – in this case Google – with an incentive to increase clicks by finding ways to make advertising as relevant as possible to its users. Search pages provide the perfect opportunity for this: if a user searches, for example, for 'bass guitar strings', then it is very clear that they are a potential buyer of bass guitar strings and related products, and by placing ads for these products on the search results page Google can hugely increase the chances of earning a click-through: this is advertising based on the user's known *intent* at the moment the ad is displayed (Battelle, 2005, pp. 166–7). Second, building on the GoTo model, Google introduced an auction system known as Adwords, in which advertisers bid for the chance to have their ad displayed alongside the results for a specific search term – and still only pay if the ad is clicked. Advertisers can bid at any time, and one of the remarkable things about Google search is that every search prompts not only the construction of an ordered set of 'organic' results tailored to that specific search but also an instant auction for the paid advertising positions on that user's results page, both typically completed within a fraction of a second (Levy, 2011, p. 93). The bid process is also conducted online, and potential advertisers can bid for small numbers of clicks, or for clicks from users located in a limited geographical area, with the result that the process is attractive to the 'long tail' of small local businesses as well as the larger advertisers that old media businesses had courted.

Google was thus able to deliver ads without driving away its users, and to deliver ads that secured relatively high click-through rates, with the result that it became the first web business to make substantial profits from advertising, and these have grown remarkably. In 2014, it earned $45 billion of revenue by selling ads on its own sites, primarily its search results pages but also, for example, on its email and You-Tube services, and a further $14 billion by selling ads on other sites (a service known as Adsense), with these two streams accounting for 89% of its total revenue (Google, 2015). Around 25% of this ($16.5 billion) was profit. As of mid-2015 it had the second-highest market capitalisation in the world, on the basis of these revenues and investors' expectations of its future earning potential (Forbes, 2015).

Over time Google's targeting of adverts has become more sophisticated, and in particular it has become more personalised to the individual user. The implications of this will be examined in a later section, but the core elements of the complex of appropriative practices at work here are already clear. First, the company offers a free service that many users find attractive. Second, it uses that service to do two things that make it an ideal vehicle for advertising: to gather information about what a user is interested in at a specific moment and to retain the attention of the user long enough to present ads that fit with that interest. Third, this enables it to sell advertising at a premium rate that reflects the quality of the leads that it generates.

Gift capitalism?

Are Google's free services gifts to their users? To answer this question we will first need to spend a little more time on the nature and varied types of gifts, picking up from the initial discussion in Chapter 4. Gifts are sometimes selfless acts of generosity, and sometimes designed to build networks of mutually obligated social relations, but they may also have other forms and purposes. As we saw in Chapter 5, for example, certain commercial software companies pay programming staff to write code that is then donated to open-source software projects such as Linux (Cammaerts, 2011; Elder-Vass, 2014). Although this is a gift, and the open-source software that results from it is given away for free, the motives behind these contributions are primarily profit oriented.

IT services companies that contribute to developing an open-source product develop deep expertise that enables them to provide support and integration services to companies that wish to use it. They can, for example, write fixes and new function for a customer (which then also become part of the open-source product) (Anderson-Gott Ghinea & Bygstad, 2011, p. 109; Weber, 2004, pp. 195–203). Red Hat, for example, markets itself as 'The world's leading provider of open-source enterprise IT products and services' (Red Hat, 2012).

This is a case of a more general form of gifts that I call *inducement gifts*. Inducement gifts are given in order to induce a further transaction or transactions that provide greater value to the giver than the original gift. This type of giving is growing rapidly as a result of the possibilities opened up by digital technology (Anderson, 2009). Unlike many other giving practices, which may be alternatives to, or in competition with, contemporary capitalism, inducement giving is giving turned to the service of capitalism. Within this cluster of practices we constantly find what Fuchs calls 'an entanglement of gifts within the commodity form' (2008, p. 171). Inducement giving is a set of non-exchange practices deep within the capitalist economy. One implication is that even thinkers whose aim is only to understand the commercial economy also need to take account of other kinds of motivation and other kinds of practice than those analysed in commodity exchange models of commerce. At the same time, there is a kind of colonisation of giving going on here, in which the commercial economy acts back on the form and usage of giving practices.

An inducement gift is not itself part of an exchange, nor does it generate a normative requirement for a reciprocal return gift. Any return by the recipient is voluntary, but the gift is nevertheless designed to produce such a return. So this is a variety of giving that may sometimes generate an element of reciprocation but a very different kind of reciprocation than that involved in pure exchange, first because it is voluntary and second because it is often far from equivalent in value. There are at least three significant varieties of inducement giving.

In the first variety the inducement gift is intended to induce subsequent exchanges in the market. We may call these *marketing gifts*. Anderson, for example, describes the strategy adopted in the United States in the early twentieth century to market Jell-O, a gelatine-based food product. Unable by law to sell their product door to door, the company's sales force gave away recipe books with recipes for using the product instead. The result was to encourage consumers to buy the product in order to try out the recipes (Anderson, 2009, pp. 9–10). Marketing gifts are a fairly widespread phenomenon in commercial economies, but they have been given a new lease of life by digital developments. One contemporary digital case is the phenomenon of 'advergaming' in which companies give away computer games that feature their products in ways designed to encourage the gamer to buy them (or ask their parents/carers to do so) (Lumpkin & Dess, 2004, p. 166). This is also the logic behind free computer games in which gamers can make accelerated progress or enhance their participation in other ways by making in-game purchases—a $2 billion market in the United States in 2011 (T. Cheshire, 2012, p. 139). Such gifts do not entail an obligation to reciprocate, but they *are* designed to induce a response that generates a return to the original giver. That response, however, is not a return gift but a market exchange in its own right, from which the original giver expects to make a profit.

The second variety of inducement gifts is *solicitation gifts*. These gifts are linked to a request for a return gift that is nevertheless entirely voluntary. For a non-digital case consider the beggar's flower: a gift given by a beggar that is then followed by a request for a return gift of money. In principle the return gift is optional, but, if one accepts the flower, reciprocation may be strongly expected by the giver and the recipient may experience strong criticism from the giver if a return gift is not made. Such cases approach quite closely to the principle of reciprocity, despite being nominally free, and one reason for this is that the beggar's flowers are a limited resource. Whether the beggar has bought the flower, grown it or picked it from the roadside, there is some cost to the beggar in replenishing the supply so he or she needs to ensure a reasonably high rate of reciprocation. When potential recipients are aware of these expectations, accepting the flower is more or less a signal of intent to reciprocate.

The effectiveness of solicitation gifts depends on the cultural associations they invoke: in particular the expectation of fair reciprocity that is built into some types of giving (see Chapter 4). Such associations can be exploited in a variety of commercial contexts to provoke returns to the original giver that carry the outward form of market exchange (unlike the return gift to the beggar) and yet are motivated in part, not by the purchaser's need for the thing purchased, but by a sense of normative obligation to the seller.

In the digital economy the virtually costless nature of digital gifts changes the dynamic of solicitation gifts radically. When the digital gift is effectively free (at least at the margin) to the giver as well as the recipient, the giver can afford to give away vast numbers of gifts even if the rate of reciprocation is extremely low. In such circumstances it is not necessary to pressure the recipient for a return and there can be a much stronger sense in which the return is voluntary for the original recipient. This is a practice that mushroomed for a while in the smartphone app market, though it has roots in the PC shareware movement.[3] Many software apps are available in two forms: a free form and a paid form. Nominally the paid form may be superior in some way – the 'freemium' business model (Anderson, 2009, pp. 26–7) – but in practice the free version is often very close in functionality to the paid version. It may, for example, do everything that the paid version does but include a start-up screen encouraging the user to upgrade to the paid version, or it may be identical to the paid version except that advertisements are displayed on certain screens. Another feature of these apps is that even the paid versions are remarkably cheap – perhaps a twentieth or a fiftieth of the price of a console game.

In cases where the paid version is markedly superior to the free version, we may regard the free version as a marketing gift, designed to induce the recipient to purchase the paid version. But in cases where the paid version is very similar to the free version, why do users upgrade? No doubt there are many reasons, but one is simply the feeling that the suppliers of the app *deserve* a reward for providing something that we experience as having significant use value. Such feelings are encouraged, though fairly subtly on the whole, by introductory messages from the developers and by occasional comments by other users. For a purer case of this phenomenon, consider the launch of the album *In Rainbows* by Radiohead:

Rather than release its seventh album into stores as usual, the band released it online with the request that you pay as much or as little as you wanted. Some chose to pay nothing... while others paid more than $20. Overall, the average price was $6 (Anderson, 2009, p. 153).

[3] An *app* is a computer program, typically for a smartphone. I follow usual practice here in calling the sites from which apps can be acquired *markets*, although the term is thoroughly inappropriate when the apps are free. At the time of writing, the solicitation model seems to be in decline in the app markets relative to the in-game purchases and advertising business models.

The return gift in these cases is itself a further free gift, but it is one that is motivated by a sense of the justice of paying something for what we have received. These are not reciprocal gifts in the sense that reciprocation is *required* by either gift in the sequence, yet they do evoke a different variety of the spirit of reciprocity.

I call the third variety of inducement gifts *loaded gifts*. These are gifts whose acceptance or use automatically entails a return that is in a sense hidden, or at least an implicit rather than an explicit element of the process. To start with a non-commercial case, some evangelizing religious groups distribute free pamphlets or even books to anyone who will take them. In taking a book, a recipient has already made a small return by indicating to the distributor that she or he might be open to the group's ideas, and going on to read it provides a further return – the possibility that the reader will be influenced to develop the contact further. Commercial cases tend to cluster around advertising. At some conferences, for example, delegates are provided with free bags to carry their papers in, but these bags often carry a logo and message from a commercial sponsor, so by using the bag a delegate becomes a mobile advertising hoarding for the sponsor. Or consider the case of free newspapers, such as the *London Evening Standard*, given away to 700,000 people a day (Preston, 2013). Free newspapers are loaded gifts because in accepting one the reader increases the newspaper's circulation figures and thus its appeal to advertisers, producing a return to the newspaper in the form of advertising revenue. This is what Anderson calls a 'three party market' (Anderson, 2009, pp. 24–5), though the commodity sale is a transaction between the newspaper and the advertiser, while the relationship between the newspaper and the reader is not a commodity relationship at all.

Google's search results are similar. Like the newspaper, the search results are free. Like the newspaper they provide an opportunity to deliver advertising, exploiting the attention of the user to the free content. And like the newspaper reader, the user of web search increases the outlet's appeal to advertisers simply by using the service. The differences, however, are equally significant. Most strikingly, the reader of a free newspaper provides very little information to the publisher about her interests. There is just one significant piece of information that marks out its readers to potential advertisers: their location. Advertisers in the *London Evening Standard*, for example, can be confident that almost all its readers will have passed through

London on the day the newspaper is published. No doubt the publishers could exploit this information more subtly – they could perhaps publish different editions for North and South London, or a special edition for distribution in the financial districts, and thus attract businesses with more local or specialised target markets, but the opportunities for targeting advertising are limited by the nature of the information available and the format of the product. Google's advantage is that its users necessarily provide a much more specific and valuable transfer of information: as a minimum, a search user provides a search string that reveals what she is interested in learning about, and thus what sorts of products she might potentially be interested in buying *at this particular moment*. Google's search results are also, therefore, loaded gifts, provided freely and yet entailing a return transfer of fundamental value to Google, since its entire business depends on exploiting these returns of information about users' needs and interests.

Still, we might wonder whether loaded gifts are really gifts at all. Newspapers given away at railway stations are indeed free in monetary terms, and there is no direct return from the reader to the publisher but only a rather vague piece of information implicit in the transaction, so they are clearly not commodities. Google's search results are equally free, but involve a rather more specific piece of information that inherently must be supplied for the search to be possible. Might we say that they are *neither* gifts nor commodities? Not all transfers are gifts or exchanges. Thefts and loans, for example, are other kinds of transfer, and there may also be other varieties. These cases help us to see that the nature of a transfer depends on the intentional attitudes of the parties towards it. A theft, for example, is different from a gift because the person from whom the item is stolen has no intention to transfer it to the recipient.

What casts doubt on the status of Google's search results as gifts is the necessary existence of a return transfer from the user, the provision of the search term. But what is the status of *this* transfer? I suggest we may see it as an *incidental* transfer. Incidental transfers occur when a recipient receives a benefit as a result of another agent's intentional action, but the intention behind that action was not to transfer the benefit concerned. Such transfers occur as a by-product of some other intended action. For example, a donor may give money to a charity for children with cancer, and incidentally contribute to paying the salaries of managers at the charity.[4] Search users' transfers to Google of information that it can use to target ads are incidental transfers: the search term is provided by the user because this is a logically necessary part of the process of searching for information about a specific topic, but in providing the search term for one purpose, the user also incidentally transfers data that creates an advertising opportunity for Google. Because the user's intent in providing the search term is to access the service rather than to pay for it, we cannot see this as a commodity exchange. But where does this leave the status of Google's provision of free search?

It helps, I think, to recognise that transfers may also be *asymmetric*, when the parties have different intentional attitudes to them. The provider, for example, may see the transfer as a gift and the recipient may see it as a loan, or vice-versa (see, for example, Heath & Calvert, 2013; Lainer-Vos, 2013). Or the victim of a fraudster may see a transfer as part of an exchange, whereas the fraudster understands it is theft. A free newspaper or a free page of search results may appear as a gift to the recipient, but his or her receipt of it results in an incidental transfer to the publisher in the form of an increase in advertising opportunities. For the publisher and for Google, this incidental transfer is the purpose of the initial offer. We might say that this is a case where a gift is made with a view to a reciprocal return, but unlike traditional gift reciprocation the return is incidental to some other action as far as the recipient is concerned, rather than a fully intended act of reciprocal transfer. Given the parallels with reciprocal giving, I suggest we are still justified in calling Google's search results a gift – a loaded gift – but like some traditional forms of reciprocal giving it is a gift with strings.

Resistance and attachment

Google's revenue thus depends on its ability to attract large numbers of users to its services, and in particular its search services, while delivering paid advertising to them. These two objectives, however, are potentially in conflict with each other, if customers are resistant to advertising. Pervasive advertising has to some extent conditioned us to

---

[4] Incidental transfers have some similarities to Rey's concept of *ambient* production, in which users produce data or other benefits without being aware of doing so (Rey, 2012, pp. 400, 410). However, transfers can still be incidental even if we are aware that they are occurring.

expect and accept it – as well as encouraging us to accept the consumerist values it embodies (Schudson, 2009) – but advertising audiences are not simply dupes. Even members of television audiences, who in some respects play a rather passive role as consumers of media by comparison with Internet users, have significant autonomy and have often used it to evade exposure to the advertising that is presented to them (Turow, 2009). They may leave the room during ad breaks to do other things, they may skip past the ad breaks on recordings of programmes or they may simply 'tune out' and ignore them. Advertisers and the advertising industry have constantly striven to overcome this – one strategy, for example, is product placement within media content such as movies and television series. But they face a set of difficulties that Eric Clemons has expressed nicely: 'There are three problems with advertising in any form, whether broadcast or online: 1. Consumers frequently do not trust advertising... 2. Consumers often do not want to view advertising... 3. And mostly, consumers do not need advertising' (2009, p. 18).

Internet audiences have considerably more autonomy than television audiences, and they are sometimes willing to exercise that autonomy to avoid advertising – sites that host overly intrusive advertising, for example, may well find users going elsewhere. Similarly, the profusion of pop-up ads led to the development of pop-up blockers and eventually the addition of pop-up blocking features to popular web browsers, and there are also more radical ad blocking programs available to web users. In general, web advertising must tread a fine line between noticeability (or it would be pointless) and intrusiveness (or it will generate avoidance activities). Some digital businesses even use customer resistance to advertising as a revenue generator. Spotify, for example, is one of many businesses that offers a choice between ad-supported and subscription-based versions of its service, and those customers that opt for the latter are paying, at least partly, to avoid advertisements. Such businesses, however, are always vulnerable to the conventional market risk of competitors undercutting their prices.

Price competition is not an issue for Google – it's hard to undercut 'free' – but free sites can also be in competition with each other, and they compete in different ways. Google's success is largely a product of its ability to compete effectively, not on price, but on the quality of the user's experience. As we have seen, its early success was a result of providing search results that were more relevant and more useful than those provided by earlier search services, but this is an advantage that has been difficult to sustain over the long term, and as other search providers have reverse-engineered Google's algorithms the difference in quality of results between Google and its major competitors has largely disappeared (see, for example, E. Davies, 2014; Hachman, 2014). It also set the standard for design of search pages, with a clean, simple, uncluttered 'pure search' design that was once distinctive – but is also now widely imitated.

Google was also a trailblazer in managing the quality, not only of its organic search results, but also of the ads it delivers (Levy, 2011, pp. 86, 91–2). Above all, it is the keyword system that is at the heart of this: earlier ads were often irrelevant to their audience, with no relation to whatever activity a user was undertaking. Combining this with an intrusive delivery style simply increased user resistance to them. By linking ads with the user's search keywords, however, Google made ads potentially useful: these ads could actually be seen as a positive service to the user (Levy, 2011, pp. 92–3). One consequence was that it was unnecessary to present them intrusively, thus allowing the simplicity and usability of the search box to be carried over to the results pages. Over time Google has experimented with a variety of formats for presenting paid ads alongside organic search results – testing, perhaps, the balance between effectiveness in securing clicks and the potentially alienating effects of ads on users.

Google has also taken its focus on ad quality further by making it a factor in the algorithms that determine which ads are served up. While Adwords is an auction-based system, it is not *purely* an auction system. If Google finds that users are clicking more frequently on the second ad on a page than the first one, for example, its algorithm may push the second placed ad up to first place, even though the advertiser bid less per click (Battelle, 2005, pp. 142–3). This penalises advertisers whose offers are less relevant to user needs, providing a more relevant service to users and helping to keep them on the site. Its short term effects on Google's revenues are unclear – it has to cut the price it receives per click as a consequence, but it may receive more clicks overall – but the policy is clearly aimed at retaining users in the longer term, sacrificing short-term revenue if necessary to do so.

Google, in other words, is just as devoted to securing the preferential attachment of its users as more conventional capitalist companies like Apple. While in the past it has gained attachment by being free and highly functional, by the minimalist aesthetic and by the subtlety of the advertising, all of these are replicable by its competitors. In circumstances like these, companies must pay careful attention to what distinguishes one service from another similar one. Continuing marginal improvements in these areas can help, if a site can always claim to be one step ahead, but over time marginal improvements tend to become less and less significant to most users.

In such circumstances, incumbency is a substantial advantage. As the 'first mover' in many areas of search and related technology, Google has established itself in many users' lives in a variety of ways that sustain continuing use. Users who have established the habit of using Google search, perhaps setting it as the default search provider in their browser, are likely to continue to use it unless and until they are presented with a prompt to change, and Google's careful management of the impression it presents to users is in part a strategy for avoiding such prompts. Its effort to retain the trust of users by its careful control over the placement and relevance of paid ads is also a significant contributor, and it even attracts an element of ethical approval from its well-publicised motto 'Don't be evil' (Google, 2012). Even humour is employed, with the 'doodles' that frequently replace the Google logo on the search page.

Google is in a business where, despite its clear current global dominance, competitive advantage is ephemeral and securing user attachment is enormously important for continuing commercial success. Perhaps the greatest threat to Google's dominance is the risk of being unseated as the default search provider when users purchase new digital devices, and thus losing the benefit of convenience and user inertia. For example, Microsoft's launch of the Windows Phone operating system and acquisition of Nokia has enabled it to marginalise Google on some of its phones, which are shipped with Microsoft's own search service Bing preinstalled as the default (Warren, 2014). Similarly, the popular open-source browser Firefox switched to Yahoo as its default search provider in the US in late 2014 (Lardinois, 2014), though at the time of writing it is too early to tell how large an effect this has had. Google, however, appears to have been aware of this risk for some time, and in particular on the mobile platform, which has recently overtaken the desktop as the source of most web searches. Google's purchase of Android in 2005 and its enormously successful promotion of it as a smartphone operating system must be seen in this light. Stephen Levy suggests that part of its motivation for this was to protect 'the opportunity to place its services' on new phones (Levy, 2011, p. 215). For Levy, the risk was that mobile networks might control the operating software on these phones and thus exclude Google from the position of default search provider. It seems just as plausible that Google was concerned that Apple's then dominance of the smartphone market would enable it to exclude Google or charge it for the position thus skimming off a substantial portion of its revenue, as it has done for other mobile content providers. By the third quarter of 2014, over 84% of new smartphones were shipping with the Android operating system, typically but not always with Google installed as the default search provider (IDC, 2015). Google's control over Android is limited by its status as open-source software, and does not extend to enforcing its own search tool as the default, but it has succeeded in removing that power from the hands of potential major competitors, and thus in removing a potentially catastrophic change to its ability to secure the preferential attachment of search users.

To secure that attachment, then, Google must ward off competitors for the attention of its users while simultaneously balancing the need to hold on to its users with the need to monetise their attention. This dynamic of developing preferential attachment while also exploiting it for commercial benefit is at the heart of contemporary forms of capitalist business, and managing the potential tension between the two is one of its central challenges.

Personalisation, privacy and power

The most recent developments in online advertising, with Google once again in the forefront, depend on the collection of ever-increasing amounts of personal data about web users. Many websites store 'cookies' on our devices that enable them to track our browsing behaviour and save the details for future reference; we make the job easy for others by registering as users for their services, providing names, addresses, phone numbers and much more; and many sites sell this data to aggregators who are able to link together evidence about our behaviour and personal details from many different sites (Pariser, 2012, pp. 42–5). Google collects not only the search terms we use, but also the data we provide to any of their other services – the content of our emails and who we send them to if we use Gmail; the places where we go (and perhaps even who we were there with) if we allow Google Maps to track our location; our social interaction with friends and colleagues if we sign up and use Google+. All this is combined to provide substantial details on our interests, contacts and preferences. Nor is Google alone in this; another prominent example is Facebook, which collects vast amount of data arising from the posts users make on it. One student who had been a Facebook user for three years discovered that Facebook held 1,222 pages of data on him (Pidd, 2011).

The primary commercial reason for assembling these profiles is to tailor advertising to be more personal and more relevant to the user. This can be of value to the user, bringing the search results that are most likely to fit their interests nearer the top of the list, particularly for the many search terms with ambiguous referents. If a user types in 'bridge', for example, they might be interested in the card game, structures built across rivers, dental prosthetics, a section of a song or the command areas of ships. In the absence of information about which of these they are most likely to be interested in, they might have to go through several screens of search results before they find something relevant, but if Google knows that they receive emails from a contract bridge club, or that they frequently search for musical terms, for example, it can use this information to prioritise results that might be more relevant to this user than to others. For Google this is one more step towards making its search results and advertising more useful and appealing to its users, and thus increasing its advertising revenues – and the payoff from providing a wide range of free services that enable it to extend the data it holds on users.

A second closely related trend has been led by Facebook (discussed in more depth in the next chapter), which has found it more difficult than Google to monetise its huge user population by hosting advertising. Search-based advertising has two great advantages. First, the search term entered tells the search provider what the user is interested in learning more about *right now*, so advertising can be targeted very precisely at the user's current needs and interests. Second, the user is expecting to be presented with a full page of information that relates to that search term, which provides a natural opportunity to include related advertising. While Facebook does have access to users' posts, and thus information about their current interests, this doesn't necessarily entail that the user wants to be presented with information, let alone advertising, about what they have just posted, and doing so can seem intrusive. Indeed, it can highlight the commercial use that is being made of what the user may see as quite private personal information, and positively antagonise users as a result, in a situation where users are often unaware of the ways in which Facebook uses its data and somewhat negative towards the advertising presented on the site (Lilley Grodzinsky & Gumbus, 2012). In some ways Facebook's challenge in balancing exploitation of user data against retaining the attachment of its users is more difficult than Google's and it has repeatedly angered users with initiatives that exposed their data in ways they had not anticipated, notably the Facebook Beacon initiative, which revealed users' activities on other sites in automated posts on Facebook (Debatin Lovejoy Horn & Hughes, 2009, p. 85).[5] Given these difficulties, Facebook has sought to use the social connections that users reveal on the site to leverage advertising opportunities. After some false starts, it seems to be making progress through the use of the 'Like' button: Facebook users can click this button to indicate their approval of a post, a web page or a product (not just on Facebook's own pages but on a wide range of other sites across the Internet). This provides Facebook with more valuable information not only about its users' preferences, but also about the preferences of their friends, which can be used to target advertising more effectively. As of 2012, Facebook users had hit the like button over a trillion times (Gerlitz & Helmond, 2013). Google, too, has sought to move into this space, with its launch of Google+ as a competitor to Facebook, though with only limited success so far.

Now the incidental transfers that users make to Google and similar sites start to take on a somewhat different character. They remain incidental transfers, but they are no longer merely transactional. A collection of every imaginable kind of data gathered from a broad range of a user's digital activity and stored indefinitely is very different from the tiny ephemeral transfer that occurs in the simplest search engines.

Perhaps the most obvious concerns that arise are related to privacy – is it acceptable in principle for a company to have data about us that

---

[5] Though it also has one substantial advantage over Google, known as the *network effect*: it is difficult for users to leave Facebook and get an equivalent service elsewhere if their friends are on Facebook but are not on other social media sites.

we do not realise it has, to sell or reveal that data to others without our awareness or explicit consent and to keep it long after we have stopped using the services from which it was gathered? These questions take on more sinister connotations when, for example, hackers are able to access the data and use it to defraud the users concerned, or when web companies reveal data about the political activities of dissident users to oppressive governments, as Yahoo did in the cases of Li Zhi and Shi Tao in China (Dann & Haddow, 2007, p. 229). Google is at risk of losing users' trust if it does not exercise considerable caution over its use of personal data (Battelle, 2005, pp. 14–15). There is already at least one competitor offering a search service that trades on this risk by assuring users that it collects no personal data (Hern, 2014).

A second set of concerns arises from Google's ability to shape the digital knowledge environment in which we are all embedded. This is nicely expressed by Eli Pariser with his theory of the *filter bubble* (Pariser, 2012). As we have seen, sites like Google and Facebook are increasingly using the personal data that they hold on each of their users to shape the information they deliver, determining, for example, the order of search results and which posts appear most prominently in a Facebook feed. Pariser is concerned that the consequence is 'to create a unique universe of information for each of us' (Pariser, 2012, p. 9) which constitutes 'a kind of invisible autopropaganda, indoctrinating us with our own ideas, amplifying our desire for things that are familiar' (Pariser, 2012, p. 15). In some areas the result might simply be to discourage us from seeking out new experiences – if your data suggests you like romantic novels, for example, you may never see an ad for sci-fi or detective stories. But in politics, Pariser suggests, democracy itself is threatened, because we will all constantly find our existing opinions and preconceptions confirmed and never be exposed to contrary views that could stimulate re-evaluation, compromise or constructive thinking (Pariser, 2012, Introduction).

Pariser's concerns are perhaps overstated (Morozov, 2011), but our knowledge environments are increasingly under the control of a small number of extremely powerful web service providers like Google and Facebook. The decisions those providers take will exert substantial influence over the discursive environment we all face and thus the decisions that *we* make (Elder-Vass, 2011). Companies like these have the capacity to censor, or subtly shift, the content that we see, and although there is little evidence that Google and Facebook use these powers in a politically contentious way at the moment, this is a risk that we must consider. The very fact that web companies are subject to the laws and governments of the countries in which they operate amplifies the risk, and there is strong evidence, for example, that web companies operating in China are complicit in that state's political censorship of the Internet (Dann & Haddow, 2007). But governments are not the only risk. Old media remains notoriously politically partisan, and old media companies have already sought to buy their way into this space, as for example when Rupert Murdoch's News Corporation bought (and subsequently sold) MySpace ('News Corp finally sells MySpace', 2011). As Siva Vaidhyanathan has argued, the level of power over global knowledge flows that is being concentrated in the hands of Google represents a major risk for the future, even if Google is currently relatively benign in its use of that power (Vaidhyanathan, 2012).

Conclusion

Google, then, is a fascinating hybrid of the gift and capitalist economies. On the one hand, it is oriented to the pursuit of profit, and obliged to be so as a result of its listing on the stock exchange and the obligations to investors that this implies. Hence it is unambiguously a capitalist company. Furthermore it earns its revenue by selling a commodity in a market: it sells clicks to advertisers using an auction model to determine the price. Hence it is unambiguously part of the commodity economy. Yet it depends utterly for its revenue on giving away a free service, or rather a series of free services, to its users, and must constantly attend to the needs and preferences of those users if it is to retain their attachment. Those gifts are loaded gifts, gifts that entail incidental transfers back to Google from its users, and thus have some similarities to exchange and to reciprocal forms of gifting, but we can understand them most plausibly as a different kind of transfer than either free gifts or commodity exchanges. Unlike commodity exchange, the return that Google expects from its users is neither monetary nor quantified. It is not negotiated, nor is it generally presented as an element of a deal that Google makes with its users, though more sophisticated users do understand that the return is occurring.

Google thus exemplifies a complex of appropriative practices that it would be difficult to explain using either of the dominant approaches to political economy. The non-commodity element of its business that provides the essential basis for the commodity element cannot be explained in terms of the market models of mainstream economics, nor can it be analysed in Marxist terms as the extraction of surplus value from wage labourers.[6] Google *can*, however, be analysed as an appropriative structure, as the site of a mutually interdependent complex of appropriative practices. These include selling advertising as a commodity, loaded gifts of services to users, incidental transfers of data from users, the accumulation of user data to support personalisation and a constant dynamic interaction between efforts to increase advertising revenue and efforts to retain and extend the attachment of users to its services.

The consequence of these practices is to produce a range of different benefits – and sometimes harms – for the different actors involved. Users benefit from useful free services but are at risk from abuse of the data collected on them; advertisers benefit by securing an audience and thus the possibility of increased sales for their products; and Google and its stockholders benefit by making immense profits. But the effects are also felt more widely. In particular, print media businesses have experienced a radical reduction in advertising revenue as advertisers have shifted their spending to digital media that can focus more precisely on their target customer groups (McKinsey & Company, 2013).

Beyond the economic question of who receives what benefits and harms, the success of Google's business model has also left it with substantial power over the flow of information over the Web, generating a significant political risk. But there are also larger ethical questions to be asked. How should we evaluate hybrid economic models like this one? Are companies like Google corrupting the gift form of economy or inventing a more generous form of capitalism? The capitalist market model is neither perfectly admirable nor utterly evil, but requires a more subtle evaluation on the basis of the benefits and harms it produces in each type of case. From the brief overview provided, the balance of benefits over harms seems substantial, but there remain ethical questions to be asked. How desirable is an economic model for the digital economy that rests on advertising and thus the

---

[6] Google does also employ staff who contribute to its success and some could perhaps be seen as exploited (Fuchs, 2014, chapter 9). Some Marxists, including Fuchs, have sought to analyse hybrid digital businesses in terms of surplus value. These attempts are criticised in the next chapter.

promotion of consumerism? How much data is it justifiable for service providers to keep on their users? And should we accept the degree of dominance over crucial services like web search that is currently exercised by Google? If this were a commodity market, a company with a market share of 88% or more in 24 out of 31 major countries (and 98% in some of them) would be attracting serious attention from anti-trust regulators. Doesn't the concentration of power involved in this degree of dominance over a free service require the same attention? Google may not be evil, but it surely does require regulation.

9 | *User content capitalism*

Introduction

This chapter turns to a different kind of hybrid economic form, though one that is often combined with the advertising form discussed in the previous chapter. The cases it discusses articulate two types of appropriative practice: first, as in the last chapter, gifts of services from commercial websites to ordinary users, and second, the unpaid creation of resources on these sites – resources that are crucial to the attractiveness and thus the commercial success of the free service itself – by some or all of those same ordinary users.

Those cases are YouTube (owned by Google), currently the dominant video-sharing site on the Internet, and Facebook, currently the dominant social networking site. At first video content on YouTube was provided entirely by ordinary users and it still obtains much of its content in this way, though it also now hosts commercially produced content. Facebook's service is centred on giving users access to material (including status updates, photos, and videos) provided by their friends on the site. Both depend to some extent, and Facebook almost entirely, on the provision of content by users to make the service attractive to other users. Both then use the traffic this generates – and the related personal information about their users – to generate revenue from targeted advertising. In principle, however, the practices discussed in this chapter could be articulated with other revenue-raising practices instead. Facebook, for example, has experimented with putting 'Buy' buttons on its pages, to produce a commission or sales-based revenue stream (Duke, 2014), and also earns revenue from partners whose games it hosts (Van Grove, 2013).

This chapter examines the appropriative practices that combine to produce this form of capitalism, marked by its dependence on user-generated content. Like most other massive web businesses, these ones are utterly dependent on attracting large volumes of user traffic to sustain the viability of their business model, and once again we will see that practices designed to secure user attachment are of the utmost importance to them. Giving services as a gift is only part of this: the services must also be attractive, and user dissatisfiers must be carefully managed to avoid driving traffic away from the site. We will also look at the relations between these sites and the more conventional capitalist business sector; to some extent they are in competition, though as major carriers of advertising they are also symbiotic. The most significant tensions arise in the area of copyright over digital content, where YouTube has faced conflict with the major media corporations and yet ultimately found mutually beneficial agreements with them.

The user contributions upon which this model of capitalism depends are often labelled *prosumption* – a kind of labour intermediate between production and consumption – and prosuming labour has often been characterised as a form of exploitation of users by the companies concerned. The last sections of the chapter criticise both the concept of prosumption and the claim that user contributions are necessarily a form of exploitation. Labelling this work as exploitation imports the Marxist model of concealed ethical evaluation criticised earlier in Chapter 3, when the evaluation of these economic forms ought to be based on a more specific assessment of who receives what benefits from them. It also seeks to impose a dogmatic model of production derived from the nineteenth century factory on a very different economic form. User-content capitalism is utterly unlike both the Marxist stereotype of industrial-style capitalism and the mainstream economist's stereotype of the market economy.

Neither commodities nor wage labour

The business model of organisations like YouTube and Facebook is a complex of appropriative practices that depends on multiple interdependent forms of transfer. Three of these are already familiar from the last chapter: commodity sales, mostly based on advertising, the provision of free services, which attract users to the site and thus create the opportunity to generate advertising revenue, and incidental transfers of personal data by users which help these sites to target advertising. The fourth, however, is distinctive: the provision of the media content that the first two practices depend upon, also done by users. None of these last three practices takes the form of commodity exchange, wage labour or indeed any other form of exchange. The services are a gift, and personal data is provided as an incidental transfer, but the provision of content by users is a more complex form, in which a gift from one user to others also produces an incidental benefit (unintended by the user) for the business operating the site: they are not a gift *to* the site but they are nonetheless appropriated by the site as a side effect of being given to other users.

As a social networking service, Facebook enables its registered users to create and maintain a *profile* on the site that includes information about themselves, photographs, and news (*status updates*) and to make connections with other users (who thus become *friends*) (Boyd & Ellison, 2007). Once two users are Facebook friends they may view each other's profile information and status updates, and other users may also have access to these, depending on the posting user's privacy settings. Facebook is now a remarkably widely and intensively used medium for social communication. In September 2014, 1.35 billion users logged in to Facebook (approaching 20% of the entire population of the world) (Facebook, 2015a), and a survey of US adults in 2014 suggests that 70% of those with Facebook accounts logged in on a daily basis (Duggan Ellison Lampe Lenhart & Madden, 2015). Over time, the service has been gradually extended. For example, the number of videos posted is currently growing rapidly – in the second half of 2014 the site hosted over 1 billion video views per day (Facebook, 2015b). Facebook has also become an important platform for playing games (Cheshire, 2013; Van Grove, 2013).

While it is possible in principle to connect with almost any other user on Facebook, the platform is used overwhelmingly to 'maintain or intensify relationships characterized by some form of offline connection' (Ellison Steinfield & Lampe, 2007, p. 1162). Facebook friends are mostly face-to-face friends as well, however occasionally, and Facebook is used primarily to increase interaction with existing contacts when they aren't physically co-present. A survey of US college students in 2010–11 showed that they found Facebook most valuable for 'Keeping up with what is happening with family and friends' and 'Sustaining good friendships', though these were closely followed by 'Being entertained' (Lilley et al., 2012, p. 86).

Although some of the content that provides these benefits is commercially provided – notably games – the vast majority of it, and in particular all the content that allows users to keep up with news about family and friends, is provided by other users. While some Facebook users post relatively little material, others post a great deal. In total, as of May 2013, there were 4.75 billion pieces of content shared each day (Noyes, 2014). No doubt both the posters and their friends benefit from these posts but so does Facebook. On the one hand, it is these posts that make the site attractive to its users, bringing in huge numbers of visitors and thus opportunities for Facebook to sell advertising space. On the other, these posts are also data about the users concerned and, as discussed in the previous chapter, Facebook collects this data and analyses it in order to categorise its users for advertisers. The more data Facebook can collect on a user the more accurately advertising can be targeted, and the more valuable that advertising opportunity is to Facebook. In this respect Facebook's introduction of a 'like' button enabling users to show their interest or approval for other users' posts was a masterstroke, providing data comparable to Google's search term data in the sense that it shows exactly what a user is interested in – data that is supremely relevant to potential advertisers. As discussed in the previous chapter, the extension of Facebook buttons to many other sites on the Internet only serves to increase the quantity and value of this data (Gerlitz & Helmond, 2013).

In many respects YouTube's business model depends on a similar mix of appropriative practices: users are attracted by a free service, those users themselves contribute much of the content that makes the service attractive, and the model is monetised by analysing user input to reveal and exploit targeted advertising opportunities. In other respects it is rather different from Facebook. The core service that attracts visitors is the ability to view free videos, mostly only a few minutes long (Ross, 2014), and a vast searchable selection of videos of every imaginable variety is available – YouTube estimates that a hundred hours of new videos are uploaded to the site every minute (YouTube, 2015). These include, for example, music videos, clips of movies and TV programmes, reviews of products, 'how to' videos, recordings of family occasions and holiday moments, political comment, educational material, and videos of pets and other animals. Like Facebook, the number of users this attracts is huge: over a billion users visit the site each month, viewing over six billion hours of video (YouTube, 2015). Their motivations vary: one study found that 'Participants viewed videos for information seeking, and viewed and shared videos for entertainment, co-viewing and social interaction' (Haridakis & Hanson, 2009, p. 317). Like Facebook, though less centrally to the user experience, there is a social element: users can leave comments below videos they have watched but they can also, outside the YouTube platform itself, discuss videos they have watched and share links to them – for example on Facebook and similar social networking platforms.

YouTube's users also play a key role in providing the content that appears on the site. It was originally launched as a platform for users to upload videos they had created themselves, and most of the videos, including some of the most popular, are still user-created,[1] though as we shall see in the next section, there are increasing amounts of commercially produced video on YouTube too. Amateur video is generally less attractive to advertisers, who are wary of its low production values and the risk of linking their products to commercially inappropriate content but it has considerable appeal to users of the site (McDonald, 2010, p. 392; Strangelove, 2010, pp. 6–7). While YouTube's revenue model depends on advertising, and most of this is placed against commercial content, the amateur content continues to bring in viewers who can then be encouraged to view ad-carrying content as well. Since 2007, YouTube has also offered advertising partnerships to some of the most successful amateur video makers on the site, allowing ads to run alongside their videos and the video maker to take a share of the advertising revenue (Cheshire, 2013; Wasko & Erickson, 2010, p. 380).

Though the provision of content by creators who receive advertising revenue in return is a straightforward commodity transaction, the provision of strictly amateur content is not, and nor is YouTube's provision of freely downloadable video to viewers. But are they gifts? As we saw in the previous chapter, not all transfers are gifts or exchanges, and the concept of *incidental transfers*, introduced there, is also very relevant here. Incidental transfers, to repeat, occur when a recipient receives a benefit as a result of another agent's intentional action, but the intention behind that action was not to transfer the benefit concerned.

---

[1] Strangelove reports estimates that 79% of content is user-generated (Strangelove, 2010, p. 10). YouTube no longer identifies the most-watched videos, but what it calls the 'top trending' video in 2014, for example, was an amateur comedy horror clip called 'Mutant Giant Spider Dog' (YouTube, 2014).

In the appropriative practices that are the focus of this chapter, I suggest we can see three broad kinds of transfer at work, though with mixed or intermediate cases. The provision of video to users by YouTube is a *gift* and sometimes even a free gift. It is possible to view YouTube videos without returning anything of value to YouTube at all – it is not necessary to enter a search term, for example, and it is even possible for users to block ads and cookies. These services are intentionally made available to users to take advantage of, and given that they are made available even when users return nothing of value, we can reasonably say that there is no obligation on the user to make a return of any sort, or to reciprocate in any way, and hence these are free gifts – though they are of course inducement gifts, intended to generate a monetary return in the aggregate (see Chapter 8), even if there is no obligation on any individual user to make a return of any form.

In practice, most users do not block cookies, and many do enter search terms on YouTube, and when they do so, they provide data that has commercial value to YouTube. As on Google's main search service, when someone enters a search term they fully intend to find a certain sort of content, but they typically have no specific intention to transfer useful information to YouTube. Such a transfer is therefore not a gift to YouTube, nor even part of an exchange, which would require that the user understood that the data supplied constituted a payment for the services received, but rather an incidental transfer, a transfer that occurs as an unintended consequence of an intended action.

It is useful in this context to distinguish between *user-generated data* and *user-created content* (Andrejevic, 2010, pp. 414–8). User-generated data is data that sites collect as a by-product of actions that the user did not intend as content provision, such as search terms on YouTube and Google. User-created content, by contrast, is material that users deliberately provide as content for others to view, such as videos uploaded to YouTube, or status updates posted on Facebook. Unlike user-generated data, uploads of user-created content are intended as transfers, but like user-generated data, they have multiple aspects. YouTube videos seem to be intended by most amateur uploaders as a kind of gift to other YouTube users (some may have hopes of some sort of return, but there is no obligation or indeed expectation placed on individual recipients to make a return). Some users creating fan videos on YouTube, for example, see their contributions as gifts to the fan community concerned (Jenkins, 2009, p. 119). But these are intended as gifts to other YouTube users, not as gifts to YouTube itself, although YouTube clearly benefits from them. They are thus *simultaneously* gifts to other YouTube users, and incidental transfers to YouTube itself.

Facebook posts seem similar, but these raise further issues. Is a message to a friend or a group of friends on the Internet an economic transfer, or is it more appropriate to see it as analogous to a conversation, as a form of communicative interaction? I suggest that there is no conflict between these two descriptions; the same action can be both. They are communicative actions, but they are also in a sense economic transactions because benefits are being created for our friends when we make our Facebook posts available to them, and this is typically part of what we intend when we post them. There is room for some ambiguity here, given the difficulties in defining the economy discussed in Chapter 2, but there is no doubt about the economic character of the transfer to Facebook itself. The benefits that are created for Facebook clearly *are* economic since it translates them into advertising revenue, and this is typically *not* part of what we intend to bring about, even if we are aware that it is a side effect of our action. Whether or not we think of Facebook posts as gifts to friends, then, they are also incidental transfers to Facebook itself.

We may also think of the transfer of data to Facebook as another asymmetric transfer. Unlike YouTube, it is impossible to use Facebook without providing user-generated data and at least some user-created content – a certain minimum is required to set up a user account. From the user's perspective, this may be an incidental transfer as part of a process that enables them to take advantage of the gift of Facebook's services, but because it can impose the requirement for the provision of profile data, and it subsequently obtains commercial benefit from that data, from Facebook's perspective this looks rather more like an exchange, a barter form of commodity exchange perhaps.

Here, then, we have a complex of non-market appropriative practices: commercial businesses providing services that are at least sometimes gifts, users of those services providing gifts for each other, and as a consequence of both using the service and giving to each other also making incidental transfers to the commercial businesses concerned. These practices are strongly articulated: without the service there would be no gifts between users, without the gifts between users there would be no incidental transfers to the service providers, and without those transfers there would be no opportunity for the service providers to articulate these non-market practices with the market practice of selling advertising. Only that last part of this complex can be understood in terms of conventional economics, and none of it in terms of Marxist political economy.

Securing attachment from contributing users

Like both Apple and Google, sites like Facebook are profit-oriented businesses whose profit depends on securing the preferential attachment of their user populations. The free services they provide to site users are the bait, and they have an interest in finding more and stronger ways to make those services attractive to users. At the same time, however, their attempts to regulate those users and extract revenue from their access to them are constantly at risk of driving them away,[2] so like Google they must perform a balancing act, taking care to avoid actions that undermine the attachment of users to the site. The degree of care they must take depends in turn on the strength of the preferential attachments they have established in their customer base. The stronger those attachments, the more they can take advantage of them, like Apple, though in the long term this strategy risks creating an opening for competing services.

Perhaps the most obvious attractor of ordinary users to these sites is the quality of content available on them. For social networking sites like Facebook, the facilities available are significant – what sorts of links friends can make with each other, and what sorts of content can be shared, for example – but the most important factor of all is simply whether the people that a user would like to interact with are themselves users of the service. On a social networking site, quality content is content that is provided by the people a user wants to interact with, and if those people aren't using the site the facilities available are irrelevant. This is known as the *network effect*, a well-known effect that long precedes the Internet – the telephone network, for example, was of little value for any given individual unless the people she wanted to talk to had telephones as well. But once a particular network has a

---

[2] Friendster, an early social networking site, antagonised many of its users by withdrawing popular facilities that did not fit with the company's view of what should be happening on the site (Boyd & Ellison, 2007, pp. 215–6).

large population, it acquires a substantial advantage over new entrants to the same space. Any new service, even if its facilities were considerably better than Facebook's, would face an uphill struggle to compete against it because people who already have a large friend network on Facebook are unlikely to leave it for a service where relatively few of their friends are users.

Scale, in other words, is a source of preferential attachment to social networking sites, but it can also have benefits for other kinds of sites. YouTube, for example, benefits from the sheer quantity of video available on it: because users can find almost any kind of material they might want on the site, they are more likely to use it than competing sites that don't have such a large range, even if some other features of those sites are better. Scale effects aren't completely decisive, though – another site, for example, might have better coverage of a particular specialist area than YouTube and it would attract away viewers with that specialist interest even if it didn't compete at all in other areas. But the more material that YouTube has, the less risk there is of this occurring.

Securing the preferential attachment of users is important not only to keep them coming back to the site, but also because these sites need to overcome user resistance to other dissatisfiers, and in particular resistance to viewing adverts. Like Google, YouTube and Facebook have seen a constant tension between increasing advertising revenue and the risk of driving away users who dislike the impact of advertising on their experience of the site. Thus, for example, YouTube decided in its early days to avoid playing 'pre-roll' ads – video adverts that a user must sit through before they can see the video they actually requested – because this would have undermined the sense of the site being a community for video-sharers (Cloud, 2006). Other advertising formats have been used at various times, such as banner ads, or advertising videos that appear at the top of lists of video search results. YouTube, despite its early concerns, has also experimented with ads running 'before, during or after videos' (Wasko & Erickson, 2010, p. 380), but these drove away users: pre-roll ads 'cause 70 percent of the audience to stop watching the video' (Strangelove, 2010, p. 6). Hence they were replaced with 'image-overlay advertising... in which a semi-transparent banner would run at the bottom of the video screen' (Wasko & Erickson, 2010, p. 380). More recently, pre-roll ads have been re-introduced, but they are either quite short, or include a 'Skip

Ad' button that the user can press after the first five seconds. YouTube, in other words, is constantly experimenting with ways to confront its users with advertising in order to find formats that don't antagonise them.

A different set of attachment issues arises for users who, rather than simply consuming content, are active members of a community of content creators. The significance of social interaction with a community is obvious on Facebook, but it also has a role to play on YouTube. YouTube users can be divided into three groups: those who upload videos, those who do not upload but do comment on videos, and those who simply view them. One analyst looking at YouTube (relatively early in its life) found that only 0.16% of visits to the site by US users involved video uploads (Tancer, 2008, p. 125). Another found that 'in 2007 over 13% of the online audience posted comments about the videos they watch' (Strangelove, 2010, p. 14). Those who post videos and comment are interacting in a way that is reminiscent of other online communities. According to Strangelove, the amateur video uploaders 'see themselves as the authentic members of the community' (Strangelove, 2010, p. 113), and other authors have seen their 'video content itself' as a 'vehicle of communication and... indicator of social clustering' (Burgess & Green, 2009, p. 58). Those who comment on videos contribute to this process of interaction, and even those who only view can contribute to the sense of community, for example by subscribing to the content provided by particular contributors. Many of the most subscribed channels are those of 'YouTube stars... whose brands were developed within YouTube's social network' (Burgess & Green, 2009, p. 59).

This sense of engagement in a community can clearly contribute to attachment to a site, and this is in turn deliberately encouraged by the provision of facilities by the site itself – the ability to make comments or to subscribe to a channel, for example – that make social links and interaction possible. But communities can also create negative experiences, and YouTube has been 'a notoriously unruly and uncivil conversational domain' (Goode McCullough & O'Hare, 2011, p. 594). To put the point more colloquially, 'youtube is infested with internet trolls' (YouTube user Dallah1990, quoted in Goode et al., 2011, p. 596) – users who find it entertaining to abuse other users in order to generate conflict (Lumsden & Morgan, 2012). These trolls are particularly prone to sexist and homophobic comments (Burgess & Green, 2009, pp. 96–7). In enabling communicative interaction, YouTube thus opened the door to abusive forms of it that act as a positive dissatisfier to participation in the community. In 2013 it prevented users from making comments unless they had Google+ accounts, thus attempting to force them to log in with a real verifiable identity. According to some commentators this was aimed at 'filtering out annoying comments on videos' (Larson, 2013), but this move seems to have backfired. There was widespread criticism of the move, with critics including one of YouTube's founders (Hern, 2013), and suggestions that it was really intended to boost user numbers on Google+, the company's competitor to Facebook. Whether or not that is the case, trolling on YouTube continues. It is not clear how far YouTube's inability or unwillingness to prevent it undermines participation on the site – users may simply ignore the comments below videos, and content creators who are disturbed by trolling can disable comments – but it is surely a latent dissatisfier that presents an opportunity to potential competitors.

UGC businesses and conventional capitalism

Despite their use of unconventional forms of transfer in giving away services and depending on user-created content, in other respects these are very conventional capitalist businesses. While YouTube's revenues and profits are not announced separately from its parent company Google, estimates suggest that it earned in the region of $3.5 billion in profit in 2013 (DeSimone, 2014). Facebook was earning over $1 billion profit per quarter by Q3 2014 (Rushton, 2014) and is valued at over $200 billion on the stock market (Bradshaw, 2014b). Like more traditional media businesses, these ones earn most of their revenue by advertising, and in consequence they not only promote the products of a wide range of other capitalist businesses, but also help to encourage consumerism and commodification more generally. These are also companies, like any other successful capitalist business, that profit at the expense of their competitors, in these cases taking revenue from conventional advertising media by providing a more engaging and more personal experience than earlier forms, notably adverts in print media. They are also out-competing alternative social networking and video sites. While the most rapid growth in social networking has started to move to other sites, Facebook has an answer: it has used its enormous financial power to buy two of its most significant competitors, Instagram and Whatsapp, spending $19 billion for the latter (Stone, 2014). Both businesses also employ significant numbers of salaried staff, though these numbers remain relatively small by comparison with the number of users who contribute content to their sites.

YouTube is perhaps less conventional in its relationship with media production businesses, particularly concerning the question of copyright. When it was founded, all video was uploaded by amateurs, who in principle owned copyright in material they had created themselves. However, many of the videos they uploaded included material that had been copyrighted by media businesses in the music, film and television industries. Some users obtained clips of TV programmes, or official music videos, and uploaded them. Others ripped tracks from CDs and MP3 files, added images or video, and uploaded them. Others recorded their own videos but had copyrighted music playing in the background (for a nice example, see Lessig, 2008, pp. 1–3). And others developed creative re-mixes of commercially copyrighted material, whether as satire, in homage to the original creators, or because that's what cultural creators have always done to develop new material (Jenkins, 2006; Lessig, 2008). When the businesses who owned the copyright in this material became aware of this, they accused YouTube of consciously encouraging and profiting from such infringements (Burgess & Green, 2009, p. 5). For these businesses, YouTube's use of this material was doubly harmful, or so they claimed: first because users were able to view their material on YouTube instead of buying it from the media companies, and second because YouTube was using it to generate advertising revenue without sharing it with the copyright owners. At one stage Viacom sued YouTube and Google for $1 billion and demanded that they remove 'upwards of 100,000 clips of Viacom content' from the site (Burgess & Green, 2009, pp. 32–3).

There is a certain irony in this, as all of the US's major media industries began as pirates themselves: Hollywood was set up on the West Coast to evade Thomas Edison's film technology patents, the music recording business didn't pay royalties to composers until forced to by a change in the law, and in the closest echo of YouTube's case, for thirty years cable TV companies in the US re-broadcast video material without any payment to its original creators (Lessig, 2004, chapter 4). In several of these cases, new industries took advantage of the failure of the law to catch up with new technological possibilities for delivering cultural content. By contrast, YouTube took advantage of the changes that *have* been made to the law to adjust to new technology. In 1998 the United States passed legislation (the Digital Millennium Copyright Act) that protected certain sorts of online service providers against charges of copyright infringement. While this seems to have been intended to protect telecommunications companies, search engines, and other providers of access to the Internet from prosecution for transmitting content that they had no control over, it was worded sufficiently openly for YouTube to claim protection under it. There were conditions on this protection: providers were only protected if they were not aware that infringement was occurring, if they were not directly gaining financially, and if they removed the material promptly once informed of it (McDonald, 2010, p. 398). YouTube has been able to interpret the law to mean that it can continue to broadcast infringing material until the copyright owner issues a 'takedown notice' specifying the details of each case that they want removed – though they have also been careful to avoid running ads against material where copyright ownership has not been established (McDonald, 2010, p. 399). There's a touch of defiance of the media corporations here, but this is defiance as a business strategy, not a principled objection to the copyright system.

Given that they can only fight a rearguard action against the constant stream of their material appearing on YouTube, the media corporations have had little choice but to take the other option available to them. As they can't beat YouTube, they have had to join it: within two years of YouTube's creation, virtually all of the major media businesses had concluded revenue-sharing agreements with it (McDonald, 2010, p. 394). These deals have two parts. First, the media corporations supply their own content to YouTube, and then share the revenue from advertising that runs against this content. But YouTube has also introduced content-identification technology, which automates the process of recognising copyrighted material once the copyright owner has supplied YouTube with 'digital fingerprints' of it. This means that material posted by ordinary users that infringes the copyright of a partner corporation can be identified much more promptly and either removed, or used to run ads against – the revenue from which will be shared, not with the poster of the material, but with the corporation owning the copyright. According to Wasko and Erickson 'It is estimated that 90 percent of copyright claims made in this manner are converted into advertising opportunities' (Wasko & Erickson, 2010, p. 381). Despite the early conflicts, then, YouTube and the content industries have shifted to a rather cosy symbiotic relationship, in which both earn substantial advertising revenue. Given that both have a strong interest in boosting those revenues, there are concerns that YouTube may use its control of the site to favour its corporate partners over the amateur content producers who continue to upload vast amounts of material – in selecting featured videos, for example, or in removing material that is critical of its partners (Strangelove, 2010, p. 108; Wasko & Erickson, 2010, p. 382).

None of this should obscure the fact that YouTube and Facebook are also very different in some ways from conventional capitalist businesses. Facebook and similar social networking sites have created new kinds of spaces where the primary focus is on free social interaction, without geographic restriction, with friends, family and acquaintances. YouTube has provided a new space for freely sharing creativity and for interacting collaboratively that stands in stark contrast to the top-down model of mass media that preceded the Internet. It has contributed to a revival of opportunities for participative culture, created by ordinary people who draw on wider cultural memes, whether commercial in origin or not, to reclaim creativity from the corporations (Jenkins, 2006; Lessig, 2008). This includes significant elements of the gift form of economy, both in the provision of content by users and in the provision of services by the sites concerned. YouTube's free music, for example, has become a significant competitor to Apple's iTunes model of charging for digital content.

There are two equally valid ways of presenting the relationship of these businesses to the capitalist model. On the one hand, this is a gift economy subjected to the interests of capital, framed in in an environment that is constantly reshaped to serve those interests. On the other, it is a kind of capitalism that has been re-formed as an appendage to new kinds of interaction with gift transactions in the foreground. This is still capitalism but it's a very different kind of capitalism. Both perspectives recognise that there is a strange hybrid at work here, with an element of capitalism interacting with elements of other forms of economy. But by occupying these spaces, and by taking the high ground generated by network effects and scale effects, these businesses have prevented purer gift economy alternatives from gaining traction. In the video space peer-to-peer file sharing could have been an alternative; in the social network space there are diversely hosted alternatives like diaspora*, but it is hard to see how either could now achieve critical mass in the face of the 'market' dominance of YouTube and Facebook.

The troublesome concept of prosumption

Recent discussions of user-generated content have employed the concept of *prosumption*, or the *prosumer*, first introduced by the futurist Alvin Toffler. Toffler used it to describe an increasing blurring of the roles of producer and consumer, as consumers increasingly took on tasks that had previously been done by employees of the businesses they were buying from (Toffler, 1981). Toffler, even before the appearance of the Internet, saw this occurring in a variety of ways, such as customers designing their own variation of a configurable product, but the best-known cases arose from the introduction of self-service in retail outlets like supermarkets, petrol stations, banks and fast food restaurants. In these cases, business processes were redesigned to reduce or eliminate tasks that required wage labour by making them the responsibility of the customer.

More recently, a number of writers have connected the concept of prosumption to developments in the digital economy, starting with the business writer Don Tapscott (1997, pp. 62–3). Most prominently in the academic literature, George Ritzer and Nathan Jurgenson have argued that digital developments herald the rise of 'prosumer capitalism' (Ritzer & Jurgenson, 2010). While they don't provide a formal definition, they stay close to the spirit of Toffler's argument when they describe prosumption as 'putting consumers to work' (2010, p. 18). They offer a long list of examples of digital prosumption, including the creation of content by unpaid users on Wikipedia, Facebook, Twitter and YouTube, writing blogs, creating characters and communities on role-playing games like Second Life, developing open-source software, providing product reviews on Amazon, and creating 'the market' on eBay and craigslist (2010, p. 19).

Having distinguished prosumption from earlier varieties of production or consumption, Ritzer and Jurgenson go on to argue that prosumption is expanding in significance, primarily under the influence of Web 2.0 – the growing orientation of the Internet to user-contributed content – and that we are now entering 'the age of the prosumer' or 'prosumer capitalism' (2010, pp. 19–21). They see digital prosumption as heralding a more interesting sort of economy, in which capitalists cannot entirely control prosumers, where prosumers cannot necessarily be said to be exploited because they choose and enjoy their contributions, and companies have to find new ways of making profit (2010, pp. 21–2). In subsequent work, Ritzer has expanded the reach of the concept of prosumption still further, redefining it to mean 'the interrelated process of production and consumption' (Ritzer, 2014, p. 3 and see fn 1), and arguing that both production and consumption should really be seen as varieties of the 'primal' process, which is prosumption (Ritzer, 2014, p. 10). Production, he says, inherently contains consumption, and consumption itself has production 'intertwined' with it. Yet at the same time as arguing that production and consumption are really just flavours of prosumption, he also continues to insist that we are seeing 'a massive expansion' of prosumption (Ritzer, 2014, p. 10).

There are elements of these arguments that overlap with the arguments of this book, but the concept of prosumption and the role it plays in Ritzer's arguments are problematic. These problems arise from a failure to interrogate the terms *production* and *consumption* before employing them in more ambitious theoretical constructions. Both Toffler's and Ritzer and Jurgenson's versions of *prosumption* depend on the activity concerned shifting between these two categories, as for example when customers start to dispense their own petrol rather than a pump attendant doing it for them. These activities seem to count as getting customers to do production because they were regarded as part of production before the change occurred, but what the prosumption theorists miss is that it is really the market boundary that defines the distinction between production and consumption (see Chapter 2). The very same physical activity counts as production when it is done by an employee as part of a process of supplying a commodity and as consumption when it is done by the purchaser of a commodity. Shifting it across a market boundary does not somehow give it an ambiguous character: none of the examples of prosumption they provide should be counted as production at all.[3]

---

[3] To use Marxist terminology, only activities that create exchange value count as production, whereas activities that create use values without creating exchange value do not (Humphreys & Grayson, 2008).

To believe that they do is to fall victim to an uncritically essentialist conception of production, which locates the character of production in the physical nature of the activities concerned rather than in the relation in which they stand to the market. This ideological conception of production is the outcome of a discursive naturalisation of the market boundary, in which activities that contribute to creating commodities are seen as more socially valuable than activities that do not, a value that is signposted by labelling them 'productive' and imbuing this label with symbolic approval. The origin of this belief then becomes lost to view, which makes it possible to *begin* from the idea that 'productive' activities are uniquely socially valuable, and proceed to argue that the market is good because it tends to orient firms to such activities and firms deserve monetary compensation because they undertake those activities. For this reversal to work, it is necessary to obscure the fact that the character of being 'productive' is defined in the first place by the market boundary, so that it can be argued that doing 'productive' things is a merit of commodity production whereas this claim is really just a tautology. Hence we get the idea that although most 'productive' activities are done by commodity producers, it would be possible for others to do them, and they would still be 'productive', while most activities that are not done by commodity producers are dismissed as unproductive, irrespective of what benefits they might produce for people. Marx's well-known distinction between productive and unproductive labour, incidentally, is a strange confection of this logic with the placement of industrial workers on a political pedestal.

This is not to deny that it might be useful to have a category called *prosumption* (or something else) that refers to activities that have recently been shifted across the market boundary into the hands of the unpaid. These are real and significant changes, and labelling them helps to expose one of the ways in which capitalists have found ways to increase profitability, but it is an error to believe that these activities continue to be a form of *production*. True, they create benefits in much the same way as activities that do count as production, but so do a vast range of other activities that are performed by people outside the market economy, as we saw in Chapter 2. But the theoretical argument that there is now a grey area between production and consumption cannot be justified in these terms. Furthermore, this is an inherently unstable category, in that it depends on linking an activity now done by consumers with some comparable activity done by producers, and what counts as prosumption therefore depends on what comparisons are allowed (cf. Glucksmann, 2013, p. 19). How recently, for example, did an activity have to be done by paid suppliers for a purchaser doing it to be a prosumer? Or how often? If one person fifty years ago paid a company to supply staff to lift grapes to their mouth, does that make the rest of us prosumers when we lift grapes to our own mouths? If it did, but fifty years was the limit, would that mean we were prosuming today when we lifted grapes but not tomorrow?

Perhaps it is because of issues like these that Ritzer has now changed his definition of prosumption. His understanding of prosumption as embracing all of both production and consumption brings it close to my account of the substantive or provisioning economy in Chapter 2, in which there is no essential distinction between production and consumption. He also quite rightly argues that the distinction between production and consumption is a historic rather than an essential one, linked to marketization of the economy (Ritzer, 2014, pp. 15–6). But he continues to argue that within the larger set of economic activity some is more production-like, some is more consumption-like, and prosumption is a growing element: all arguments that depend on the failure to interrogate the concepts of production and consumption criticised above.

Nevertheless, we may still ask whether there is a kind of role that doesn't fit neatly into the binary division between producers and consumers implicit in the dominant economic discourse, and whether the notion of a prosumer helps us to identify it. The kind of role exemplified by collecting one's own meal at a fast food restaurant doesn't seem to be significantly different from the role of a consumer more generally, but *some* of the activities identified by Ritzer and Jurgenson are distinctive. However, they are not distinctive because they involve shifting a task from one side of the market boundary to another, but because they entail roles that are different from either that of the traditional consumer or the paid worker. Here I have in mind the kind of role that has been discussed extensively earlier in this chapter. Facebook users, for example, are not taking over a role formerly performed by wage labourers when they post status updates and photos of their friends on their Facebook pages, but they *are* doing something that doesn't correspond with conventional concepts of the producer or the consumer. On the one hand they are neither employed nor paid by Facebook and hence unlike the conventional producer; but on the other they are creating content and relinquishing at least some control over it to a commercial company providing them with a service, unlike the stereotypical consumer. To avoid confusion with the concept of the prosumer, let me call the occupants of roles like this one *co-creators*: co-creators are unpaid creators who contribute content to commercial businesses.[4] This kind of role predates the digital economy, indeed some of Ritzer and Jurgenson's own pre-digital examples are cases of it – callers who phone in to radio shows, and people who appear on reality TV shows, for example – but it is a role that seems to have expanded enormously through the practice of providing user-generated content on commercial websites.

As we have seen, this role is of central importance to a whole class of major digital businesses, but it is a role that cannot plausibly be explained in terms of either mainstream economics or Marxist political economy. Some Marxists, however, have striven to bring it within their scope by arguing that co-creators – or prosumers – are the subjects of exploitation.

Are amateur content contributors exploited?

Christian Fuchs, for example, argues that Facebook users and other digital prosumers are exploited. On his reading of Marx, anyone who contributes labour is exploited if they are (a) coerced; and also (b) paid less, in strictly monetary terms, than the contribution that their labour makes to the creation of exchange value. In a familiar Marxist argument he asserts that wage labour is coerced because workers will suffer deprivation and even death if they are unable to earn a wage, but it is rather harder to extend this to the case of co-creators. Fuchs argues that they are 'coerced by ideological violence' (Fuchs, 2014, p. 90) because if they do not join Facebook they will suffer social isolation (Fuchs, 2014, p. 91). This is hardly a compelling argument, but on my reading Marx's notion of exploitation does not depend on coercion anyway, so the second part of the argument is perhaps more important: he argues that prosumers, through some mix of providing data about themselves and spending time as the audience for the advertising that they experience as a result, constitute an 'Internet prosumer commodity' (Fuchs,

---

[4] This term has some history in the business literature (e.g. Prahalad & Ramaswamy, 2000). I do not mean to endorse all the usages of it there.

2014, p. 93) that generates exchange value for companies like Facebook but is paid nothing in return. He recognises that they may obtain some use value from free services, but insists that this is not a real wage, because wages must give 'access to a general equivalent of exchange' or in other words, money (Fuchs, 2014, p. 105). By discounting other benefits, he arrives at the result that 'Internet prosumer labour is infinitely exploited by capital. This means that capitalist prosumption is an extreme form of exploitation in which the prosumers work completely for free' (Fuchs, 2014, p. 104). The rate of exploitation is infinite because the amount of value generated for the capitalist business is divided by the wage received, which is zero. The implication for Fuchs, mathematically at least, is that Facebook users are *more* exploited than wage labourers, such as the assembly workers in Foxconn's Chinese factories. If this is where Marx's concept of exploitation leads, it merely demonstrates its own redundancy as an ethical barometer.

Not all thinkers in the Marxist tradition, however, are convinced by this logic: many are open to more creative ways of using his work. As Hesmondhalgh has pointed out, for example, digital prosumers are clearly not exploited in the same way as sweatshop workers (Hesmondhalgh, 2010, p. 271). They do receive rewards for their effort, though not financial ones, and Hesmondhalgh dismisses the idea that wages are 'the only meaningful form of reward' (Hesmondhalgh, 2010, p. 278). On the basis of a similar argument, Rey concludes that co-creators are indeed exploited since their work generates profits for the businesses to which they contribute, but not infinitely, since they do receive some rewards in kind which must be taken into account (Rey, 2012, p. 402). 'The more useful content is to the prosumer' he says, 'the less exploitative prosumption is' (Rey, 2012, p. 415). Both Hesmondhalgh and Rey, however, still cling to versions of Marx's labour theory of value and exploitation,[5] which was rejected in Chapter 3 above. Rey takes for granted that the profits of Facebook must be produced by the work done by co-creators and therefore that they are exploited if there are any profits made, since the existence of profits, on Marx's theory, can only occur if workers are paid less than the full value of what they produce.

---

[5] Although Hesmondhalgh quite rightly insists that these debates must be 'informed by ethical thinking and by attention to the specifics of particular forms of work and leisure experience' (Hesmondhalgh, 2010, p. 279).

This argument however, like Fuchs's, requires a little fudging of Marx's theory, because for Marx it is only the labour of wage labourers, and indeed only wage labourers engaged in a subset of activities he labelled 'productive', that creates value. Including work done by unpaid users in the equation opens up a question that believers in the labour theory cannot afford to ask: if these new factors also contribute to creating value, why not also include all the others, such as the technology used by the site, the programming work done to create that technology, the entrepreneurial efforts of the site creators, the marketing work done to sell advertising on it, and the contributions of the advertisers themselves, when identifying what contributes to the creation of value? As I argued in Chapter 3, the assertion that all value is derived from (wage) labour is thoroughly unscientific; it is an ethically driven article of faith that is utterly inadequate as an account of the causal processes that produce exchange values under capitalism. Nor is it viable as an ethical position: even if it were true that all value is created by labour this would not entail that workers ought to receive all the value that they create.

Still, unpaid user contributors of content and data do play a crucial causal role in the processes that generate substantial profits for these sites, and we are entitled to ask whether they are exploited in the more useful, explicitly ethical, sense of that term. To answer we must in turn ask a question about appropriation: who makes what contributions to the production of benefit from these sites, and who receives those benefits? In brief, as we have seen, the users of these services obtain benefits in the form of, for example, improved opportunities to communicate with their friends and free access to media content such as videos, while the site providers, or at least the more successful ones, benefit by making revenue from advertising and other opportunities to sell services to their users. Then we come to the ethical question: are the benefits that they receive, in this case the free services provided by these sites, a fair recompense for the input that users make into the profitability of companies like Facebook and Google? At one level, these users freely choose to use these sites, suggesting they believe the deal is a fair one. We could still make a case for exploitation, however, if those users were unaware of important elements of the situation that they would object to if they were aware of them: if the terms of the deal were unfair in a way that they had not understood.

We could construct such a case, for example, by combining two interesting arguments from Andrejevic and Rey respectively. Andrejevic questions various attempts to characterise prosumers as exploited, then suggests that they have missed something important: 'the distinction ... between user-created content and user-generated data' discussed earlier in this chapter (Andrejevic, 2010, p. 418). The latter data, he suggests, is the real issue, because it is extracted in a context 'that structures the terms of access to productive resources in ways that compel submission to detailed forms of monitoring and information gathering' (Andrejevic, 2010, p. 418). While these users have a certain amount of control over their user-created content, they have none over the data that is generated as a side effect of their activity on the site, indeed there is a sense in which they are alienated from that data – they are separated from it and have no control over the process or the way the data is used (Andrejevic, 2010, pp. 418–9). Rey too sees this as a form of alienation and adds the point that 'users are often unaware of the full extent of the information that they are producing' - a phenomenon he calls 'ambient production' (Rey, 2012, p. 410). Indeed there is empirical evidence that many Facebook users are not fully aware of the ways in which their data is made available to advertisers, and have negative attitudes towards the advertising that appears as a consequence (Lilley et al., 2012). We could therefore argue that co-creators are exploited because they create data that generates benefits for the company without being fully aware that this is occurring and indeed that this is largely concealed from them, hence their consent and participation are obtained under false pretences.

I question whether we should call this exploitation – it may be, for example, that most of these users would continue to contribute even if they knew the full extent of the data being collected and the benefits it generates for the site owners, and would consider this a reasonable reward to them for providing the services the users enjoy. Indeed, the concealment argument must be questioned on the grounds that the profitability and high stock market valuations of Facebook and Google are well known, as is the fact that their profits are derived from advertising to site users and that this advertising is tailored to users. No doubt some users are unaware of this, and many may be unaware of the sheer extent of data collection that is occurring, but it's not clear that this is enough to justify claims that these users are unfairly receiving less than they ought for their contributions.

Nevertheless, there are significant ethical issues here: in particular, we should have certain rights over the data that is held about us, and I would also argue that we should have access to environments that are not polluted by a stream of consumerist advertising. My objection here is only to the attempt to corral these into the sterile and only marginally relevant Marxist category of exploitation. Ethical criticism, as I suggested in Chapter 3, always implies that there is a better alternative, and the better alternative here would not be sites which commodified the provision of content and data by paying users until all profit was eliminated. As Hesmondhalgh puts it, this would be 'internalising capitalism's own emphasis on commodification' (Hesmondhalgh, 2010, p. 278). Even Fuchs argues, not for this alternative, but for 'the creation of non-commercial non-profit websites' (Fuchs, 2014, p. 89). The ideal implicit in these criticisms is not an alternative in which users are paid, but one in which they have full awareness and control over the data being held about them, and are not bombarded with unwanted advertisements as a condition of using the service.

Conclusion

This chapter has analysed contemporary forms of digital capitalism that depend on the work done by unpaid users who contribute content and incidentally generate valuable data about their own interests and characteristics: content and data that underpin the services provided by these companies and their profitability. This is a hybrid form of capitalism and collaborative production, involving gifts, commodities and incidental transfers that have been configured into new complexes of appropriative practices. It produces enormous profits for the most successful companies, while enormous numbers of users take advantage of the free services they deliver. It is a form that challenges taken for granted assumptions about the boundaries of production and the economy, and the focus of the two dominant forms of political economy on commodity production through the employment of wage labour.

Like many of the other economic forms considered in this book, this hybrid points towards the need to reconfigure our theories of the economy. Theories of prosumption, however, focus on the wrong issues. There is not some third category between production and consumption: rather, we need to recognise that these terms only have meaning in the context of the discourse of the market economy. Nor do attempts to fit prosumption back into the old box of Marx's theory of exploitation help us to make sense of either the economic practices or the ethical issues involved. Instead they distract attention away from the genuinely interesting feature of user content capitalism: that it is *nothing like* a market and *nothing like* wage labour. This chapter offers a more productive approach, by beginning to analyse the appropriative practices involved in these hybrids, their implications and their interactions with other economic forms, and their ethical implications. There is no clear case for asserting that co-creators are exploited, indeed most obtain real benefits from their participation, but there are other grounds for criticising the existing capitalist forms of this hybrid: in particular, they abuse their control over user-generated data and subject us to a stream of consumerist advertising. Still, this is one of the less malign forms of capitalism, and one merit of the approach developed in this book is that it allows us to make such judgements: capitalism is neither inherently evil nor inherently desirable, but each case must be judged in terms of its consequences.

10 | Conclusion

Introduction

To make it possible to think beyond the economic systems we have today – and even just to understand the economy we already have – we need a new kind of political economy. We need a political economy that recognises that commodity production is not the only form of economic activity and is therefore able to address the full diversity of existing and possible economic forms, rather than trying to force them all into a dogmatic mould. We need a political economy that recognises the fundamentally social – and indeed material – nature of economic activity and examines the practices through which it operates, not as a sideshow to a more formal, more fundamental, economics but rather as the theoretical foundation for a more realistic study of the economy. We need a political economy that evaluates economic actions and practices against explicit ethical standards that reflect the actual needs of people, not against ideological principles that purport to reflect long-term common benefit. We need a political economy that helps us to see viable routes towards a better economy rather than denying the need for one, as mainstream economics does, or placing a better economy impossibly out of reach, as traditional Marxism does.

This book proposes some elements of such a political economy: a political economy of socio-material structures and practices – which I abbreviate to a *political economy of practices*. In this approach, the economy is defined as a *provisioning economy*, which includes all those activities that create or deliver benefits to people whether or not they operate through commodity exchange. These activities take a variety of forms, each of which can be analysed – and this is the central theoretical innovation of the book – as an interacting set or complex of *appropriative practices*, where an appropriative practice is a normatively standardised way of acting that affects who receives what benefits from provisioning activity. Capitalism is not one such form but a range of different complexes of appropriative practices that share one central feature: activity in capitalist forms is ultimately driven by the need to accumulate ever-increasing amounts of capital. Our economy, however, is not only the site of capitalism but also of a wide range of other complexes of appropriative practices, including gift economy and hybrid forms. Given that economic forms and appropriative practices determine who receives what benefits, critical analyses of such forms and practices are necessarily based on ethical principles regarding who *should* receive what benefits, whether those principles are explicit or hidden. This book advocates principles agreed through open discursive processes like those described by Habermas and Nussbaum: in particular, the principle that the basic needs of all human beings should be met and their essential capabilities protected. Judging economic alternatives on this basis is what makes this a *political* economy, and it is primarily by judging between real *existing* economic forms and moving towards a mix that reduces the more harmful alternatives and supports the more beneficial ones that we will achieve a better economy.

This concluding chapter begins by saying a little more about the political economy of practices as a perspective for theorising the economy and then turns to the digital economy, showing how the cases discussed in Part III – and others like them – illustrate the book's claims about economic diversity. It ends where any book about political economy should: by considering what this all means for changing the world.

How to theorise the economy

Embrace diversity

The contemporary global economy is enormously diverse, and not just because of varying levels of economic development between different countries and regions. In almost every country of the world a substantial sector of the economy is run by profit-oriented businesses, another substantial sector by the state and a third operates as a gift economy, with a broad range of variation within each of these sectors and a broad range of hybrid forms that sit between them. But the dominant ways of thinking about the economy treat it as a monolith: a uniformly commodity economy, characterised by mainstream economists as a market economy and by their Marxist critics as a capitalist economy.

While both traditions recognise the existence of a state sector, it is derided as an inefficient distortion by mainstream purists and as a creature of the capitalist class in traditional Marxism, and largely ignored in their theorisation of the economy. Nor does either of these traditions recognise the significant role of the gift economy in contemporary society.

As J.K. Gibson-Graham have argued, both of these traditions, despite the major differences between their theoretical and political approaches, have contributed to the construction of a discursive regime that identifies the very concept of the economy with commodity production by capitalist businesses. The everyday concept of the economy is defined by buying and selling and by national income statistics that measure only what is bought and sold. The related concepts of *production*, *consumption* and *the market* have all been naturalised as if these were the right and only ways to talk about the economy, and the very notion that volunteering, for example, or giving blood or cooking a meal at home might be economic activities seems faintly absurd under the influence of this discursive regime.

Yet if we fail to challenge this, we close off the possibility of thinking of the economy as being radically different from this monolithic model. This has two serious consequences. First, it obstructs the recognition of real non-market forms of economy as viable alternatives for the future. Traditional Marxists, of course, do advocate an alternative economy, but one that is only vaguely imagined, entirely untested and utterly implausible as a viable way forward. The rest of us need to see more practical alternatives before we can believe that another economy is possible. And second, it prevents us from seeing the reality of the diverse economy that *already* surrounds us, and thus the very real viability of moving towards less marketised forms of economy by expanding and developing the non-market forms that already exist.

Thus we need a different kind of political economy, a kind that recognises the existence of a broad range of economic forms, not as marginal to the market, but as equally significant, and as a reservoir of already-viable alternatives.

Define the economy by provisioning

The notion that we can have non-market forms of economy, however, would be incoherent if we continued to accept that the economy is defined by the market relation. We cannot think more openly and flexibly about forms of economy unless we define the economy itself in other terms. As a number of thinkers in heterodox economic traditions have argued, we should define the economy, not in terms of the market, but in terms of *provisioning*: those activities are economic that provide the goods and services that people need. On this understanding cooking a meal, for example, counts as provisioning and thus as economic whether it is done for wages and creates a commodity for sale in a restaurant, or done in the home to feed one's family.

This definition of the economy depends on what we are prepared to count as needs: if we define *needs* too narrowly we exclude activities that are clearly economic, such as the production of luxury goods that have no significant functional value, even though we might question the quality of the 'needs' that they meet. If we define them too broadly, then it might seem that *all* human activity meets needs and should therefore be construed as economic. In Chapter 2, therefore, I argued for a definition of the provisioning economy as those activities that provide goods and services through commodity exchange, plus the provision of equivalent goods and services through other social practices. This is a political definition, which plays the tactical role of opening our eyes to the possibility of non-market economic practices. But this is not a weakness: the existing mainstream definition of the economy is also a political one, in that it tends to support our existing economic system, although that political nature is disguised by its discursive dominance.

Appropriative practices

Having recognised economic diversity, we also need to find ways to analyse different economic forms. Once again the existing traditions of political economy are of little help here. Mainstream economics is fixated on the market form and has no tools for making sense of other forms. Marxists recognise that economic forms vary between historical periods, but tend to see one economic form as necessarily dominant in each period and others as merely subsidiary to it, or as historical anachronisms: hangovers from earlier dominant forms or nascent future forms. Instead, we need a framework for political economy that enables us to theorise a broad range of coexisting economic forms in the full range of their diversity and hybridity.

This book's primary theoretical contribution is to propose that we analyse each economic form in terms of the *appropriative practices* that it entails. A practice is a standardised way of acting, usually standardised as a consequence of normative pressures not only from other people (or rather, from *groups* of people that I call *norm circles*) but also sometimes by the influence of standardised material objects (including computer systems) used in the practice. An *appropriative* practice is one that significantly affects the allocation of benefits and/or disbenefits from processes of provisioning. Thus, for example, wage labour is an appropriative practice, in which workers receive a wage and thus part of the benefits of the provisioning process in return for their work in that process. For another example, income tax is an appropriative practice, in which a part of the benefits (or rather benefit-carriers) payable to wage earners is diverted to funding the state. For a third, feeding one's children is an appropriative practice, in which they receive benefits as a result of the actions of their parents or carers.

I focus on appropriative practices for two reasons. First, because the allocation of benefit and disbenefit from economic processes is the fundamental *ethical and political* concern of studies of the economy, whether we label that concern as inequality, exploitation, poverty, or indeed prosperity or flourishing. And second, because the orientation of economic actors to acquiring or distributing benefits makes appropriative practices central to *explanations* of economic action and interaction.

The most significant economic forms, however, are not defined by single appropriative practices, but rather by interrelated and interacting *complexes* of practices. Thus, for example, the form of capitalism analysed by Marx is a complex that combines the appropriative practices of capital accumulation, wage labour and commodity production. But we may equally describe other economic forms as different and perhaps overlapping complexes of appropriative practices. We could define 'public service' for example as a complex that combines the appropriative practices of taxation, wage labour and the provision of free services to citizens. Or 'family commodity production' as a complex that combines unpaid family labour with commodity production.

By freeing ourselves from the dogmatism of the prevailing political economies we can begin to make sense of the diversity of actual economic forms, and to see how each form is produced by social and indeed material forces that shape the normative practices that underpin it. This is a vision of the economy as fundamentally diverse and fundamentally social.

A moral political economy

The study of the economy is the study of who gets what: a necessarily ethical question. Yet the established political economies have an uneasy relationship with ethics. Mainstream economics is generally presented as a purely technical enterprise, which assumes that people's values can be read into their purchasing preferences and that economics can therefore sidestep ethical questions by focusing on how best to satisfy those preferences. But this stance subordinates the needs of the less wealthy to the desires of those who have the resources to satisfy their preferences in the market. Traditionally, although it is ultimately driven by an ethical vision, Marxist political economy has practiced a different ethics of subordination, placing an imaginary future utopia on a political pedestal and subordinating all ethical questions to the pursuit of its achievement.

By contrast, the political economy of practices advocated in this book is explicitly ethical. It recognises that economic decisions are not technical decisions and therefore must be shaped by ethical judgements – not remotely, by virtue of allegiance to some distant political principle, but proximately, by considering the actual benefits and harms that are likely to result and by evaluating the distribution of those benefits and harms. Such evaluations depend in turn on ethical standards.

There is no objectively correct set of ethical principles, and our actual ethics develop continuously through a complex process of social interaction, in which social power has a substantial influence. Jurgen Habermas has provided us with good reasons for preferring principles that arise from, or are confirmed in, honest open processes of debate where all points of view can be heard and the outcome is not distorted by the differential power of some participants. Such processes, or at least the closest approximations to them that have been managed so far, in fora like the United Nations and in studies like those done by Martha Nussbaum, support the principle that we should value all humans and ensure they have the key human capabilities required to sustain life and dignity. This book advocates a transformation of our economy that makes this possible.

A scientific political economy

Any worthwhile political economy, however, must do more than take ethical positions on questions of appropriation. It must also analyse how appropriative processes work, how they produce certain types of results and how they could be changed to produce different types of results. It must, in other words, be scientific as well as ethical. Both the prevailing traditions of political economy see themselves as scientific, but neither can deliver on this claim. Mainstream economics is divided between a theoretical moment, which substitutes highly abstracted and mathematised models for study of the real world, and an empiricist moment, which produces linear statistical models of economic variables with little consideration of the mechanisms and complex interactions that might lie behind the phenomena being measured. Marxist political economy substitutes philosophical dogma, notably the labour theory of value and its teleological theory of history, for a study of the sheer variety of causal interactions occurring in contemporary economies.

The political economy of practices is informed by a critical realist social ontology. From this perspective, societies, including economies, are open systems in which multiple causal forces interact to produce outcomes. The scientific study of the economy requires us to identify the causal powers that interact to produce events and explain the mechanisms that lie behind those causal powers. Those explanations are to be found primarily by investigating the persistently structured ways in which people interact with each other, and with material objects, to form social entities with causal powers. Appropriative practices, for example, are shaped by normative pressures, and groups of people and objects whose interactions are shaped by such practices form appropriative structures with substantial impacts on the benefits and harms that people receive from provisioning activity.

The diverse digital economy

The third part of this book focused on complexes of appropriative practices in the digital economy, and this section will summarise the implications for the book's larger argument. Like the economy more generally, the contemporary digital economy is the site of a profusion of different economic forms, including many fascinating hybrids of more familiar forms. Digital products – such as encyclopaedia entries, news articles, music recordings and videos – have a very different cost structure than conventional material products, given that the cost of replication is trivially small, and this has opened up the possibility of an economy of abundance that is governed in very different ways than the economies of scarcity to which we are accustomed. Opportunities for gift forms of economy abound, but this space is also a prime target for the ever-expanding appetite of capital. At its current early stage of development, the digital economy is therefore both a major site of proliferation of economic forms and a battleground between competing forms. This book has illustrated some of those forms using a handful of cases, and I will start to widen the focus by mentioning some others later, but this remains a set of illustrations of my argument, rather than an attempt to give a comprehensive view of the digital economy.

The digital gift economy

The World Wide Web is built on digital gifts: web pages are digital files that are transferred over the Internet to the computers and smartphones of the people who access them, and the overwhelming majority of the pages that we access with our browsers are free. Not only is the cost of transferring a typical web page vanishingly small, but what is transferred is always a *copy* of the original object, leaving the original available for indefinitely many further transfers. Neither the originator of the file nor other potential users lose access to it when one user downloads it. This transforms the economics of giving. Donors need no longer ration their giving or make careful decisions about who they are going to give to. Instead, digital information can be made freely available to anyone that wants it, at virtually no cost beyond the labour required to create it in the first place.

The most interesting cases of the gift economy on the Internet take things a step further, organising widely distributed groups of contributors to create large and sometimes complex resources for others to access freely: collaborative commons. Chapter 7 discussed Wikipedia, one of the pre-eminent cases: the largest encyclopaedia the world has ever seen, created entirely through voluntary contributions by self-organising individuals, who find the work of editing it satisfying enough in its own right to need no wage to compensate for the time spent on it. Its editors are co-ordinated by a normative, regulatory and technical framework that preserves the quality of the overall product with a remarkably light organisational touch. The gift economy orientation is completed by the funding model, with all of Wikipedia's financial costs covered by donations, mostly from its users – or at least that relatively small subset of its users that is both prosperous enough and committed enough to Wikipedia's gift economy model to contribute to its costs. This is one of the most heavily used resources on the Internet, created by gifts of labour, funded by gifts of money and provided to its users as gifts of information.

Although Wikipedia is the most prominent example of the digital gift economy, it is only one of many. Perhaps the most closely comparable is the open-source software movement (Elder-Vass, 2014, 2015c). Although some open-source projects count commercial companies amongst their major contributors, the basic model is rather similar to Wikipedia's: volunteers select tasks to undertake and freely donate their time to performing them, creating a product that is then made available freely for anyone to use. There are some differences: for example, open-source software projects require a central authority to co-ordinate releases, even though individual work packages are self-directed by individual programmers. Nevertheless, open-source software projects depend on a very similar complex of appropriative practices to Wikipedia's: what Benkler calls collaborative peer production.

Voluntary sector political commentary sites like the UK's Open Democracy are also similar, while some gift economy structures represent rather different mixes of appropriative practices. Peer-to-peer file-sharing services devolve hosting to users themselves and thus eliminate the central costs and much of the central organisation of these collaborative sites. Many of them also disregard copyright law, bringing in a very different set of appropriative issues, notably the contested claims by commercial copyright owners to control copying of certain digital material. Other services use digital means to facilitate non-digital giving, notably Freecycle, with 7 million members across 85 countries, which enables users to advertise physical things they want to give away (Freecycle, 2015). Pre-digital forms of giving have also migrated to some extent onto the Internet, such as sponsorship sites which make it easier for individuals undertaking sponsored fund-raising activities to collect donations.

Despite the hegemonic discourse of the monolithic capitalist market economy, then, the gift economy is alive and well in the digital space.

The digital commodity economy

Capitalism, of course, is also alive and well, but it is no more monolithic than the gift economy. If we may define capitalism as the economic form that is devoted to the accumulation of capital, it may be combined with a variety of other appropriative practices, each combination representing a different variety of capitalism. The most conventional of the varieties discussed in this book is represented by Apple, currently the biggest company in the world by market capitalisation. Apple designs and sells for profit a mix of physical and digital products, and the physical ones are mass-produced in factories with cheap labour and alienating work practices. To this extent it conforms with a number of stereotypical understandings of capitalist business, yet neither the neoclassical nor Marxist models give adequate explanations of its scale or profitability.

While Apple's profits do benefit from the low wages paid to manufacturing workers, as Marxists might expect, this by no means explains the full extent of its profits. Once we take a causal rather than a dogmatic approach to explaining those profits we must recognise a range of other contributing factors. In contrast with the Marxist model, for example, entrepreneurship has played a major role in Apple's success: the focus of Steve Jobs on design, usability, marketing and image has generated massive preferential attachment to its products and enabled Apple to charge premium prices which other manufacturers, with equivalent labour contributions, are unable to do. Nor is mainstream economics any better placed to explain Apple's success. Apple does not compete on price; it makes profits by exercising control over its markets: by building preferential attachment from its users, by exploiting legal provisions regarding intellectual property rights to exclude competitors and by exploiting its control over the hardware it creates to fence off related markets from competitors, such as those for apps and music downloads. We can explain Apple's success far more plausibly as the product of a complex of interacting appropriative practices, at least some of which have been shaped by Apple itself.

Just as Wikipedia defines only one possible model of the digital gift economy, however, Apple defines only one possible model of the digital commodity economy. Other businesses in this sector have combined somewhat different but overlapping sets of appropriative practices. Amazon, for example, has deliberately *opened* markets around its products, creating a platform where its competitors – or at least its smaller competitors – can offer the same products, sometimes more cheaply, on Amazon's own website. Amazon takes a commission on those sales, gains valuable information about market categories and increases the flow of customers to its own site by positioning it as a competitive marketplace, so there is nothing benevolent about this strategy (Jopson, 2012).[1] Arguably it is just a different way of building preferential attachment amongst its customers.

The hybrid digital economy

Although the profit model is in competition with the gift model in the digital economy, the two have also been profusely hybridised as commercial companies seek out unconventional strategies for profiting from the Web. Thus, for example, Google has built an enormously profitable business by giving away free services to its users – web search, email and maps, for example. These services are gifts to its users, but a different kind of gifts than those we receive from Wikipedia. Like the reciprocal gifting documented by Mauss, the inducement gifts given by companies like Google are designed to produce a return, but unlike reciprocal gifts, the primary return does not come from the recipient of the gift. Instead, Google's return comes in the form of advertising revenue, earned when it serves up content-relevant advertising to the users of its services. Content relevance, in turn, is achieved by making use of the information supplied by the user to tailor advertising to the user's interests. That information itself is not supplied by the user with the intention of giving Google assistance in tailoring its ads, but rather is an incidental transfer from the user, a by-product of some other intention.

Google's profitability, therefore, arises from a complex of appropriative practices that includes a gift of services from Google to the

---

[1] Nor does the idea of a 'market' which is under the control of one of its participants sit particularly easily with neoclassical dreams of perfect competition.

user, an incidental transfer from the user to Google and a commodity sale of advertising by Google to its advertiser. This is even less like the neoclassical model of the economy than Apple's business. Unlike Apple, manufacturing labour is nowhere to be seen, and most of Google's processes are automated, so Marxist accounts of profit as based on the exploitation of wage labour are no more relevant. And unlike Apple, Google's business depends not on a conventional sales relationship with the primary users of its services but on a gift relationship, which then enables a sales relationship with a different set of users: the users of its advertising services. The success of the latter is entirely dependent on the success of the former, and so Google must compete in one space to succeed in another, but it does not compete on price, because Google and all its major competitors provide this service for nothing: instead they compete for the attachment of the user.

Facebook and YouTube also give away services to attract users so that they can make money by hosting advertising, but in addition they employ a second form of gifting: they depend on users providing free content to the site (status updates, photos, videos, etc.), and it is this content that makes the site attractive to other users. For the users who provide this content, it may be a gift, but if so it is a gift to their friends or fellow users of the site concerned, and only incidentally is it also a transfer to the site owners, so we must add a further appropriative practice to the mix exploited by Google if we are to make sense of how these sites make money.

These hybrids are unquestionably examples of a capitalist economic form: the companies concerned make substantial profits and indeed are under considerable pressure to do so from their shareholders. But they also employ elements of a gift economy form, and making sense of the resulting hybrids requires a new kind of political economy.

Interacting economic forms

The chapters in Part III have focussed on individual organisations that illustrate particular forms, but from time to time they have also touched on the question of how interactions between different organisations, and between organisations that instantiate different economic forms, generate emergent effects. This opens up the possibility of a *macro* political economy of practices, a political economy that addresses systematic patterning of the behaviour of larger economic systems or subsystems, but this book makes only some very small steps in this direction. We have seen, for example, gift economy enterprises competing with commodity economy enterprises, hybrid enterprises competing with each other in giving away services as gifts, capitalist businesses seeking to avoid taxes and hybrid enterprises trying to give away intellectual property that belongs to other capitalist enterprises but ending up sharing revenues with them.

I have not touched at all on other possible forms such as the public service model, but this too interacts with other forms: in the United Kingdom, for example, the role of the BBC in giving away digital content has been politically contentious as capitalist media businesses have seen it as undermining their prospects of selling equivalent content. Nor have I touched on the criminal digital economy, which employs yet another set of appropriative practices, sometimes at the expense of ordinary individuals and sometimes at the expense of states and businesses.

Still, it remains to be seen whether a truly macro-political economy of practices is possible. It would have to begin from a very different place than conventional macroeconomics, which is tied to statistics that measure only the monetary economy and thus cannot see the rest of the provisioning economy. And it would primarily be concerned with very different issues from macroeconomics: not levels of national income but levels of need satisfaction; not wealth but well-being; not the size of the commodity economy but the relative roles of different economic forms and their effects on each other. The economic questions we ask reflect our political objectives, and these ones are oriented to changing our economy to better meet human needs. The mainstream's questions, by contrast, are about how to stimulate the endless growth of the commodity economy regardless of human needs.

How to change the economy

How, then, might we go about changing the economy to better meet human needs? Recognising the diversity of our existing economy provides grounds for some limited optimism about the possibility of significant economic change. The domination of our economies by capitalism is less than it might seem from the prevailing discourses of the economy, and it must be possible to build alternatives alongside capitalist economic practices since many alternative forms are already thriving. This perspective allows us to transcend the binary choice between total capitalism and its total overthrow that has often been characteristic of Marxist politics (though there are encouraging signs of Marxist thinkers who are also looking for alternatives to this binary). Instead, we could change our economy by progressively altering the mix of economic forms, steadily reducing the more harmful forms of capitalism and building more human forms of economy alongside. Indeed, it is only if we do build alternatives alongside capitalism that viable alternative economic futures can be developed, and we should welcome the work of thinkers like Erik Olin Wright and Yochai Benkler who are examining some of the ways in which this could occur.

A role for capitalism

On the other hand, however, this optimism must be qualified. As we have seen, alternative appropriative practices can themselves be entangled in capitalist forms, and ultimately the viability of alternative forms will depend not only on growing them within our existing economy but also on finding ways to criticise and curtail the role of capitalist appropriative practices. Capitalism, despite being only part of our contemporary economy, is still capable of generating massive harms – notably extreme exploitation, alienation, inequality, massive distortions in the use of resources, environmental damage and support for oppressive political regimes. It is still backed by enormous political and discursive power, and it constantly tends to subvert alternatives to its thirst for profit.

Once we recognise that capitalism itself is diverse, however, we may find that there are some forms of it, suitably regulated, that make a positive contribution overall to our well-being. Given this possibility, we can no longer simply dismiss all capitalism on the grounds of Marx's spurious theory of exploitation. Instead of applying the formulaic dogma of Marx's labour theory of value, we need to evaluate forms of capitalism by identifying their real tendencies and assessing their actual effects against explicitly stated and justified ethical standards. When we do so I believe we will find, for example, that forms of capitalism that rest on the provision of free content by users are considerably less harmful than those that rest on the extraction of minerals by slave labourers in Africa (Fuchs, 2014, pp. 172–81) and those that rest on the creation of unstable financial assets. These forms can be separated. They are not all parts of one monolith, and they should be treated differently: lightly regulated, heavily regulated or abolished entirely depending upon their impact on human flourishing.

A role for the gift economy

Alongside the less harmful remnants of the capitalist economy, we need to support the development of other forms. The state has an important continuing role to play in the provision of essential services that are made available to all irrespective of their ability to afford them, and in the provision of public goods that we all benefit from. Non-capitalist commodity forms should also continue to be important: family businesses and co-operatives, for example. But the gift economy, particularly if we include large parts of the household economy, is already as important as these, and the digital gift economy is particularly promising. As we have seen, the gift economy is particularly suited to the distribution of digital goods, with their trivial marginal costs, and innovative forms of collaborative production have flourished there, with benefits not only for the users but also for the creators of the content that they share.

Nevertheless, there are also good reasons to restrain claims for the potential of the digital gift economy. One limitation arises from the same factors that give the digital gift economy its advantages: virtually costless distribution of gifts that entails no sacrifice by the donor is *only* a characteristic of digital information goods. There is little reason to believe that similar economic processes might roll back the *non-digital* market economy in the way that the open-source movement has generated a tendency for the decommodification of software.[2] Indeed, the digital gift economy itself clearly depends on other sectors of the economy that are currently dominated by the market: for example, the hardware and networks that make the digital gift economy possible are themselves physical products created in the commercial economy, and independent programmers that contribute to open-source software must have other sources of income to support them, which are often derived from the commercial economy (Barbrook, 2005).

[2] Benkler has expressed a similar caution (Benkler, 2002, p. 381) but also identified some interesting cases of non-digital goods where giving seems to be efficient even in terms derived from conventional economics (Benkler, 2004, pp. 275–7).

Certain elements of the digital gift economy also face attempts at outright suppression by government, acting in the interests of pre-digital media corporations. Most notably, governments have been persuaded by lobbyists for these corporations to extend copyright protection in an attempt to prevent the free distribution of vast amounts of digital media products (Gillespie, 2007, chapter 4; Lessig, 2004). Open-source software seems likely to escape this, partly because of some clever work on copyleft licensing, but perhaps more so, ironically, because of the many ways in which it has become embedded in commercial business. Many IT businesses have found ways to make money out of open-source software, and at least some major open-source software products are predominantly developed at the expense of such companies (Elder-Vass, 2015c). But this is only half of the picture: we must also recognise that commercial companies are amongst the largest beneficiaries of the financial savings that arise from *using* free open-source software – these savings are a major reason for the massive 'market' shares of products like Linux and Apache.

Such entanglements warrant scepticism towards suggestions in the literature that phenomena like open-source software herald the replacement of capitalism (Berry, 2008, p. 98). But once we recognise the diversity of the economy, we no longer need all-or-nothing alternatives to capitalism. The issue we face is not a choice between a gift economy and a commodity economy; the issues are *how much* of the economy will take a gift form, *what kinds* of gift form, *how much* will take a commodity form and *what kinds* of commodity form.

Towards an open future

Let me end, not by re-summarising a chapter that is already a summary, but by asking what role a book like this can play in advancing such changes. Books alone do not change the world; any impact they might have depends upon influencing people, and movements of people, but where are the movements that might back a progressive shift towards a gift economy? Part of the problem we confront is what David Harvey calls a 'double blockage': 'the lack of an alternative vision prevents the formation of an oppositional movement, while the absence of such a movement precludes the articulation of an alternative' (D. Harvey, 2011, p. 227). As Harvey rightly says, the solution to this double blockage is inevitably iterative: the relation between these two absences 'has to be turned into a spiral' (D. Harvey, 2011, p. 227).

That spiral is already in progress, though its overall direction is uncertain. There are already movements working towards aims compatible with the ideas expressed in this book, for example Green parties, the Occupy movement, many of the groups that combine in the World Social Forum, and the movements against austerity policies in Europe. And there are already huge numbers of people participating in gift forms of economy. Though many of them do not even recognise that they *are* forms of economy, these are people who could be persuaded to back further growth of these forms. There are already, too, writers expressing ideas that complement those in this book, for example those who have contributed to the Convivialist Manifesto (Clarke, 2014), and those whose work is collected in *The Human Economy* (Hart et al., 2010). This book and the political economy of practices that it advocates are, at best, another turn of the spiral, one that encourages a more open but more realistic alternative vision of a future that could enable more of us to flourish rather than being subjected to a logic of pointless accumulation that ultimately benefits no-one.

We cannot know exactly what kind of economy and what kind of society this will lead us to, not least because there is no end point and no single overriding logic to social development but rather a continuing process of change in a fundamentally open system. The mix of economic forms within that system will inevitably develop in response to emerging possibilities but it is up to us, collectively, to find ways to encourage those forms that seem most beneficial for all human beings in the light of ethical debate. We will only be able to engage productively in such a process by abandoning monolithic visions of nirvana and working instead towards multiple partial real utopias. This is not a step backwards but a step forwards for progressive politics: we must reject the dogmas of both of the old political economies and instead engage creatively with our diverse economy and its open future.

Bibliography

Aaltonen, A., & Lanzara, G. F. (2015). Building Governance Capability in Online Social Production: Insights from Wikipedia. *Organization Studies*, 36(12), 1649–73.

Ackerman, B., Alstott, A., & Van Parijs, P. (2006). *Redesigning Distribution*. London: Verso.

Adloff, F., & Mau, S. (2006). Giving, Social Ties, Reciprocity in Modern Society. *European Journal of Sociology*, 47(1), 93–123.

Aglietta, M. (2000). *A Theory of Capitalist Regulation*. London: Verso.

Albert, M. (2003). *Parecon: Life After Capitalism*. London: Verso.

Alexa.com. (2015). Top 500 Global Sites. Retrieved from www.alexa.com/topsites

Althusser, L., & Balibar, É. (2009). *Reading Capital*. London: Verso.

Anderson, C. (2009). *Free: The Future of a Radical Price*. New York: Random House.

Anderson-Gott, M., Ghinea, G., & Bygstad, B. (2011). Why Do Commercial Companies Contribute to Open Source Software? *International Journal of Information Management*, 32(2), 106–17.

Andrejevic, M. (2010). Exploiting YouTube: Contradictions of User-generated Labour. In P. Snickars & P. Vonderau (Eds.), *The YouTube Reader* (pp. 406–23). Stockholm: National Library Sweden.

Apple Boss Explains Ban on Flash. (2010, April 29). BBC.

Archer, M. S. (1995). *Realist Social Theory: The Morphogenetic Approach*. Cambridge: Cambridge University Press.

Arthur, C. J. (2001). The Spectral Ontology of Value. In A. Brown, S. Fleetwood, & J. Roberts (Eds.), *Critical Realism and Marxism* (pp. 215–33). London: Routledge.

Assiter, A., & Noonan, J. (2007). Human Needs: A Realist Perspective. *Journal of Critical Realism*, 6(2), 173–98.

Banaji, J. (2012). *Theory as History*. Chicago, IL: Haymarket Books.

Barbrook, R. (2005). The Hi-Tech Gift Economy. *First Monday*.

Barman, E. (2007). An Institutional Approach to Donor Control: From Dyadic Ties to a Field-Level Analysis. *American Journal of Sociology*, 112(5), 1416–57.

Battelle, J. (2005). *The Search*. London: Nicholas Brealey.

Baytiyeh, H., & Pfaffman, J. (2010). Volunteers in Wikipedia: Why the Community Matters. *Educational Technology and Society*, 13(2), 128–40.

Becker, G. (1990). *Treatise on the Family*. Cambridge, MA: Harvard University Press.

Beckert, J. (2009). The Great Transformation of Embeddedness. In C. Hann & K. Hart (Eds.), *Market and Society: The Great Transformation Today* (pp. 38–55). Cambridge: Cambridge University Press.

Beckert, J. (2013). Capitalism as a System of Expectations Toward a Sociological Microfoundation of Political Economy. *Politics & Society*, 41 (3), 323–50.

Benkler, Y. (2002). Coase's Penguin, or, Linux and The Nature of the Firm. *Yale Law Journal*, 112(3), 369–446.

  (2004). Sharing Nicely. *Yale Law Journal*, 114(2), 273–358.

  (2006). *The Wealth of Networks*. New Haven: Yale University Press.

  (2013). Practical Anarchism. *Politics and Society*, 41(2), 213–51.

Benton, T. (1984). *The Rise and Fall of Structural Marxism: Louis Althusser and His Influence*. London: Palgrave Macmillan.

Berking, H. (1999). *Sociology of Giving*. London: Sage.

Bernstein, J. (2011, January 31). Wikipedia's Benevolent Dictator. *New Statesman*, 35–7.

Berry, D. (2008). *Copy, Rip, Burn*. London: Pluto.

Bhaskar, R. (1975). *A Realist Theory of Science* (1st ed.). Leeds: Leeds Books.

  (1979). *The Possibility of Naturalism*. Brighton: Harvester.

  (1986). *Scientific Realism and Human Emancipation*. London: Verso.

  (1993). *Dialectic: The Pulse of Freedom*. London: Verso.

  (1994). *Plato etc*. London: Verso.

  (1998). *The Possibility of Naturalism* (3rd ed.). London: Routledge.

Bird-David, N., & Darr, A. (2009). Commodity, Gift and Mass-gift. *Economy and Society*, 38(2), 304–25.

Boltanski, L., & Chiapello, E. (2005). *The New Spirit of Capitalism*. London: Verso.

Boltanski, L., & Thévenot, L. (2006). *On Justification: Economies of Worth*. Princeton: Princeton University Press.

Boulding, K. E. (1973). *The Economy of Love and Fear*. Belmont, CA: Wadsworth.

Bourdieu, P. (1984). *Distinction: A Social Critique of the Judgement of Taste*. London: Routledge & Kegan Paul.

  (1990). *The Logic of Practice*. Cambridge: Polity.

  (2002). The Forms of Capital. In N. W. Biggart (Ed.), *Readings in Economic Sociology* (pp. 280–91). Oxford: Blackwell Publishers Ltd.

Boyd, D., & Ellison, N. B. (2007). Social Network Sites: Definition, History, and Scholarship. *Journal of Computer-Mediated Communication*, 13(1), 210–30.

Bradshaw, T. (2014a, August 6). Apple and Samsung Settle Non-US Patent Disputes. *Financial Times*.

(2014b, September 9). Facebook Market Value Tops $200bn. *Financial Times*.

Brenner, R., & Glick, M. (1991). The Regulation Approach. *New Left Review*, I(188), 45–119.

Brown, A., & Spencer, D. A. (2014). Understanding the Global Financial Crisis: Sociology, Political Economy and Heterodox Economics. *Sociology*, 48(5), 938–53.

Burczak, T. A. (2006). *Socialism After Hayek*. Ann Arbor, MI: University of Michigan Press.

Burgess, J., & Green, J. (2009). *YouTube: Online Video and Participatory Culture*. Cambridge: Polity Press.

Callon, M., Méadel, C., & Rabeharisoa, V. (2002). The Economy of Qualities. *Economy and Society*, 31(2), 194–217.

Callon, M., & Muniesa, F. (2005). Economic Markets as Calculative Collective Devices. *Organization Studies*, 26(8), 1229–50.

Cammaerts, B. (2011). Disruptive Sharing in a Digital Age: Rejecting Neoliberalism. *Continuum: Journal of Media and Cultural Studies*, 25(1), 47–62.

Caplow, T. (1984). Rule Enforcement Without Visible Means: Christmas Gift Giving in Middletown. *American Journal of Sociology*, 89(6), 1306–23.

Cassidy, J. (2002). *Dot.Con: Greatest Story Ever Sold*. London: Allen Lane.

Cauz, J. (2013). Encyclopædia Britannica's President on Killing Off a 244-Year-Old Product. *Harvard Business Review*, 91(3), 39–42.

Chamberlin, E. (1956). *The Theory of Monopolistic Competition* (7th ed.). Cambridge, MA: Harvard University Press.

Channick, R. (2014, September 10). Encyclopaedia Britannica Sees Digital Growth, Aims to Draw New Users. Retrieved from www.chicagotribune.com/business/ct-britannica-digital-0911-biz-20140910-story.html.

Charities Aid Foundation. (2012). World Giving Index. Retrieved from www.cafonline.org/PDF/WorldGivingIndex2012WEB.pdf.

Cheal, D. J. (1988). *The Gift Economy*. London: Routledge.

Chen, B. X. (2008, November 17). Why Apple Won't Allow Adobe Flash on iPhone. Retrieved from www.wired.com/2008/11/adobe-flash-on/

Chernilo, D. (2007). *A Social Theory of the Nation-State*. Abingdon: Routledge.

Cheshire, T. (2012). Test. Test. Test. Wired UK, 132–9.

(2013, February). Talent Tube: How Britain's New YouTube Superstars Built a Global Fanbase. *Wired UK*, (02.13), 88–97.

Clarke, M. (Trans.). (2014). *Convivialist Manifesto: A Declaration of Interdependence*. Duisburg: Käte Hamburger Kolleg / Centre for Global Cooperation Research.

Clemons, E. (2009). Business Models for Monetizing Internet Applications and Web Sites: Experience, Theory, and Predictions. *Journal of Management Information Systems*, 26(2), 15–41.

Clippinger, J., & Bollier, D. (2006). A Renaissance of the Commons. In R. Ghosh (Ed.), CODE: Collaborative Ownership and the Digital Economy (pp. 259–86). Cambridge, MA: MIT Press.

Cloud, J. (2006, December 25). The YouTube Gurus. *Time*.

Coase, R. H. (1937). The Nature of the Firm. *Economica*, 4(16), 386–405.

Cohen, G. A. (1978). *Karl Marx's Theory of History: A Defence*. Oxford: Clarendon Press.

Conway, D. (1987). *A Farewell to Marx: An Outline and Appraisal of His Theories*. Harmondsworth: Penguin.

Cowell, F. A. (2006). *Microeconomics: Principles and Analysis*. Oxford; New York: Oxford University Press.

Curran, D. (2014). The Challenge of the Financial Crisis for Contemporary. *Sociology*, 48(5), 1048–54.

Cutler, T., Hindess, B., Hussain, A., & Hirst, P. Q. (1977). *Marx's Capital and Capitalism Today* (Vol. 1). London: Routledge & Kegan Paul.

Dalby, A. (2009). *The World and Wikipedia: How We are Editing Reality*. Somerset: Siduri Books.

Dann, G. E., & Haddow, N. (2007). Just Doing Business or Doing Just Business: Google, Microsoft, Yahoo! and the Business of Censoring China's Internet. *Journal of Business Ethics*, 79(3), 219–34.

Davies, E. (2014, July 28). Google Results or Bing Results - Which Do You Prefer? Retrieved from www.hallaminternet.com/2014/google-searches-bing-searches-prefer/

Davies, M. (2007). *Property*. Abingdon: Routledge-Cavendish.

Debatin, B., Lovejoy, J. P., Horn, A.-K., & Hughes, B. N. (2009). Facebook and Online Privacy: Attitudes, Behaviors, and Unintended Consequences. *Journal of Computer-Mediated Communication*, 15(1), 83–108.

DeMartino, G. (2003). Realizing Class Justice. *Rethinking Marxism*, 15, 1–31.

DeSimone, E. (2014, July 8). New Study: YouTube Profits Far Below Expectations for 2013. Retrieved from http://newmediarockstars.com/2014/07/new-study-youtube-profits-far-below-expectations-for-2013/

Douglas, M. (2002). Foreword: No Free Gifts. In M. Mauss (Ed.), *The Gift* (pp. ix–xxiii). London: Routledge.

Duggan, M., Ellison, N. B., Lampe, C., Lenhart, A., & Madden, M. (2015, January 9). Social Media Update 2014. Retrieved from www.pewinternet .org/2015/01/09/social-media-update-2014/

Dugger, W. M. (1996). Redefining Economics: From Market Allocation to Social Provisioning. In C. J. Whalen (Ed.), *Political Economy for the 21st Century* (pp. 31–43). New York: M.E. Sharpe.

Duhigg, C., & Kocieniewski, D. (2012, April 28). Apple's Tax Strategy Aims at Low-Tax States and Nations. *The New York Times*.

Duke, S. (2012, September 30). The Untaxables. *Sunday Times*, p. 5. London.
    (2014, August 17). Welcome to Zuck's Big Online Bazaar. *Sunday Times*, p. 7. London.

Duke, S., & Gadher, D. (2012, October 14). Apple avoids up to £570m in British tax. *Sunday Times*, p. 11. London.

Ehrbar, H. (2007). The Relation Between Marxism and Critical Realism. In J. Frauley & F. Pearce (Eds.), *Critical Realism and the Social Sciences: Heterodox Elaborations* (pp. 224–39). Toronto: University of Toronto Press.

Elder-Vass, D. (2007a). A Method for Social Ontology. *Journal of Critical Realism*, 6(2), 226–49.
    (2007b). Reconciling Archer and Bourdieu in an Emergentist Theory of Action. *Sociological Theory*, 25(4), 325–46.
    (2008). Searching for Realism, Structure and Agency in Actor Network Theory. *British Journal of Sociology*, 59(3), 455–73.
    (2009). *Towards a Social Ontology of Market Systems* (CRESI Working Paper No. 2009-06). Colchester: University of Essex.
    (2010a). Realist Critique Without Ethical Naturalism or Moral Realism. *Journal of Critical Realism*, 9(1), 33–58.
    (2010b). *The Causal Power of Social Structures*. Cambridge: Cambridge University Press.
    (2011). The Causal Power of Discourse. *Journal for the Theory of Social Behaviour*, 41(2), 143–60.
    (2012). *The Reality of Social Construction*. Cambridge: Cambridge University Press.
    (2014). Commerce, Community and Digital Gifts. In R. F. Garnett, P. Lewis, & L. Ealy (Eds.), *Commerce and Community: Ecologies of Social Cooperation* (pp. 236–52). Abingdon: Routledge.
    (2015a). Disassembling Actor-Network Theory. *Philosophy of the Social Sciences*, 45(1), 100–21.
    (2015b). Free Gifts and Positional Gifts: Beyond Exchangism. *European Journal of Social Theory*, 18(4), 451–68.
    (2015c). The Moral Economy of Digital Gifts. *International Journal of Social Quality*, 5(1), 35–50.

(2015d). *The Social Structures of Money*. Available from author.

Ellerman, D. P. (1991). Myth and Metaphor in Orthodox Economics. *Journal of Post Keynesian Economics*, 13(4), 545–64.

Ellison, N. B., Steinfield, C., & Lampe, C. (2007). The Benefits of Facebook 'Friends'. *Journal of Computer-Mediated Communication*, 12, 1143–68.

Elmer-DeWitt, P. (2013, July 21). How Much Revenue Did iTunes Generate for Apple Last Quarter? Retrieved from http://fortune.com/2013/07/21/how-much-revenue-did-itunes-generate-for-apple-last-quarter/

Elson, D. (1979). The Value Theory of Labour. In D. Elson (Ed.), *Value: The Representation of Labour in Capitalism* (pp. 115–80). London: CSE Books.

Encyclopædia Britannica. (2006, March). Fatally Flawed: Refuting the recent study on encyclopedic accuracy by the journal Nature. Encyclopædia Britannica.

Engelskirchen, H. (2007). Why is this Labour Value? In J. Frauley & F. Pearce (Eds.), *Critical Realism and the Social Sciences: Heterodox Elaborations* (pp. 202–23). Toronto: University of Toronto Press.

England, P. (1993). The Separative Self: Androcentric Bias in Neoclassical Assumptions. In M. A. Ferber & J. A. Nelson (Eds.), *Beyond Economic Man* (pp. 37–53). Chicago: University of Chicago Press.

Facebook. (2015a). Company Info. Retrieved from http://newsroom.fb.com/company-info/

Facebook. (2015b, January 7). What the Shift to Video Means for Creators.

Faulkner, P. (2007). Closure. In M. Hartwig (Ed.), *Dictionary of Critical Realism* (pp. 56–7). Abingdon: Routledge.

Fleetwood, S. (2001). What Kind of Theory is Marx's Labour Theory of Value? In A. Brown, S. Fleetwood, & J. Roberts (Eds.), *Critical Realism and Marxism* (pp. 57–87). London: Routledge.

Fleetwood, S. (2011). Laws and Tendencies in Marxist Political Economy. *Capital and Class*, 36(2), 235–62.

Folbre, N., & Hartmann, H. (1994). The Persistence of Patriarchal Capitalism. In H. Fraad, S. Resnick, & R. Wolff (Eds.), *Bringing it All Back Home* (pp. 57–62). London: Pluto.

Forbes. (2015, May 6). The World's Biggest Public Companies. Retrieved from www.forbes.com/global2000/list/#header:marketValue_sortreverse:true

Forte, A., Larco, V., & Bruckman, A. (2009). Decentralization in Wikipedia Governance. *Journal of Management Information Systems*, 26(1), 49–72.

Foster-Carter, A. (1978). The Modes of Production Controversy. *New Left Review*, I(107), 47–77.

Fraad, H., Resnick, S., & Wolff, R. (1994). *Bringing it All Back Home*. London: Pluto.

Freecycle. (2015). History and Background Information. Retrieved from www.freecycle.org/about/background

Frenkel, K. A. (2012, March 15). Encyclopaedia Britannica Is Dead, Long Live Encyclopaedia Britannica. Retrieved from www.fastcompany .com/1824961/encyclopaedia-britannica-dead-long-live-encyclopaedia-britannica

Friedan, B. (1963). *The Feminine Mystique*. New York: Norton.

Froud, J., Johal, S., Leaver, A., & Williams, K. (2014). Financialization across the Pacific: Manufacturing Cost Ratios, Supply Chains and Power. *Critical Perspectives on Accounting*, 25(1), 46–57.

Fuchs, C. (2008). *Internet and Society*. New York: Routledge.

(2014). *Digital Labour and Karl Marx*. New York: Routledge.

Garnett, R. F. (2007). Philanthropy, Economy, and Human Betterment. *Conversations on Philanthropy*, IV, 13–35.

(2014). Commerce and Beneficence: Adam Smith's Unfinished Project. In R. F. Garnett, P. Lewis, & L. T. Ealy (Eds.), *Commerce and Community: Ecologies of Social Cooperation* (pp. 56–76). Abingdon: Routledge.

Garside, J. (2012, May 30). Apple's Efforts Fail to End Gruelling Conditions at Foxconn Factories. Retrieved from www.theguardian.com/technol ogy/2012/may/30/foxconn-abuses-despite-apple-reforms

Gasper, D. (2004). *The Ethics of Development*. Edinburgh: Edinburgh University Press.

Geiger, R. S., & Ribes, D. (2010). The Work of Sustaining Order in Wikipedia: The Banning of a Vandal. In *Proceedings of the 2010 ACM Conference on Computer Supported Cooperative Work* (pp. 117–26). New York, NY, USA: ACM.

Geras, N. (1985). The Controversy About Marx and Justice. *New Left Review*, 150, 47–85.

Gerlitz, C., & Helmond, A. (2013). The Like Economy: Social Buttons and the Data-intensive Web. *New Media & Society*.

Gibbs, S. (2014, December 4). Apple Deleted Music from Users' iPods Purchased from Rivals, Court Told. *The Guardian*.

Gibson-Graham, J. K. (2006a). *A Postcapitalist Politics*. Minneapolis: University of Minnesota Press.

(2006b). *The End of Capitalism (As we knew it)*. Minneapolis: University of Minnesota Press.

Gibson-Graham, J. K., Cameron, J., & Healy, Stephen. (2013). *Take Back the Economy: An Ethical Guide for Transforming Our Communities*. Minneapolis: University of Minnesota Press.

Giles, J. (2005). Internet Encyclopaedias Go Head to Head. *Nature*, 438 (7070), 900–1.

Gillespie, T. (2007). *Wired Shut: Copyright and the Shape of Digital Culture*. Cambridge, MA: MIT Press.

Gimenez, M. E. (1997). Review of Bringing it all Back Home by Fraad, Resnick & Wolff. *Cultural Logic*, 1(1).

Glucksmann, M. (2012). *Cottons and Casuals*. Abingdon: Routledge.

Glucksmann, M. A. (2013). *Working to Consume: Consumers as the Missing Link in the Division of Labour* (Monograph).

(2014). Bake or Buy? Comparative and Theoretical Perspectives on Divisions of Labour in Food Preparation Work. *Anthropology of Food*, (S10).

Godbout, J., & Caillé, A. (1998). *The World of the Gift*. Montreal: McGill-Queen's University Press.

Goldsmith, J. L., & Wu, T. (2006). *Who Controls the Internet? Illusions of a Borderless World*. New York: Oxford University Press.

Goode, L., McCullough, A., & O'Hare, G. (2011). Unruly Publics and the Fourth Estate on YouTube. *Participations*, 8(2), 594–615.

Google. (2012, April 25). Code of Conduct. Retrieved from http://investor.google.com/corporate/code-of-conduct.html

(2015). 2014 Financial Tables. Retrieved from https://investor.google.com/financial/tables.html

Graeber, D. (2011). *Debt: The First 5,000 years*. New York: Melville House.

Granovetter, M. (1985). Economic Action and Social Structure: The Problem of Embeddedness. *American Journal of Sociology*, 91, 481–510.

Gray, R. (2013, August 7). The Apps that Apple Does Not Want You to Use.

Gregory, C. A. (2000). Value Switching and the Commodity-free Zone. In A. Vandevelde (Ed.), *Gifts and Interests* (pp. 95–113). Leuven: Peeters.

Gruchy, A. G. (1987). *The Reconstruction of Economics*. Westport CT: Greenwood Press.

Habermas, J. (1990). *Moral Consciousness and Communicative Action*. Cambridge: Polity Press.

(1993). *Justification and Application*. Cambridge: Polity.

(2003). *Truth and Justification*. Cambridge: Polity.

Hachman, M. (2014, September 22). The 4 Reasons I Switched from Google to Bing. Retrieved from www.pcworld.com/article/2685215/the-4-reasons-i-switched-from-google-to-bing.html

Hann, C. (2010). Moral Economy. In K. Hart, J.-L. Laville, & A. D. Cattani (Eds.), *The Human Economy* (pp. 187–98). Cambridge: Polity Press.

Hansen, S., Berente, N., & Lyytinen, K. (2009). Wikipedia, Critical Social Theory, and the Possibility of Rational Discourse. *The Information Society*, 25(1), 38–59.

Hardin, G. (1968). The Tragedy of the Commons. *Science*, 162(3859), 1243–8.

Haridakis, P., & Hanson, G. (2009). Social Interaction and Co-Viewing with YouTube: Blending Mass Communication Reception and Social Connection. *Journal of Broadcasting & Electronic Media*, 53(2), 317–35.

Harrison, J. (1973). The Political Economy of Housework. *Bulletin of the Conference of Socialist Economists*, 35–52.

Hart, K., Laville, J.-L., & Cattani, A. D. (2010). *The Human Economy*. Cambridge: Polity Press.

Hartwig, M. (2007). *Dictionary of Critical Realism*. Abingdon: Routledge.

Harvey, D. (2011). *The Enigma of Capital: And the Crises of Capitalism*. London: Profile Books.

Harvey, M. (2010). Introduction: Putting Markets in their Place. In M. Harvey (Ed.), *Markets, Rules and Institutions of Exchange*. Manchester: Manchester University Press.

Harvey, M., & Geras, N. (2013). *Marx's Economy and Beyond (Monograph)*. Colchester: CRESI, University of Essex.

Healy, K. (2006). *Last Best Gifts*. Chicago: University of Chicago Press.

(2011, October 10). A Sociology of Steve Jobs. Retrieved from http://kieranhealy.org/blog/archives/2011/10/10/a-sociology-of-steve-jobs/

Heath, S., & Calvert, E. (2013). Gifts, Loans and Intergenerational Support for Young Adults. *Sociology*, 47(6), 1120–35.

Heilbroner, R. L. (2000). *The Worldly Philosophers: The Lives, Times, and Ideas of the Great Economic Thinkers* (7th ed.). London: Penguin.

Hern, A. (2013, November 8). YouTube Co-founder Hurls Abuse at Google Over New YouTube Comments. Retrieved from www.theguardian.com/technology/2013/nov/08/youtube-cofounder-why-the-fuck-do-i-need-a-google-account-to-comment

(2014, April 4). DuckDuckGo: the Plucky Upstart Taking on Google with Stealth Searches. Retrieved from www.theguardian.com/technology/2014/apr/04/duckduckgo-gabriel-weinberg-secure-searches

Hesmondhalgh, D. (2010). User-generated Content, Free Labour and the Cultural Industries. *Ephemera*, 10(3/4).

Hindess, B., & Hirst, P. (1972). *Mode of Production and Social Formation*. London: Macmillan.

Hochschild, A. (1989). *The Second Shift: Working Families and the Revolution at Home*. New York: Penguin.

(2012). *The Managed Heart: Commercialization of Human Feeling* (3rd Revised edition). Berkeley: University of California Press.

Hodgson, G. M. (1988). *Economics and Institutions*. Cambridge: Polity.

(1999). *Economics and Utopia*. London: Routledge.

(2009). On the Problem of Formalism in Economics. In E. Fullbrook (Ed.), *Ontology and Economics: Tony Lawson and his Critics* (pp. 175–88). London: Routledge.

Humphreys, A., & Grayson, K. (2008). The Intersecting Roles of Consumer and Producer: A Critical Perspective on Co-production, Co-creation and Prosumption. *Sociology Compass*, 2(3), 963–80.

IDC. (2015). Smartphone OS Market Share, Q3 2014. Retrieved from www.idc.com/prodserv/smartphone-os-market-share.jsp

Ingham, G. (2006). Economy. In B. S. Turner (Ed.), *The Cambridge Dictionary of Sociology* (pp. 157–8). Cambridge: Cambridge University Press.

Internet Live Stats. (2014). Google Search Statistics. Retrieved from www.internetlivestats.com/google-search-statistics/

Isaacson, W. (2011). *Steve Jobs: The Exclusive Biography*. London: Little, Brown.

Jenkins, H. (2006). *Convergence Culture: Where Old and New Media Collide*. New York: New York University Press.

(2009). What Happened Before YouTube. In J. Burgess & J. Green (Eds.), *YouTube: Online Video and Participatory Culture*. Cambridge: Polity Press.

Jessop, B. (2001). Capitalism, the Regulation Approach, and Critical Realism. In A. Brown, S. Fleetwood, & J. Roberts (Eds.), *Critical Realism and Marxism*. London: Routledge.

Johnson, B. (2010, February 18). Wikipedia Wins the Google Lottery - But Why? *The Guardian*.

Johnson, J. (2011, March 2). My Gadget Guilt: Inside the Foxconn iPhone Factory. *Wired UK*, (April), 101–7.

Jopson, B. (2012, July 8). From Warehouse to Powerhouse. *Financial Times*.

Kahneman, D. (2012). *Thinking, Fast and Slow*. London: Penguin.

Keen, S. (2011). *Debunking Economics* (Rev. and expanded.). London: Zed Books.

Kinna, R. (2014, April 1). *Practising (for) Utopia*. Retrieved from https://philosophersforchange.org/2014/04/01/practising-for-utopia/

Kirman, A. P., & Vriend, N. J. (2000). Learning to Be Loyal. A Study of the Marseille Fish Market. In D. D. Gatti, M. Gallegati, & A. P. Kirman (Eds.), *Interaction and Market Structure* (pp. 33–56). Berlin Heidelberg: Springer.

Klein, N. (2007). *The Shock Doctrine*. London: Penguin.

Kolakowski, L. (1981). *Main Currents of Marxism Volume 1: The Founders*. (P. S. Falla, Trans.) (New ed.). Oxford: Oxford University Press.

Kopelev, L. (1979). *No Jail for Thought* (New ed.). Harmondsworth: Penguin.

Krippner, G. R., & Alvarez, A. S. (2007). Embeddedness and the Intellectual Projects of Economic Sociology. *Annual Review of Sociology*, 33, 219–40.

Kropotkin, P. (2006). *Mutual Aid*. Mineola, NY: Dover.

Kuhn, T. S. (1970). *The Structure of Scientific Revolutions* (Second Edition). University of Chicago Press: Chicago.

Kurzweil AI. (2014, February 20). Are Bots Taking over Wikipedia? Retrieved from www.kurzweilai.net/are-bots-taking-over-wikipedia

Lainer-Vos, D. (2013). *Sinews of the Nation*. Cambridge: Polity.

Lardinois, F. (2014, December 1). Firefox 34 Launches With Yahoo As Its Default Search Engine. Retrieved from http://social.techcrunch.com/2014/12/01/firefox-34-launches-with-yahoo-as-its-default-search-engine/

Larson, S. (2013, September 24). Want To Comment On YouTube? You'll Need a Google+ Account First. Retrieved from http://readwrite.com/2013/09/24/youtube-google-plus-comment

Lashinsky, A. (2012). *Inside Apple: The Secrets behind the Past and Future Success of Steve Jobs's Iconic Brand*. London: John Murray.

Laville, J.-L. (2010a). Plural Economy. In K. Hart, J.-L. Laville, & A. D. Cattani (Eds.), *The Human Economy* (pp. 77–83). Cambridge: Polity Press.

(2010b). Solidarity Economy. In K. Hart, J.-L. Laville, & A. D. Cattani (Eds.), *The Human Economy* (pp. 225–35). Cambridge: Polity Press.

Lawson, C. (forthcoming). *Technology and Isolation*. Cambridge: Cambridge University Press.

Lawson, T. (1997). *Economics and Reality*. London: Routledge.

(2009a). On the Nature and Roles of Formalism in Economics: Reply to Hodgson. In E. Fullbrook (Ed.), *Ontology and Economics: Tony Lawson and his Critics* (pp. 189–231). London: Routledge.

(2009b). Provisionally Grounded Critical Ontology: Reply to Vromen. In E. Fullbrook (Ed.), *Ontology and Economics: Tony Lawson and his Critics* (pp. 335–53). London: Routledge.

(2014). The Nature of Heterodox Economics. In S. Pratten (Ed.), *Social Ontology and Modern Economics* (pp. 97–126). Abingdon, Oxon; New York, NY: Routledge.

Leahy, T. (2013). Considering exploitation, surplus distribution and community economies in the work of Gibson-Graham. Retrieved from http://www.gifteconomy.org.au/

Lessig, L. (2004). *Free Culture*. New York: Penguin.

(2006). *Code: And Other Laws of Cyberspace, Version 2.0*. New York: Basic Books.

(2008). Remix. Retrieved from http://archive.org/details/LawrenceLessigRemix

Levy, S. (2011). *In the Plex*. New York: Simon & Schuster.

Light and Death. (2010, May 27). *The Economist*.

Lilley, S., Grodzinsky, F. S., & Gumbus, A. (2012). Revealing the Commercialized and Compliant Facebook User. *Journal of Information, Communication and Ethics in Society*, 10(2), 82–92.

Lukes, S. (1985). *Marxism and Morality*. Oxford: Oxford University Press.

Luk, L. (2013, November 27). iPhone 5S Wait Time Drops as Foxconn Boosts Production.

Lumpkin, G. T., & Dess, G. G. (2004). E-business Strategies and Internet Business Models. *Organizational Dynamics*, 33(2), 161–73.

Lumsden, K., & Morgan, H. M. (2012). 'Fraping', 'Sexting', 'Trolling' and 'Rinsing': Social Networking, Feminist Thought and the Construction of Young Women as Victims or Villains.

Macari, M. (2012, November 7). Apple Finally Gets its Patent on a Rectangle with Rounded Corners. *The Verge*. Retrieved from http://www.theverge.com/2012/11/7/3614506/apple-patents-rectangle-with-rounded-corners

Martins, N. O. (2013). *The Cambridge Revival of Political Economy*. London; New York: Routledge.

Marx, K. (1954). *Capital, Volume 1*. London: Lawrence & Wishart.

(1959). *Capital, Volume 3*. London: Lawrence & Wishart.

(1973). *Grundrisse: Foundations of the Critique of Political Economy (Rough Draft)*. Harmondsworth: Penguin.

(1978a). Economic and Philosophical Manuscripts of 1844. In R. C. Tucker (Ed.), *The Marx-Engels Reader* (pp. 66–125). New York: WW Norton.

(1978b). Preface to a Contribution to the Critique of Political Economy. In R. C. Tucker (Ed.), *The Marx-Engels Reader* (2nd ed., pp. 3–6). New York: WW Norton.

(1978c). The Eighteenth Brumaire of Louis Bonaparte. In R. C. Tucker (Ed.), *The Marx-Engels Reader* (2nd ed., pp. 594–617). New York: WW Norton.

Marx, K., & Engels, F. (1978). Manifesto of the Communist Party. In R. C. Tucker (Ed.), *The Marx-Engels Reader* (2nd ed., pp. 469–500). New York: WW Norton.

Matthaei, J. (1994). Surplus Labor, the Household, and Gender Oppression. In H. Fraad, S. Resnick, & R. Wolff (Eds.), *Bringing it all Back Home* (pp. 42–9). London: Pluto.

Mauss, M. (2002). *The Gift*. London: Routledge.

McClain, N., & Mears, A. (2012). Free to Those Who Can Afford it. *Poetics*, 40, 133–49.

McDonald, P. (2010). Digital Discords in the Online Media Economy: Advertising versus Content versus Copyright. In P. Snickars & P. Vonderau (Eds.), *The YouTube Reader* (pp. 387–405). Stockholm: National Library Sweden.

McGoey, L. (2015). *No Such Thing as a Free Gift: The Gates Foundation and the Price of Philanthropy*. London: Verso Books.

McGuigan, J. (2009). *Cool Capitalism*. London: Pluto Press.

McKinsey & Company. (2013). *Global Media Report 2013: Global Industry Overview*.

McLellan, D. (1980). *The Thought of Karl Marx*. London: Macmillan.

McNamara, P. (2014, January 22). How Apple and Pepsi Fumbled their 2004 Super Bowl Ad Play. Retrieved from www.networkworld.com/article/2226187/software/how-apple-and-pepsi-fumbled-their-2004-super-bowl-ad-play.html

Mertes, T. (2004). *A Movement of Movements*. London: Verso.

Miller, D. (1998). *A Theory of Shopping*. Ithaca, NY: Cornell University Press.

Mirowski, P. (1991). *More Heat than Light: Economics as Social Physics, Physics as Nature's Economics*. Cambridge University Press.

(2013). *Never Let a Serious Crisis Go to Waste: How Neoliberalism Survived the Financial Meltdown*. London; New York: Verso Books.

Mitchell, T. (2005). Economists and the Economy in the Twentieth Century. In G. Steinmetz (Ed.), *The Politics of Method in the Human Sciences* (pp. 126–41). Durham, NC: Duke University Press.

Molyneux, M. (1979). Beyond the Domestic Labour Debate. *New Left Review*, I(116), 3–27.

Morgan, J. (2005). Ought and Is and the Philosophy of Global Concerns. *Journal of Critical Realism*, 4(1), 186–210.

(2014). What's in a Name? Tony Lawson on Neoclassical Economics and Heterodox Economics. *Cambridge Journal of Economics, Advance access*, 1–23.

Morgan, J. T., Bouterse, S., Walls, H., & Stierch, S. (2013). Tea and Sympathy: Crafting Positive New User Experiences on Wikipedia. In *Proceedings of the 2013 Conference on Computer Supported Cooperative Work* (pp. 839–48). New York, NY, USA: ACM.

Morozov, E. (2011, June 10). Book Review - The Filter Bubble - By Eli Pariser. *The New York Times*.

Nature. (2006). Editorial: Britannica Attacks... and We Respond. *Nature*, (440), 582.

Nee, V. (2005). The New Institutionalisms in Economics and Sociology. In N. J. Smelser & R. Swedberg (Eds.), *The Handbook of Economic Sociology* (2nd ed., pp. 49–74). Princeton, N.J.: Princeton University Press.

Negru, I. (2010). The Plural Economy of Gifts and Markets. In R. F. Garnett, E. K. Olsen, & M. Starr (Eds.), *Economic Pluralism* (pp. 194–204). Abingdon: Routledge.

Nelson, J. A. (1993). The Study of Choice or the Study of Provisioning? Gender and the Definition of Economics. In M. A. Ferber & J. A.

Nelson (Eds.), *Beyond Economic Man* (pp. 23–36). Chicago: University of Chicago Press.

(2006). *Economics for Humans*. Chicago: University of Chicago Press.

News Corp Finally Sells MySpace. (2011, June 29). *BBC*.

Ngai, P., & Chan, J. (2012). Global Capital, the State, and Chinese Workers the Foxconn Experience. *Modern China*, 38(4), 383–410.

Niederer, S., & van Dijck, J. (2010). Wisdom of the Crowd or Technicity of Content? Wikipedia as a Sociotechnical System. *New Media & Society*, 12(8), 1368–87.

Nielsen, K., & Ware, R. (Eds.). (1997). *Exploitation* (2nd Revised ed.). Atlantic Highlands, N.J.: Prometheus Books.

Noyes, D. (2014, October 29). The Top 20 Valuable Facebook Statistics - Updated October 2014. Retrieved from http://zephoria.com/social-media/top-15-valuable-facebook-statistics/

Nussbaum, M. C. (2000). *Women and Human Development: The Capabilities Approach*. Cambridge: Cambridge University Press.

Orlowski, A. (2012, December 20). Wikipedia Doesn't Need your Money - So Why Does it Keep Pestering You? Retrieved from www.theregister.co .uk/2012/12/20/cash_rich_wikipedia_chugging/

Osteen, M. (2002). Introduction. In *The Question of the Gift: Essays Across Disciplines* (pp. 1–41). London: Routledge.

Ostrom, E. (1990). *Governing the Commons: The Evolution of Institutions for Collective Action*. Cambridge: Cambridge University Press.

O'Sullivan, D. (2009). *Wikipedia: a New Community of Practice?* Farnham: Ashgate.

Pariser, E. (2012). *The Filter Bubble: What The Internet Is Hiding From You*. New York: Penguin.

Pettinger, L. (2011). 'Knows How to Please a Man': Studying Customers to Understand Service Work. *The Sociological Review*, 59(2), 223–41.

Pidd, H. (2011, October 20). Facebook Could Face €100,000 Fine for Holding Data that Users have Deleted. Retrieved from www.theguardian.com/technology/2011/oct/20/facebook-fine-holding-data-deleted

Piketty, T. (2014). *Capital in the Twenty-First Century*. Cambridge, MA: Harvard University Press.

Polanyi, K. (2001). The Economy as Instituted Process. In M. Granovetter & R. Swedberg (Eds.), *The Sociology of Economic Life* (pp. 31–50). Boulder, CO: Westview Press.

Ponniah, W. F. F. and T. (2003). *Another World Is Possible: Popular Alternatives to Globalization at the World Social Forum*. London; New York: Zed Books.

Pountain, D., & Robins, D. (2000). *Cool Rules: Anatomy of an Attitude*. London: Reaktion Books.

Power, M. (2004). Social Provisioning as a Starting Point for Feminist Economics. *Feminist Economics*, 10(3), 3–19.

Prahalad, C. K., & Ramaswamy, V. (2000). Co-opting Customer Competence. *Harvard Business Review*.

Preston, P. (2013, July 7). Standard Shows Free Content Can Compete with the Paywall Brigade. *The Guardian*.

Purcher, J. (2011, May 26). Apple Files Trademark Infringement Lawsuit Against whiteiphone4now.com. Retrieved from www.patentlyapple.com/patently-apple/2011/05/apple-files-trademark-infringement-law suit-against-whiteiphone4nowcom.html

Pyyhtinen, O. (2014). *The Gift and its Paradoxes*. Farnham: Ashgate.

Ramos, K. (2014, September 25). Oh, the Irony! iPhone 6 Copies the Nexus 4. Retrieved from www.computerworld.com/article/2687612/oh-the-irony-iphone-6-copies-the-nexus-4.html

Reagle, J. (2010). *Good Faith Collaboration*. Cambridge, MA: MIT Press.

Red Hat. (2012). The World's Leading Provider of Open Source Enterprise IT Products and Services. Retrieved from www.redhat.com/rhecm/rest-rhecm/jcr/repository/collaboration/jcr:system/jcr:versionStorage/fb405b2d0a0526023d2a9fc5eedad019/2/jcr:frozenNode/rh:resourceFile

Reeve, A. (Ed.). (1987). *Modern Theories of Exploitation*. London: Sage.

Return On Now. (2013). 2013 Search Engine Market Share by Country - Resources. Retrieved from http://returnonnow.com/internet-marketing-resources/2013-search-engine-market-share-by-country/

Rey, P. J. (2012). Alienation, Exploitation, and Social Media. *American Behavioral Scientist*, 56(4), 399–420.

Ritzer, G. (2014). Prosumption: Evolution, Revolution, or Eternal Return of the Same? *Journal of Consumer Culture*, 14(1), 3–24.

Ritzer, G., & Jurgenson, N. (2010). Production, Consumption, Prosumption: The Nature of Capitalism in the Age of the Digital 'Prosumer'. *Journal of Consumer Culture*, 10(1), 13–36.

Robbins, L. (1932). *An Essay on the Nature and Significance of Economic Science*. London: Macmillan.

Roemer, J. E. (1994). *A Future for Socialism*. London: Verso.

Rosenzweig, R. (2006). Can History be Open Source? *Journal of American History*, 93(1), 117–46.

Ross, P. (2014, May 29). YouTube For Smart Social Marketers. Retrieved from www.socialbakers.com/blog/2190-youtube-for-smart-social-marketers

Rushton, K. (2014, October 28). Facebook Now has as Many Users as China has People. *The Telegraph*. London.

SACOM. (2012, May 30). Sweatshops are Good for Apple and Foxconn, But Not for Workers. Retrieved from www.sacom.hk/?p=947

Sandel, M. (2013). *What Money Can't Buy*. London: Penguin.

Sanghera, B., & Bradley, K. (2015). Social Justice, Liberalism and Philanthropy: the Tensions and Limitations of British Foundations. In B. Morvardi (Ed.), *New Philanthropy and Social Justice: Debating the Conceptual and Policy Discourse* (pp. 175–90). Bristol: Policy Press.

Satgar, V. (Ed.). (2014). *The Solidarity Economy Alternative: Emerging Theory and Practice*. Scottsville, South Africa: University of KwaZulu-Natal Press.

Sayer, A. (1992). *Method in Social Science*. London: Routledge.

(1995). *Radical Political Economy*. London: Wiley.

(1997). Critical Realism and the Limits to Critical Social Science. *Journal for the Theory of Social Behaviour*, 27(4), 473–88.

(2003). (De)Commodification, Consumer Culture, and Moral Economy. *Environment and Planning D: Society and Space*, 21, 341–57.

(2004a). Moral Economy. Retrieved from www.lancs.ac.uk/fass/sociology/papers/sayer-moral-economy.pdf

(2004b). Moral Economy and Political Economy. Retrieved from www.comp.lancs.ac.uk/sociology/papers/sayer-moral-economy-political-economy.pdf

(2011). *Why Things Matter to People*. Cambridge: Cambridge University Press.

(2015). *Why We Can't Afford the Rich*. Bristol: Policy Press.

Schofield, J. (n.d.). Have You Stopped Editing Wikipedia? And if so, is it Doomed? Retrieved from www.theguardian.com/technology/blog/2009/nov/25/wikipedia-editors-decline

Schrift, A. D. (1997). Introduction: Why Gift? In *The Logic of the Gift*. New York: Routledge.

Schudson, M. (2009). Advertising as Capitalist Realism. In J. Turow & M. Mcallister (Eds.), *The Advertising and Consumer Culture Reader* (1 ed., pp. 237–55). New York: Routledge.

Schumpeter, J. A. (1994). *Capitalism, Socialism and Democracy*. London: Routledge.

(2000). Entrepreneurship as Innovation. In R. Swedberg (Ed.), *Entrepreneurship: The Social Science View* (pp. 51–75). Oxford; New York: Oxford University Press.

Searle, J. R. (1995). *The Construction of Social Reality*. London: Allen Lane.

(2010). *Making the Social World*. Oxford: Oxford University Press.

Shah, A. (2012, May 31). Apple, Foxconn Slammed by SACOM on Worker Abuse in China. Retrieved from www.pcworld.com/article/256590/apple_foxconn_slammed_by_sacom_on_worker_abuse_in_china.html

Shirky, C. (2009). *Here Comes Everybody*. London: Penguin.

Silverman, M. (2012, March 16). Encyclopedia Britannica vs. Wikipedia [INFOGRAPHIC]. Retrieved from http://mashable.com/2012/03/16/encyclopedia-britannica-wikipedia-infographic/

Simon, H. (1972). Theories of Bounded Rationality. In C. B. McGuire & R. Radner (Eds.), *Decision and Organization* (pp. 161–76). Amsterdam: Elsevier Science Publishing Co Inc., U.S.

Sippel, R. (1997). An Experiment on the Pure Theory of Consumer's Behaviour*. *The Economic Journal*, 107(444), 1431–44.

Smelser, N. J., & Swedberg, R. (2005). Introducing Economic Sociology. In N. J. Smelser & R. Swedberg (Eds.), *The Handbook of Economic Sociology* (2nd ed., pp. 3–25). Princeton, N.J.: Princeton University Press.

Sparsam, J. (2013). Explanatory Isomorphism Between Economics and New Economic Sociology. Jens Beckert's Sociology of Markets. Jena.

Stalder, F. (2010). Digital Commons. In K. Hart, J.-L. Laville, & A. D. Cattani (Eds.), *The Human Economy* (pp. 313–24). Cambridge: Polity Press.

Standing, G. (2014). *The Precariat: The New Dangerous Class*. London: Bloomsbury Academic.

Stiglitz, J. (2013). *The Price of Inequality*. London: Penguin.

Stone, B. (2014, February 19). Facebook Buys WhatsApp for $19 Billion. *BusinessWeek: Technology*.

Strangelove, M. (2005). *The Empire of Mind: Digital Piracy and the Anti-capitalist Movement*. Toronto: University of Toronto Press.

(2010). *Watching YouTube: Extraordinary Videos by Ordinary People*. Toronto; Buffalo, NY: University of Toronto Press.

Tancer, B. (2008). *Click: What Millions of People Are Doing Online and Why It Matters*. New York: Hyperion Books.

Tapscott, D. (1997). *Digital Economy: Promise and Peril in the Age of Networked Intelligence* (New edition.). New York: McGraw-Hill Inc., US.

Testart, A. (1998). Uncertainties of the 'Obligation to Reciprocate': A Critique of Mauss. In W. James & N. J. Allen (Eds.), *Marcel Mauss: A Centenary Tribute* (pp. 97–110). New York: Berghahn Books.

Thompson, E. P. (1971). The Moral Economy of the English Crowd in the Eighteenth Century. *Past & Present*, (50), 76–136.

Thompson, E. P. (1991). *Customs in Common*. New York: The New Press.

Titmuss, R. (1997). *The Gift Relationship*. New York: The New Press.

Tkacz, N. (2011, January 20). The Spanish Fork: Wikipedia's Ad-fuelled Mutiny (Wired UK). *Wired UK*.

Toffler, A. (1981). *The Third Wave*. New York: Bantam.

Turow, J. (2009). Advertisers and Audience Autonomy at the End of Television. In J. Turow & M. Mcallister (Eds.), *The Advertising and Consumer Culture Reader* (1 ed., pp. 402–9). New York: Routledge.

Vaidhyanathan, S. (2012). *The Googlization of Everything*: Berkeley, CA: University of California Press.

Van Grove, J. (2013, July 10). Forget Zynga: Facebook's Games Business Stronger than Ever. *CNET*.

Varian, H. R. (2010). *Intermediate Microeconomics: A Modern Approach* (8th International student ed.). New York, NY: W. W. Norton & Company.

Vascellaro, J. E. (2012, August 25). Apple Wins Big in Patent Case. *Wall Street Journal*.

Waldfogel, J. (1993). The Deadweight Loss of Christmas. *American Economic Review*, 83(5), 1328–36.

Warren, T. (2014, July 15). Microsoft Won't Let you Set Google as Default Search on Some New Lumias. Retrieved from www.theverge.com/2014/7/15/5900895/microsoft-wont-let-you-set-google-default-search-new-lumias

Wasko, J., & Erickson, M. (2010). The Political Economy of YouTube. In P. Snickars & P. Vonderau (Eds.), *The YouTube Reader* (pp. 372–86). Stockholm: National Library Sweden.

Weber, S. (2004). *The Success of Open Source*. Cambridge, MA: Harvard University Press.

Welch, C. (2007). Complicating Spiritual Appropriation. *Journal of Alternative Spiritualitis and New Age Studies*, 3, 97–117.

Wertheimer, A., & Zwolinski, M. (2013). Exploitation. In E. N. Zalta (Ed.), *The Stanford Encyclopedia of Philosophy* (Spring 2013.).

White, H. (1981). Where Do Markets Come From? *American Journal of Sociology*, 87, 517–47.

Wikimedia. (2014a, September 11). English Wikipedia at a Glance. Retrieved from http://stats.wikimedia.org/EN/SummaryEN.htm

(2014b, October 31). Wikipedia Statistics: Site Map. Retrieved from http://stats.wikimedia.org/EN/Sitemap.htm

(2014c, December 1). Wikipedia Statistics: Edits Per Article. Retrieved from http://stats.wikimedia.org/EN/TablesArticlesEditsPerArticle.htm

Wikimedia Foundation. (2011). Donor Survey 2011 Wikimedia Germany: 1. Detailed Results. Retrieved from http://upload.wikimedia.org/wikipedia/meta/e/e8/Detailed_results.pdf

(2014, October 16). Fundraising/2013-14 Report. Retrieved from http://meta.wikimedia.org/wiki/Fundraising/2013-14_Report

Wikimedia Foundation, & KPMG. (2014, September 19). Financial Statements, June 30, 2014 and 2013. Wikimedia Foundation.

Wikipedia. (2011, October 31). User:XLinkBot/FAQ. In *Wikipedia, the Free Encyclopedia*.

(2014a, November 28). Wikipedia: List of Wikipedians by Number of Edits. Retrieved from http://en.wikipedia.org/wiki/Wikipedia:List_of_Wikipedians_by_number_of_edits

(2014b, December 11). Encyclopædia Britannica. In *Wikipedia.*

(2014c, December 11). Wikipedia: Expectations and Norms of the Wikipedia Community. In *Wikipedia.*

(2014d, December 13). Talk: Pierre Bourdieu. In *Wikipedia.*

(2014e, December 13). Wikipedia: Five Pillars. In *Wikipedia.*

(2014f, December 15). Wikipedia: What Wikipedia is Not. In *Wikipedia.*

(2014g, December 17). Wikipedia: Size Comparisons. In *Wikipedia.*

(2014h, December 31). Wikipedia: Civility. In *Wikipedia.*

(2015a, January 4). Wikipedia: Administrators. In *Wikipedia.*

(2015b, January 4). Wikipedia: Consensus. In *Wikipedia.*

(2015c, February 20). Wikipedia: Flagged Revisions. Retrieved from https://en.wikipedia.org/w/index.php?title=Wikipedia:Flagged_revisions&oldid=647967320

Wilkinson, R., & Pickett, K. (2010). *The Spirit Level: Why Equality is Better for Everyone.* London; New York: Penguin.

Williams, C. C. (2003). Evaluating the Penetration of the Commodity Economy. *Futures, 35,* 857–68.

Williams, R. (1976). *Keywords.* London: Fontana/Croom Helm.

Wolff, J. (1999). Marx and Exploitation. *Journal of Ethics,* 3, 105–20.

Woodiwiss, A. (2003). *Making Human Rights Work Globally.* London: Glasshouse Press.

Wright, E. O. (2010). *Envisioning Real Utopias.* London: Verso.

Wu, T. (2012). *The Master Switch: The Rise and Fall of Information Empires.* London: Atlantic Books.

Yarow, J. (n.d.). The Astounding Growth Of iPhone Profits. Retrieved from www.businessinsider.com/chart-of-the-day-apples-gross-profit-per-product-2012-8

Young, J. S., & Simon, W. L. (2006). *iCon: Steve Jobs: The Greatest Second Act in the History of Business.* New York: John Wiley & Sons.

YouTube. (2014, December 9). #YouTubeRewind 2014: Celebrating What You Created, Watched and Shared.

(2015). Statistics. Retrieved from www.youtube.com/yt/press/statistics.html

Zelizer, V. A. (1994). *The Social Meaning of Money.* New York: Basic Books.

Zittrain, J. (2008). *The Future of the Internet.* London: Penguin.

Index